METROPOLIS 1985

RAYMOND VERNON was director of the New York Metropolitan Region Study from its beginning in 1956 to its conclusion in 1959. Now professor of international trade and investment at the Graduate School of Business Administration, Harvard University, he was co-author with Edgar M. Hoover of *Anatomy of a Metropolis*, the first book in this series. Mr. Vernon has held various positions in the Securities and Exchange Commission, in the Department of State, and in private business, and is the author of a number of works in the fields of corporation finance, international trade, and urban economics.

NEW YORK METROPOLITAN REGION STUDY

RAYMOND VERNON, DIRECTOR

MAX HALL, EDITORIAL DIRECTOR

A Study undertaken by the Graduate School
of Public Administration, Harvard University,
for Regional Plan Association, Inc.

1. *Anatomy of a Metropolis* by Edgar M. Hoover and Raymond Vernon

2. *Made in New York* by Roy B. Helfgott, W. Eric Gustafson, and James M. Hund, with an introduction by Max Hall

3. *The Newcomers* by Oscar Handlin

4. *Wages in the Metropolis* by Martin Segal

5. *Money Metropolis* by Sidney M. Robbins and Nestor E. Terleckyj, with the collaboration of Ira O. Scott, Jr.

6. *Freight and the Metropolis* by Benjamin Chinitz

7. *One-Tenth of a Nation* by Robert M. Lichtenberg, with Supplements by Edgar M. Hoover and Louise P. Lerdau

8. *1400 Governments* by Robert C. Wood, with Vladimir V. Almendinger

9. *Metropolis 1985* by Raymond Vernon

Technical supplement: *Projection of a Metropolis* by Barbara R. Berman, Benjamin Chinitz, and Edgar M. Hoover

METROPOLIS 1985

An Interpretation of
the Findings of the
New York Metropolitan
Region Study by
RAYMOND VERNON

ANCHOR BOOKS
DOUBLEDAY & COMPANY, INC.
GARDEN CITY, NEW YORK
1963

Charts by H. I. Forman

Reprinted by arrangement with
Harvard University Press

FOREWORD

This volume is an interpretation of the principal findings of a series of books on the forces that shape metropolitan areas. In particular, the series has to do with the forces that shape the largest and most complex area in the United States, a 22-county expanse which takes in parts of three states but which, for convenience, we term the New York Metropolitan Region.

In 1956, the Regional Plan Association, a nonprofit research and planning agency whose purpose is to promote the coordinated development of these 22 counties, requested the Graduate School of Public Administration of Harvard University to undertake a three-year study of the Region. The challenging task was to analyze the key economic and demographic features of the Region and to project them to 1965, 1975, and 1985.

The resulting studies have been reports to the Regional Plan Association. At the same time, they have been designed to be of service to a much broader audience. Most Americans now live in metropolitan areas; indeed ever-increasing proportions of the world's populations are gravitating to metropolitan clusters. Their well-being depends to a considerable extent on how these areas develop. Yet the scholar's understanding of the currents underlying the rise of such areas seems grossly inadequate.

As a study of these underlying currents, this project

has been neither a blueprint for action nor an analysis of metropolitan government. It has had no recommendations to make about the physical structure of the Region or about the form or activities of the governmental bodies there. At the same time, it has been a necessary prelude to future planning studies of the Region and to well considered recommendations for governmental action. Its end product, presented in this volume, is an analysis of the Region's probable development, assuming that the economic and demographic forces in sight follow their indicated course and assuming that the role of government is largely limited to existing policies.

The results of the Study, it is hoped, will be applied in many ways. Governments and enterprises in the Region should be in a better position to plan their future programs if they become more closely aware of the economic environment in which they may expect to operate. Other metropolitan areas, it is already evident, will benefit from the methodology and conclusions the Study has developed.

From the first, there was a general recognition that the main part of the Study would have to be done by a group located within the New York Metropolitan Region and devoted exclusively to the project. Such a group was assembled in New York. The work that followed was a complex partnership. The New York staff functioned in close harness with members of the Harvard University faculty. It drew on the faculties of other universities, including Columbia University, Fordham University, Hofstra College, New York University, and Rutgers University. It obtained the help of dozens of governmental organizations in the Region, and literally hundreds of private groups and individuals. It made use of the materials which the Regional Plan Association had pulled together in prior years.

It is not easy to account for all the elements that

went into this summary volume nor into the other volumes in the series. The Regional Plan Association performed an indispensable function in conceiving and sponsoring the idea of a study. The Ford Foundation and the Rockefeller Brothers Fund generously provided financial support. Added support for specific aspects of the Study came from the Merrill Foundation for the Advancement of Financial Knowledge, Inc., and from the Twentieth Century Fund. The usual formula in such a situation obviously applies; credit for the Study's results must be shared with those who helped to bring it about, but the onus of error or omission lies with us.

EDWARD S. MASON
for the Graduate School
of Public Administration,
Harvard University

CONTENTS

CONTENTS

CHARTS

MAP

New York Metropolitan Region

TABLES

METROPOLIS 1985

1

Metropolis Today

Everyone agrees that the metropolitan behemoth surrounding New York Bay is on the move. But there are considerable differences of view over the direction in which it is moving.

To some, New York evokes images of growth and vitality—of the glistening façades of Park Avenue's office buildings, the domes and arches of the International Airport, the campuslike industry of Westchester and Middlesex Counties. To others, New York suggests a process of decay and retrogression—the stagnant populations and outmoded streets of a worn-out city, the snail's crawl of snarled traffic, the crime and social dislocation of a battered melting pot.

The goal of the New York Metropolitan Region Study has been to get behind these sometimes contradictory, always bewildering impressions and to identify the major forces which are at work in shaping the New York area's economic life. With these forces identified, our aim has been to project into future decades the likely pattern of development of the sprawling area as a whole and of its major parts as well—New York City at its center, the other old cities spaced through its 22 coun-

TABLE 1 Distribution of Employment in New York Metropolitan Region and U.S., by Major Categories, 1956

	Region		United States		Region as per cent of U. S.
	Employment (thousands)	Per cent of total	Employment (thousands)	Per cent of total	
Total employment[a]	6,409.8	100.0	62,538.9	100.0	10.2
Employment in national-market activities, total	2,436.2	38.0	24,358.5	39.0	10.0
Manufacturing	1,647.3	25.7	13,898.3	22.2	11.8
Wholesaling	83.4	1.3	212.1	0.3	39.3
Finance	131.3	2.1	376.6	0.6	34.9
Business and professional services	385.1	6.0	1,652.0	2.6	23.3
Public utilities	73.2	1.1	403.5	0.7	18.1
Retail trade and consumer services	114.5	1.8	863.1	1.4	13.3
Government	—	—	461.8	0.7	—
Contract construction	1.4	[b]	15.0	[b]	9.2
Agriculture and mining	—	—	6,476.1	10.3	—

Employment in					
local-market activities,[c] total	3,973.6	62.0	38,180.4	61.0	10.4
Manufacturing	239.6	3.7	2,414.3	3.9	9.9
Wholesaling	360.0	5.6	2,862.1	4.6	12.6
Finance	187.4	2.9	1,360.5	2.2	13.8
Business and professional services	592.7	9.2	4,287.5	6.9	13.8
Public utilities	420.6	6.6	3,645.9	5.8	11.5
Retail trade and consumer services	1,260.0	19.7	13,507.6	21.6	9.3
Government	633.0	9.9	6,734.4	10.8	9.4
Contract construction	227.8	3.6	2,486.1	4.0	9.2
Agriculture and mining	52.5	0.8	882.0	1.4	6.0

Note: Because of rounding, percentages do not necessarily add to totals.
[a] The total employment shown is less than that given in Edgar M. Hoover and Raymond Vernon, *Anatomy of a Metropolis* (Cambridge: Harvard University Press, 1959; New York: Doubleday, Anchor Books, 1962), for a number of technical reasons, the principal reason being that we could not allocate to the present classifications a number of self-employed persons. For other notes and sources on the estimates presented in this table, see Robert M. Lichtenberg, *One-Tenth of a Nation* (Cambridge: Harvard University Press, 1960), Table 1 and Appendices B and G.
[b] Less than 0.1 per cent.
[c] Includes also "sectional-market" activities serving markets within a few hundred miles.

ties, and the hundreds of suburban and semirural communities which make up the rest of the Region.

We are concerned, therefore, with the past, the present, and the future of the New York Metropolitan Region. But the past is complex, and the future is murky. We have chosen, therefore, to begin the process of exploration with the present. And to narrow the focus even further, we shall concentrate upon the picture of the Region as a whole before we get down to a consideration of its various parts.

There is no need to dwell very long on all the "firsts" which the New York Metropolitan Region represents in the United States. The 7,000 square miles which we define as the Region—an area radiating forty miles or more from the Empire State Building—is the most populous metropolitan area in the nation. The number of its jobs, the magnitude of its output, the variety of its industry, the population density of its central city, the size of its governments' budgets, and a score of other measures all place it in the leading position among the nation's urban areas. Most readers are familiar enough with the New York area's primacy in the nation's urban life. There are other facts about the Region, however—key facts in the analysis of its past and future—which are not so evident.

First of all, it is of critical importance for our purposes to understand just how the New York area's inhabitants earn their livelihood. In fact, our emphasis on the employment structure of the New York Region permeates the analysis. There is an old cliché in economic analysis which helps to explain our emphasis— the assumption that population follows economic opportunity. As our story develops, it will be apparent that there are half a dozen major qualifications of this simple proposition, some obvious, some fairly subtle. By and large, however, if we can achieve an understanding of the economic opportunities which an area like the New York Region affords, this will provide a powerful guide to the size and character of its future population. More than that, the nature of a Region's economic opportunities also tells us something of the area's income level, its consumption wants, even its land use. Employment, therefore, is the take-off point for our analysis.

How do the inhabitants of the New York Metropolitan Region earn their living? Table 1 gives a first glimpse of the situation as it existed in 1956. In this table, the New York area's employment is shown in two groups: jobs in so-called "national-market" activities, that is, jobs devoted to the generation of goods or services which characteristically are "exported" over broad market areas; and jobs in "local-market" activities, namely, those which generate goods and services of the sort which are typically consumed in the area where they are produced. In somewhat oversimplified terms, we can think of the national-market jobs as those through which the rest of the world exerts its direct influence on New York, sometimes by providing New York with opportunities for increased business, sometimes by shrinking New York's business opportunities. The local-market jobs, on the other hand, respond largely to changes which go on inside the Region.

So much for introduction. What the table shows is that about two-fifths of the employment of the New York Metropolitan Region was in national-market activities in 1956, while the remainder was in activities of a local sort. And though we tend to think of the New York Region principally as a national center for business and finance, nonetheless the Region's largest stake in national-market jobs lays in the field of manufacturing; in fact, about two out of every three national-market jobs in the Region were manufacturing jobs. "Business and professional services"—a term which here includes New York's famed central offices, as well as its national advertising agencies and other national services—ran second, but a poor second. No other group was of any great numerical importance. In cold employment magnitudes, New York's famed national wholesaling centers, its fabulous theatres, art galleries, hotels, and nightclubs, make insignificant contributions to its total employment, when compared with its national-market manufacturing.

Table 1 also helps us look at these national-market activities in another dimension. Its extreme righthand column shows New York's relative position in the nation for each category of national-market employment. Here we see that the New York area does indeed provide a dominant share of the country's national-market activities in wholesaling, in business and professional services, and in finance. So our picture of the New York area comes back into focus. The New York area is a national leader in all these fields, as our later discussion will show; but its leadership in these fields is much less important to its economic existence than its less obvious contributions in manufacturing pursuits.

In fact, so important is the manufacturing sector to the New York area's economic life that it will help, even at this introductory stage in our discussion, to begin pointing to the factors which explain the existence of so large a manufacturing group in the New York area. Table 2 makes a modest contribution in that direction by presenting a breakdown of employment in the Region's 400 or so national-market manufacturing industries, with each industry classified according to the major factor that seems to explain its locational pattern in the nation. Neatly arranged by rows and columns, the figures in Table 2 give off an aura of credibility to which they are not altogether entitled, for the classification in the table is subject to many substantial qualifications.[1] Nonetheless, the classification, as we shall see in later chapters, does have considerable analytical value.

The table shows that "transport-sensitive industries" —industries whose location is dominated by transport-cost considerations—are far less important in the New York Metropolitan Region than they are in the nation. This is largely a reflection of the Region's handicap as a center for the distribution of goods to national markets.

TABLE 2 Distribution of Employment in National-Market Manufacturing Industries Classified by Major Locational Factor,[a] New York Metropolitan Region and U. S., 1954

	Region	U. S.
All national-market industries ..	100.0%	100.0%
Transport-sensitive	15.9	42.2
Labor-sensitive	9.4	9.5
External-economy	44.6	17.3
"Footloose"	14.7	16.3
Unclassified	15.4	14.7

[a] So far as possible, the dominant locational motive is that which is characteristic of the industry on a national basis. See Robert M. Lichtenberg, *One-Tenth of a Nation* (Cambridge: Harvard University Press, 1960), Chapter 2 and Appendix B.

Sources: U. S. *1954 Census of Manufactures* and estimates of New York Metropolitan Region Study.

The Region offers a better account of itself in the "labor-sensitive" industries, that is, the industries critically reliant on labor factors in their location. But "labor factors" is a broad term. What the table does not show is that the Region's forte is in providing a site for industries to which skilled labor is critical, whereas industries tend to avoid the New York Region when their prime need is low-wage unskilled labor.

The biggest manufacturing group by far, however, is one which goes under the ambiguous heading of "external-economy industries." Thereby hangs a very complex tale, to which a considerable part of this book is devoted. The shortest way to describe the locational imperative of establishments in these external-economy industries is that they have a compelling need to be close to other firms in order to make sales or hold down costs.

In one context or another—in wholesaling, in finance, and in other fields—we shall be coming back to this concept. Much of the New York Region's activity is located in New York rather than elsewhere simply because other activities providing essential external economies are there as well. But does not this formulation flagrantly beg the question? Why did the "other activities" go to the New York area in the first place? Why not Chicago, New Orleans, or San Francisco?

So we turn to history in the search for an explanation, trying to identify what is chicken and what is egg —and above all, which came first.

2

Origins of a Metropolitan Region

"To bring New York down to date," E. B. White says, "a man would have to be published with the speed of light."

The New York Region's development does seem to set a dizzy pace—a pace so swift that one wonders whether an effort to foresee its course some decades ahead is utterly foolhardy. To get a measure of the pace, we need only look at the Region as it existed only thirty or forty years ago. At that time, the 7,000 square miles which we now define as the New York Metropolitan Region appeared so different in structure and development that one might have questioned whether the concept of a single Region was very useful. In those days, the established cities in the Region were well separated from one another, surrounded by farm and open field. Suburbs existed, to be sure; but for the most part they clung close to the railway stations. Today, only a few decades later, a huge expanse of New Jersey, the New York State mainland, the Connecticut shore, and Long Island manifest an almost unbroken development.

But a much longer look at history suggests that there has been a certain order and continuity in the development of the New York Region. One thing led to another, in a chain whose links stretch back to that $24 real estate investment and forward to a future whose character this book will try to define. We do not resort to history for its own sake, but shall be looking for clues to the pattern of the Region's past development and suggestions of its course from this point forward.

THE FIRST CITY

Historians are a trifle unsure why New York lunged forward as the nation's first city in the early part of the nineteenth century. When the Revolutionary era had ended, Boston and Philadelphia still had been strong candidates for the first-city role.

The westward movement and overland transport undermined Boston's claim. As long as travel had been mainly by sea, it had not greatly mattered that Boston lay well off the center of the growing nation. From any tidewater point in the South's plantation country, for instance, a sea voyage to Boston was not much more onerous than one to Philadelphia or New York. But with the arrival of post roads, then canals, then railroads, Boston's remoteness was a growing handicap. Whether for the gathering of people or the shipment of goods, some more central location was bound to gain in power.

But why New York? Philadelphia was the nation's capital from 1790 to 1800. Its population in 1790 was 42,000, largest in the republic. It took an early lead in banking, insurance, and the trading of securities. It had major publishers, a good port, and a rich hinterland. At the turn of the century, one might well have forecast its increasing dominance.

The disposition among historians is to lay New York's

rise to the Erie Canal; to the ice-free conditions of the East River, kept clear by its churning tides; and to a comparatively unobjectionable sand bar at the mouth of New York's harbor—a sand bar more manageable than that at the mouth of the Delaware. There is also a disposition to give credit to something in the fluid social structure of New York's life, an indefinable quality which even then attracted off-beat businessmen in search of their fortunes.

At any rate, whether or not New York's social structure was part of the lure, its early growth was almost certainly based on a lead in foreign trade. This is an old story, which does not need much retelling. From 1800 to 1830, the value of the Port's foreign trade grew fourfold. New York's proportion of the nation's foreign trade rose from 9 per cent to 37 per cent. Behind that growth lay daring innovations in commerce: for example, the introduction in 1818 of regularly scheduled transatlantic sailings, and the deliberate interposition of New York as an entrepôt between the agricultural South and Europe.

In a pattern which will appear many times during this account, growth fed on growth. For a time, New York's unique scheduled sailings, its "ship brokers," and its wholesalers could be matched nowhere else. Those who used the New York Port could hold down their costs of doing business by relying on these facilities, these "external economies" which establishments obtain through sharing the services of specialists external to themselves.

During the middle decades of the century, though New York's role as the national gateway continued to expand, its own heavy dependence on the sea was already beginning to shrink. The Erie Canal had opened up a new route through which New York could tap the wheatlands and forests of the Middle West. Bits and pieces of rail line were also beginning to be put in place, adding another means by which raw materials could be shipped east and manufactured products could move west to the new territories.

Thus, new avenues to the west did not hurt the New York area—at least not in that antebellum era. Like most transportation innovations, canals and railroads came first to the old centers of activity, to the areas of New York, Boston, and Philadelphia, but most of all to New York. As a point for goods collecting and goods distributing, New York's rail-canal system and its harbor facilities could not be matched. The early lead in foreign trade was parlayed into a giant march. The New York Port grew spectacularly, pulling away from its rivals on the East Coast. By the outbreak of the Civil War, the New York Port was handling 62 per cent of the nation's foreign trade business.

Still, long before the Civil War, one could see that New York's existence would eventually depend as much on domestic commerce as on the sea. Activities which had sprung from the Port were already beginning to develop an independent reason for existence. The wholesaling of goods, for instance, had originally been dependent on the Port because most of the goods handled by wholesalers had been foreign in origin. Later, however, wholesalers took to handling domestic products in growing quantities. By the 1860's their reliance on the railway and canal network stretching along the coast and into the hinterland to the west must have been at least as great as their reliance on the Port.

So, too, with finance. New York took the lead in marine insurance because shipwreck, fires at sea, mutiny, and piracy were among the earliest insurable catastrophes; but later on, the companies which had grown on marine business came to thrive on domestic property risks. Similarly, the Region's lead in banking could be traced partly to the importance of foreign commerce as a generator of bank business. But it was not long before the financial community was relying upon land-based business for its growth.

If we look at the internal structure of the New York Metropolitan Region during this pre-Civil War period, examining the way in which its various sub-areas developed, the early importance of the sea is once more in evidence. For two centuries after the Dutch had chosen to mount their guns on the Battery at the tip of Manhattan, habitation around the New York area clung fairly closely to the waterways. In 1825, when the Erie Canal became a reality, Manhattan, Brooklyn, Newark, Jersey City, and Hoboken were the main clusters of population, each arranged around its waterfront and each built up to fairly high densities. There were little colonies elsewhere in the area as well, strung out through the length of agricultural Long Island, up the picturesque Hudson Valley, and in the bays and lesser rivers of the New Jersey hinterland. Almost everywhere the living arrangements were aimed at making the best use of the navigable bodies of water and at reducing the movement of goods and people by land. As a result, space was at a premium in the little crowded cities of the Region, even in the early decades of the nineteenth century. Goods were received, processed, and distributed close to the waterside. Homes were squeezed into constricted areas, to be in walking distance of docks, counting houses, mills, and tanneries. By 1850, horse-drawn traffic in front of Trinity Church at Broadway and Wall Street was already in a snarl.

The development of the Region and its various parts was also affected by the special role played by immigration. For some decades before the Civil War, immigration to the United States had been mounting to new levels. The high concentration of shipping in New York's harbor meant inevitably that the Scots, Irish, and Germans who made up the great immigrant waves of the era were dumped in great numbers on New York's waterfront. Short of funds and ignorant of labor conditions in the interior, many of them stayed. The greatest clusters clung to Manhattan, where obsolescent pre-Revolutionary housing was already being abandoned by the middle classes moving uptown to the Washington Square area and to 14th Street. Other groups fanned out into the old structures which already could be had in Williamsburg and Greenpoint in Brooklyn. Still others found shelter in Newark, already two hundred years old. A few built shanty towns in Harlem and in the open fields above Manhattan's 42nd Street, before the days when the building codes and the zoning laws would rule out that kind of escape from slum crowding.

By the time of the Civil War, therefore, the old cities where the immigrants came to rest were plentifully supplied with cheap labor, some of it fairly skilled labor which had been exposed to the discipline of urban living and to a workshop existence in Europe's industrial towns. By contrast, the newer areas of the country were grossly undermanned and unable to divert much manpower away from the soil.

Accordingly, Germans staffed the tanneries of Newark and the flour mills and early work-clothes shops of Manhattan; Irishmen, drawn out of a more agrarian background, supplied the common labor of the cities; altogether, they gave a seemingly entrenched position to New York's manufacturing economy. Packed densely in the old housing of the City, they went to work on foot or by horse car to the nearby shops.

THE POSTBELLUM PERIOD

From the Civil War to the twentieth century's beginning, the New York Metropolitan Region's economic life was a story of continuous adjustment to change—adjustment by expansion in new fields to overcome growing disadvantages in old ones.

Labor supply was not one of those disadvantages. The flow of immigration continued through the decades; the origins of the immigrants changed, to be sure, from northern and western Europe to southern and central Europe, but the effect on the labor market was to provide ample replacements for the workers in the Region who were beginning to move to jobs higher in the wage scale.

Transportation now began to exert a different kind of influence on the New York area's role in the nation's economy. As the railroads stepped up their speed and reach, particular portions of the country began to show far greater tendencies to specialize in one kind of production or another. Raw materials now could be collected from farther off, but an even more important result was that final products could be shipped for great distances. The flour mills of New York, which once had ground western wheat, found themselves squeezed by the competition of Minneapolis and Buffalo. Local iron mines and foundries, spotted through the New Jersey reaches of the New York Metropolitan Region as we now conceive it, succumbed to the competition of richer raw materials elsewhere. New York City, once a center of meat-packing, lost ground to Chicago and other midwestern packing centers as refrigerated cars began to haul fresh beef to eastern markets. Tanneries declined in eastern cities like Newark, as the Midwest's supply of hides and tanning extract created new competition from that source.

The new-found freedom of plants to draw their materials over long distances and to ship their products to vast markets stimulated another trend, the move toward large factories. New ways of making steel, flour, leather, and cloth on a large scale forced small producers to the wall; local factories supplying local markets grew less common as many industries became centralized. The outlines of a great "industrial belt" took shape,

35

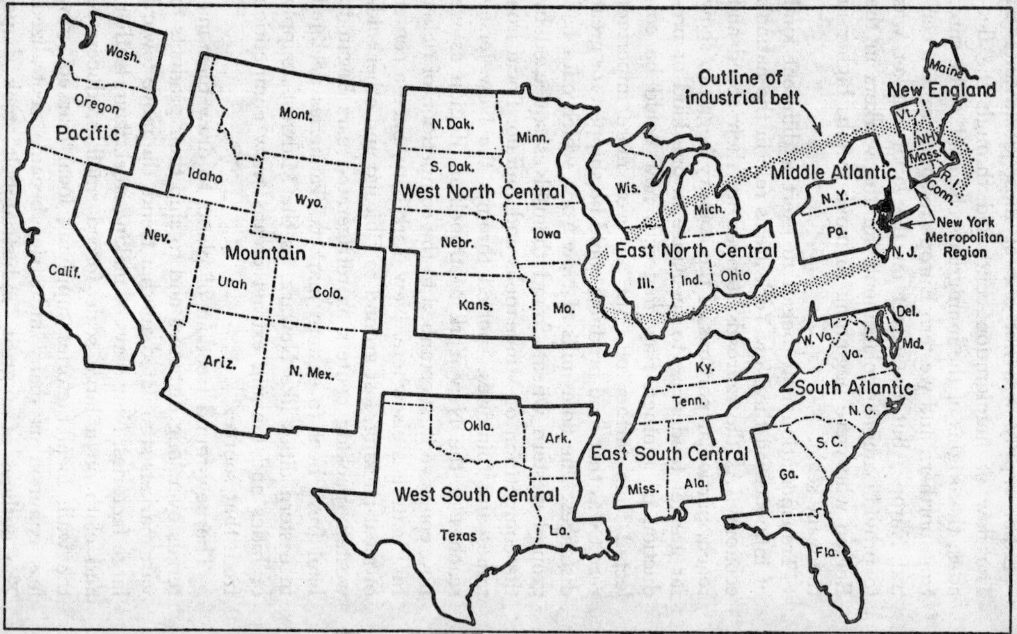

CHART 1 The Industrial Belt and the Nine Census Divisions of United States

spreading from Boston and New York to Chicago, and supplying manufactured goods not only to the belt itself but also to the more agrarian areas of the South, the Great Plains, and the Far West. Chart 1 shows the industrial belt and also the nine Census divisions which will figure in some of our later charts.

Transportation changes, therefore, forced new specializations for the New York area. Because New York was by now well to the east of the center of the nation's markets and was getting farther from the center with each decade, the specializations took the form of products having comparatively high value per pound, products for which shipping costs were no serious handicap. With labor plentiful, the New York area took to producing men's work clothes, women's aprons, cigars, and other products with comparatively low shipping costs.

The New York area adjusted in still another way during this postbellum period, namely, by corralling increasing amounts of the office work which America was beginning to generate. Here the key to the growth of the New York area was its early start in wholesaling and finance. Each new increment in office activity, from the founding of Metropolitan Life in 1868 to the great mergers of the late 1890's, was tied by its communication needs to the office activity that had settled in the New York area earlier. And all of them were readily serviced by the literate urban workers, densely packed nearby in the crowded housing of Manhattan and other residential centers.

Turning inward to the Region's various parts once again, one can easily discern some of the effects of the forces just described. The last forty years of the nineteenth century saw the building of the tenements in the City's oldest sections and the increase in population densities to two or three hundred thousand per square mile in some areas of Manhattan. In this period, too, the spanning of the Region's major rivers began—a development which was to hasten the migration of people from Manhattan outward. And all this time the central business district spread steadily northward up Broadway.

Meanwhile the railroads were beginning to affect the configuration of the Region. As long as the waterways had been a prime means for moving goods in the area, Manhattan had derived economic benefit from being an island, and factories had lined its shores on the East River and Hudson River. The railroads introduced a new geographical bias. The lines connecting with the West and South, on reaching the New Jersey shore of Upper New York Bay and the Hudson River, were obliged to stop there until man could find the means to bridge the river or tunnel under it. By 1900, some nine railroads had built terminal facilities on the New Jersey side, while only two railroads brought freight directly into the four easterly boroughs of New York City from outside the Region, and only one directly into Manhattan. Accordingly, plants with major freight-moving requirements were increasingly favoring the New Jersey side of the Region. At first, this preference retarded growth in Manhattan only, but later its effects were felt in Brooklyn and Queens as well.

At the same time quite a different force was operating in some industries—the need for more space. The stench-producing and waste-generating industries felt the need first—the abattoirs, heavy chemical plants, copper refineries, and oil refineries. Their choice of sites in the outbound move determined the character of large areas of the Region. Newtown Creek in Brooklyn drew one cluster, Hunts Point in the Bronx another, the wide-ranging Jersey meadows a third, and the banks of the waterways between Staten Island and New Jersey a fourth. Every such cluster of heavy industry generated its drab colonies of workers' homes nearby, built up in fairly heavy densities no more than a short trolley ride's distance from the plant. But between clusters the land still lay open or sparsely settled.

OLD CITIES AT THEIR PEAK

From 1900 to 1929, the incredible growth that had been the dominant trait of America was unabated. Populations spilled westward toward the Pacific Coast and the Southwest. The proportion of the nation's population residing on the Pacific Coast and in the states of Arizona, New Mexico, Oklahoma, and Texas rose from 8 per cent to 14 per cent between 1900 and 1930. Still, in that era, the Middle Atlantic states (New York, New Jersey, and Pennsylvania) managed to keep pace with the nation's population growth and even to exceed that growth by a small margin, as the left half of Chart 2 shows. And the New York Metropolitan Region, lying nearly all in the Middle Atlantic states, also exceeded the national rate of growth. Besides, the big metropolitan areas of the nation were growing faster than the sections in which they were located. The left-hand portion of Chart 3 shows the performance of metropolitan areas in relation to their Census divisions between 1900 and 1930. The New York Metropolitan Region, as a big metropolitan area in a fast-growing section of the nation, showed especially large population increases; during those three decades the Region's population grew 111 per cent, while that of the Middle Atlantic division grew 70 per cent and that of the nation 62 per cent.

Despite that record, however, powerful forces continued to challenge the dominance of the "old" industrial strongholds. New manufacturing centers of importance began to appear outside the "industrial belt." The emergence of these centers between 1900 and 1930 was related, of course, to the westward dispersion of population. Many forces motivated that dispersion, including the search for better agricultural land and min-

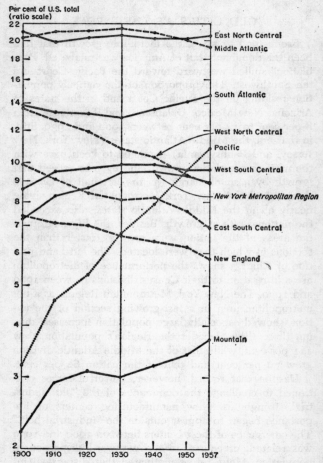

CHART 2 Distribution of Population by the Nine Census Divisions of United States, 1900–1957

Per cent of U.S. total (ratio scale)

East North Central
Middle Atlantic
South Atlantic
West North Central
Pacific
West South Central
New York Metropolitan Region
East South Central
New England
Mountain

1900 1910 1920 1930 1940 1950 1957

Sources: U. S. Censuses of Population and *Current Population Reports*, Series P–25, No. 186.

eral wealth; but the widespread new markets, once in being, began to create enough business to allow regional manufacturing plants to spring up, plants which could undersell producers who shipped goods into the area from the remote industrial belt. These were not like the little plants which fifty years earlier had dotted the countryside of the country's older sections, but were comparatively large modern establishments capable of exploiting some of the advantages of large-scale production. The effect of these developments is mirrored in Chart 4, showing the distribution of America's manufacturing workers over a period of about a century. The combined share of the Middle Atlantic and New England divisions has dropped from 72 to 35 per cent of the total since 1860. The share of the North Central division increased greatly and then stabilized. The South and West have continued to come forward in manufacturing importance.

Of course, the forces at work were much more complex than this simple vignette suggests. For instance, during the period before 1929 the labor market of the New York area underwent some fundamental changes. For the first fifteen years or so of the new century, immigration continued, providing green hands for the area's low-wage industries. But World War I cut off mass migration from Europe, and legislation in the early 1920's gave permanence to the barriers. As a result, the pools of labor existing at rock-bottom wages in the Region's old cities lost their big source of replenishment. At the same time, the progress of labor organization was gradually cutting down the freedom of some industries to tap these pools.

Meanwhile, developments on the nation's farms during the first decades of the twentieth century were turning a scarcity of labor into a surplus. Agricultural productivity soared, almost matching the growth rates in factories. Since the demand for agricultural products

CHART 3   Population in Large Metropolitan Areas
as Proportion of Their Corresponding Census Divisions, 1900–1950

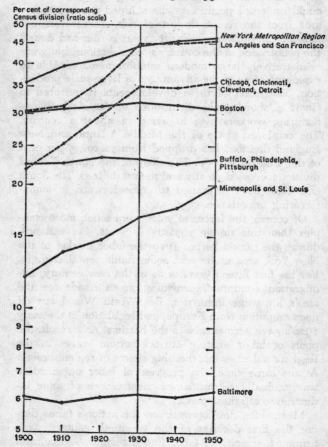

Per cent of corresponding
Census division (ratio scale)

New York Metropolitan Region
Los Angeles and San Francisco

Chicago, Cincinnati,
Cleveland, Detroit

Boston

Buffalo, Philadelphia,
Pittsburgh

Minneapolis and St. Louis

Baltimore

Note: Except for New York and Boston, lines show Standard Metropolitan Areas as used by Census. For Boston, the four-county industrial area is shown.

Sources: Donald J. Bogue, *Population Growth in Standard*

was comparatively slow-growing, the increase in productivity was creating reservoirs of idle labor, ready to be recruited for work in factories.

CHART 4 Geographic Distribution of U. S. Manufacturing Employment

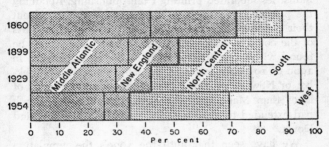

Note: In 1955, 83 per cent of North Central's manufacturing employment was in East North Central (see Chart 1 for map); 55 per cent of "South" was in South Atlantic and the rest divided equally between East South Central and West South Central; and 87 per cent of "West" was in the Pacific division.

Sources: For 1860, George Rogers Taylor, *The Transportation Revolution 1815–1860* (New York, 1951), p. 247. For other years, U. S. Department of Commerce, *Long-Term Regional Trends in Manufacturing Growth: 1899–1955*, Area Trend Series No. 2 (February 1958).

The coming of the motor truck made it easier to tap low-wage labor near the old manufacturing centers. Though in 1910 truck haulage barely existed, by 1920 there were 1,100,000 trucks on the road, and by 1929 there were 3,400,000. Plying a beat from downtown New York, trucks began to link the City's apparel salesrooms with the sewing shops in areas where labor costs

---

Metropolitan Areas, 1900–1950 (Washington, D. C.: Housing and Home Finance Agency, 1953), Appendix, and *Statistical Abstract of the United States* for various years.

were lower; some of this labor was found in the sluggishly growing agricultural areas to which we referred, and some was found in the depressed coal-mining region of Pennsylvania. Just as the apparel industry separated sewing from selling, so the book and magazine industries separated printing from publishing. Retaining the publishing function in Manhattan, they farmed out their printing to locations of lower cost in other parts of the country. Sometimes these "other parts" could be found within the Region itself as we now know it; in 1900 or 1910, for instance, the labor markets of Brooklyn or Newark provided lower rates for some kinds of labor than Manhattan. By 1930, however, the search had extended to more outlying parts like Plainfield and Dover.

We have seen that until the 1930's the population of the New York Metropolitan Region was growing faster than that of the nation. The Region's labor force, too, seems to have expanded at a pace which matched the nation's growth. Something was taking up the slack. The "something," of course, was the Region's heavy emphasis on office activities—on finance, central offices, and other business services—and its comparatively slim commitment to agriculture and mining. The manpower requirements for office activities were growing everywhere so much faster than those for manufacturing (and so very much faster than those for agriculture or mining) that any area heavily committed to office activities and substantially lacking in agricultural and mining pursuits was bound to show unusual growth. In fact—and this is an important point to which we shall return more than once—such an area did not even have to expand its office jobs as rapidly as the nation was doing in order to show a relatively rapid total job growth; its specialization in this fast-growing segment of national activity was enough to buoy its total growth

rate. This is what seems to have been happening in the
New York Metropolitan Region.*

While the Region's place in the nation's economy
was changing, the relation of the various parts of the
Region to one another was changing fully as fast. From
1900, when construction of the first subway began, to
1931, when the George Washington Bridge opened for
traffic, the movement of people within the Region was
transformed. The subways and "els" pushed across the
Harlem River to the Bronx and across the East River
to Brooklyn and Queens; tunnels were thrust under the
Hudson River to New Jersey; and bridges proliferated,
supplementing and ultimately displacing the ferries.

The new means of transport offered an escape for
some people from the aging structures of the old cities
where their parents had first settled. As a result, in
these early decades of the twentieth century, the major
cities of the Region—New York, Newark, Jersey City,
Bridgeport, Yonkers, Paterson, and Elizabeth—began to
show signs of a slowing up in population growth. In
fact, the very oldest parts of these older areas began to
lose in population. By 1910, a few ancient sections of
Manhattan were already beginning to show population
declines as boarders decamped from their temporary
resting places on beds in the kitchen and as children
came of age and set up their own families "uptown" in
Harlem and the Bronx. By 1920, as Chart 5 shows,
Manhattan as a whole was experiencing an absolute
decline in population. The chart shows, too, that Manhattan's "central business district" (everything south of
Central Park), containing the oldest areas on the island,
was falling precipitately in population.

* The data prior to 1929 are too fragmentary to demonstrate this point directly. This conclusion therefore is derived
inferentially from various fragments of information. But there
is no serious doubt of its accuracy. For a more satisfactory
test of the hypothesis in a later period, see the next chapter.

Meanwhile, obsolescence was pushing some groups farther outward into what we shall call the Inner Ring of the Region's counties. The lower panel of Chart 5 shows that in the first three decades of the century the Inner Ring increased its population at a faster rate than the other two main zones of the Region: the Core and the Outer Ring.* Though the five-cent fare was a powerful attraction to remain in the City for the many who worked at modest jobs in the lofts, stores, and offices of Manhattan and Brooklyn, it was much less of an attraction to people with higher incomes. For these, there was the suburban service of the Delaware, Lackawanna & Western to East Orange; there was the New York Central's express service to Scarsdale and White Plains; there was the New Haven's fast ride to Pelham; and so on in various directions. Spaciousness could be bought at the price of an expensive but not too time-consuming train ride. As long as one could settle within easy walking distance of the suburban station, the suburbs were an escape to an environment where children could play and where gardens—and peers—could be cultivated.

Finally, there were the very rich—small in number but important in their ability to command precious space close to the central business district of the City if they chose. Well before the period we are now examining, throughout the history of the City, the very rich had maintained homes close to the center of things. Indeed, in order to be a part of the social life of the City in the pre-automobile age, a family found it in-

* For a map of the three zones, see Chart 11. The Core consists of the four major boroughs of New York City and Hudson County immediately across the Hudson River. The Inner Ring consists of the fifth borough of New York City (Richmond) and the counties of Union, Essex, Passaic, Bergen, Westchester, and Nassau. The Outer Ring consists of the counties of Monmouth, Middlesex, Somerset, Morris, Rockland, Orange, Dutchess, Putnam, Fairfield, and Suffolk.

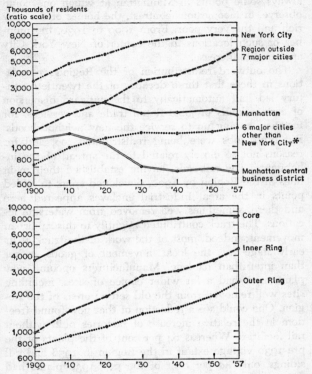

CHART 5 Population by Parts of New York Metropolitan Region, 1900–1957

Thousands of residents
(ratio scale)

New York City
Region outside 7 major cities
Manhattan
6 major cities other than New York City*
Manhattan central business district

Core
Inner Ring
Outer Ring

* Newark, Jersey City, Bridgeport, Yonkers, Paterson, and Elizabeth. The 1957 estimates for the four New Jersey cities are based on births and deaths only, and do not take account of migration; complete data would probably show that the six cities as a group, between 1900 and 1957, either gained very little population or actually declined.

Source: U. S. *Census of Population,* 1900 through 1950. The 1957 estimates are based on U. S. Special Census of April 1, 1957 (Series P–28, No. 1036), and on population estimates by state departments of health.

dispensable to have a town house within carriage ride of the opera, the theatres, and the hotels. So there were always some points in Manhattan at which one could observe, in incongruous contrast, the homes of the very rich and the very poor. From 1900 to 1930, the number of such locations in the center of New York City appeared to increase.

The outward redistribution of the Region's populations in these first three decades of the twentieth century led half automatically to the outward dispersion of certain kinds of jobs. Retail trade and services, for instance, sprang up to service the new neighborhoods. But other jobs were being redistributed too, and for reasons not so closely related to the spread of the inhabitants. The railroads, having established their main lines in the Region by 1900, developed spurs to added points in the area. Industrial enclaves appeared here and there, sometimes well removed from waterside locations. The truck contributed mightily to this suburban movement; indeed, most of the work of the truck at its early stage was the local movement of goods, rather than interurban haulage. Manufacturers opening new plants now had a far wider choice of sites, including sites well removed from the old settled areas of the Region. One could see a reflection of that new-found freedom in the relative increase of factories built without rail facilities. Whereas 64 per cent of the plants of the pre-1930 vintage extant in the Region in 1956 had rail sidings, only 40 per cent of the post-1930 plants had them.

The truck gave business not only a new release from the old city centers but also a new incentive to move, for the streets of the old cities were no less obsolescent than the houses and factories. But the truck had still another effect. The early preference which industry had shown for the New Jersey side of the Region, based on the railroad facilities on the Hudson River's western shore, began to be overcome in the 1920's. No longer tied to the rails, manufacturers could begin to think of shipping to Philadelphia or Baltimore from locations in Queens or the Bronx.

This was not a dramatic reversal nor a complete one. Railroads still had to be used for the longer hauls, leaving some advantage on the New Jersey side. Besides, the truck's effect on the competition between the two river banks did not all run one way. Though plants shipping to national markets had favored the west bank of the Hudson in the pretruck era, plants and warehouses distributing locally to the New York area's stores and homes had tended to favor the east bank. The truck helped to overcome that bias as well, making it feasible to distribute to Manhattan, Yonkers, and Long Island City from a depot in Bayonne or the Jersey meadows. From a transport viewpoint, therefore, the truck tended to homogenize the Region's land area, making one place less unlike another. The newfound freedom offered by the truck, therefore, sped the tendency for industry to grow more rapidly in the newer areas of the Region wherever they might be. Manufacturers now could search out not only more efficient sites but also cheaper or more docile labor. And, as suggested earlier, sometimes they found such labor within the counties of the New York Metropolitan Region.*

The combination of new-found transport freedom and comparative labor conditions led to a relatively rapid growth of industry outside the older portions of the

* Reliable measures of wage rates in different parts of the Region prior to the 1920's are not to be had. The only data available are the annual wages of production workers, by counties, for 1899, 1954, and four intervening dates. These data show that in 1899 wages in the counties of the Region outside Manhattan were much lower than those in Manhattan and that they remained so for the thirty years thereafter. Subsequently, however, as we point out later, a considerable change took place.

Region. Chart 6 shows that between 1919 and 1956 the number of manufacturing jobs more than doubled in the portions of the Region outside its seven biggest cities. In contrast, the number of manufacturing jobs in Manhattan, while fluctuating in response to such national forces as depression and war, never got much beyond the 1919 mark. New York City performed only a little better. The six other cities of the Region did not even come back up to their 1919 level in later years.

Yet the Core of the metropolitan area remained attractive, even indispensable, for at least one critical kind of function, especially in manufacturing: that of spawning untried little firms. The old cities in the area afforded an environment in which a number of ingredients could be had: there was the ambitious immigrant, conscious of the fact that his foreign speech and background might hold him back in the competitive scramble on someone else's payroll; there was run-down rentable space, beginning to be discarded by plants which were departing for the open spaces or by wholesalers abandoning the old waterside areas; there were contractors and suppliers galore, of all types and specialties, willing to subcontract any job or supply any service or material. Wherever an industry existed in which a small plant would not be hopelessly outclassed by a larger one—in women's dresses, for instance, but not in electric lamps—the immigrant businessman or his son could see a chance for success. Jobs in these categories, therefore, continued to buoy the economic existence of the older portions of the Region, especially of lower Manhattan.

THE MODERN ERA

As we come down to the three decades of the Region's history since 1929, we are already alerted to some

CHART 6 Manufacturing Production Workers by
Parts of New York Metropolitan Region,
1869–1956

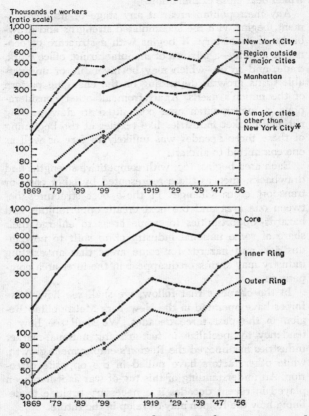

* Newark, Jersey City, Bridgeport, Yonkers, Paterson, and
Elizabeth.

Note: "Neighborhood, hand and building" industries were
included before 1899 and excluded after 1899. For 1899,
however, the figures were available both ways.

Source: For 1869 to 1947, U. S. *Census of Manufactures;*
for 1956, data collected by state departments of labor under
unemployment insurance programs, adjusted for comparability to the Census series.

of the critical forces working on the Region as a whole which bear close examination.

Any metropolitan area, at any stage of its development, begins with the accumulated strengths and drawbacks of its history. It begins with a structure of economic activity—a mixture of manufacturing, office work, trade, and so on—which may be favorable or unfavorable to its growth, depending on the changing pattern of the nation's needs. Apart from all other considerations, a metropolitan area committed to slow-growing national-market industries like textiles at the beginning of these three decades was unlikely to fare as well as one committed to aircraft.

Each area begins, too, with competitive strengths and drawbacks, such as those represented by labor costs or transport costs. Changes in these cost structures between one area and the next create opportunities and hazards—opportunities for some areas to enlarge their share of some national industry or to shift to new industries, and hazards for some areas that an existing industry may shrink or disappear in the inter-area competition.

In the chapters that follow, we shall see how these forces have operated in the New York Metropolitan Region in the past three decades. We shall see how a tendency to specialize in fast-growing national-market industries has buoyed the Region's employment growth, while other factors have pulled in the opposite direction. An understanding of this tug-of-war as it has been played in recent decades is a necessary prelude to defining how the Region may develop in the future.

3

Growth in the Region's Industries

In tracing the evolution of an area, it is always something of a distortion to mark the end of one era and the beginning of another. One era flows into another with a continuity which denies such arbitrary phasing. But, for the analyst concerned with the future economic performance of the New York Metropolitan Region, 1929 does mark a kind of turning point. From this date on, hard quantitative data begin to be sufficiently plentiful so that he can ask and effectively answer some difficult questions about the underlying basis for the Region's growth.

In our review of history we saw two different kinds of forces at play on the New York Metropolitan Region. Part of the Region's growth seemed to depend on changes in the nation's wants for some product to whose output the Region was heavily committed. New York's prior commitment to the manufacture of ready-to-wear clothing, for instance, was a factor in its growth late in the nineteenth century, when the nation's demand for such clothing mushroomed. Another part of the Region's growth, however, seemed to depend on the improvement or deterioration of its competitive position in some existing line. The Region is seen enlarging its position as a port of entry in the first half of the nineteenth century, for instance, partly at the expense of many smaller ports. And it is seen losing a share of its port business later on, to the competition of other big port centers.

We are led to ask, therefore, how much of New York's growth in recent decades could be ascribed to the fact that it possessed a "mix" of comparatively fast-growing industries, and how much of its changing position could be ascribed to a shift in its competitive position in the nation.

The distinction is critical to our story. For, in the pages that follow, we shall be demonstrating time and again that the New York Region's total employment performance can be thought of as the net product of two countervailing tendencies—a strong mix and a weak competitive position.[1] In most of this chapter, we shall concentrate on the question of mix, leaving until later an exploration of the forces behind the New York area's changing competitive position.

THE MIX OF GOODS AND SERVICES

By 1929, the evolutionary process which we highlighted in Chapter 2 had produced an economic structure for the New York Metropolitan Region quite different from that of the nation. Already the Region's economy was heavily committed to certain specialized types of office activity, such as the activity associated with finance and with the central offices of industrial corporations; and its commitment to agriculture and mining had shrunk almost to the vanishing point.

Figures adequately reflecting the Region's pattern of specialization do not exist for as early as 1929, but those for 1956 shown in Table 1 will serve well enough to illustrate the point. Though the Region had only 10 per cent of the nation's national-market jobs in the aggregate, the Region contained 39 per cent of the nation's national-market wholesaling jobs, 35 per cent of the national-market finance jobs, and 23 per cent of the national-market jobs in business and professional services. Specialization in offices has exerted a boosting effect on the employment growth of the Region. For, during the last thirty years, as in the thirty years prior, national employment grew much faster in such lines as finance, real estate, and business services than it did in manufacturing, mining, or agriculture.

The foregoing figures, however, do not reflect the full strength of the mix of the New York Region's economy. We shall demonstrate in the pages ahead that many of its manufacturing activities, its wholesale trades, its office activities, even its retail lines, have certain distinguishing traits which tend to set them apart from activities similarly labeled in the nation as a whole. In the field of manufacturing, in particular, the Region's uniqueness has added to the strength of its employment mix. In 1929, for instance, there were quite a number of manufacturing industries concentrated in the Region which were destined to show rapid national growth in the decades ahead. Examples were radio manufacturing, electric lamps, medical instruments and supplies, scientific instruments, and children's coats and outerwear. Even industries like blouses, waterproof outergarments, artists' materials, leather goods, hairwork, and lapidary, though not increasing their output spectacularly, were destined to show considerable employment growth. In sum, the Region's manufacturing mix has been so strong that if every national-market industry in the Region had grown in employment as fast as its national counterpart, the Region's total growth in national-market manufacturing jobs would have outdistanced the nation's growth in such jobs.

Table 3 presents the comparison on which this conclusion is based.[2] The figures pertain to a somewhat smaller area than the 22-county New York Metropolitan Region, but by all tests the smaller area represents the Region with a high degree of accuracy for present purposes. This table shows the growth rate which the New York area's employment could have been expected to achieve if each of the national-market manufacturing industries covered by the table had grown at the same rate as the nation in the same industries. We call the resulting hypothetical growth rate for the New York area its "expected" growth rate—though some have argued they would hardly have "expected" it. In any case, the table shows that the expected rate for the New York area was faster than the growth rate for the nation as a whole in two of three periods between 1929 and 1954, and was almost identical with the nation in the other period. Taking the 1929–1954 period as a unit, we see that the expected growth rate of the New York area's mix of national-market industries was considerably higher than the nation's growth rate for national-market industries.[3]

For many who claim familiarity with New York's economy, this conclusion will go down hard. The conclusion that the New York area's national-market manufacturing employment would have grown faster than United States national-market manufacturing employment if each splinter had grown like the nation—this is a view which flies in the face of well-entrenched preconceptions to the contrary. We tend to think of the kind of consumer soft-goods industries in which the New York area specializes as industries with comparatively slow growth characteristics; yet when employment is our measurement the contrary proves to be the case. As Table 3 shows, the New York area's mix consisted of the faster-growing segments of the consumer-goods industries and the faster-growing segments of other industries as well. So, even though consumer soft goods are prominent in the area's economy, the economy's reliance on the faster-growing splinters of consumer goods

TABLE 3   U. S. Actual Growth Rate and New York Area's[a] "Expected" Growth Rate of Employment in National-Market Manufacturing Industries, 1929–1954

Percentage change in employment

	1929– 1954[b]	1929– 1939	1939– 1947	1947– 1954
All national-market industries				
U. S. actual	+65.3	+0.1	+53.3	+7.8
New York expected	+82.8	+6.9	+50.0	+14.0
Predominantly consumer goods				
U. S. actual	+46.0	+12.2	+26.6	+2.8
New York expected	+66.0	+18.5	+30.0	+7.8
Predominantly intermediate goods				
U. S. actual	+77.0	+0.5	+60.6	+9.7
New York expected	+97.6	−0.6	+65.3	+20.0
Mixed consumer and intermediate				
U. S. actual	+67.2	−15.5	+83.0	+8.1
New York expected	+88.7	−10.8	+84.1	+14.9

[a] In this table and the other tables in this chapter, "New York area" means something less than the 22-county New York Metropolitan Region, because manufacturing statistics by groups of industries are not available for the entire Region for the earlier years. For 1929 to 1947, "New York area" means the 12-county "New York Industrial Area" which contained 87 per cent of the Region's manufacturing employees in 1947. For 1947 to 1954, it means the 17-county Standard Metropolitan Area, which contained 92 per cent of the Region's manufacturing employees in 1954.

[b] Figures obtained by linking sub-periods.

Source: Underlying data from U. S. *Census of Manufactures.* Techniques of computations explained in Robert M. Lichtenberg's book in this series, *One-Tenth of a Nation* (Cambridge: Harvard University Press, 1960), Appendices C and D.

and the faster-growing splinters of other industries produces the over-all result.[4]

EMPLOYMENT GROWTH AND INCOME GROWTH DISTINGUISHED

There is more, however, to the story of the Region's industry mix. Though the Region's manufacturing industries are of the kind which has enjoyed comparatively rapid job growth in the nation, they are not the kind which has generated an equally rapid growth in income—in payrolls, in profits, and in taxes—relative to the nation.

This conclusion comes from an analysis very like the kind we have just presented. However, instead of analyzing the *employment* growth rates of the New York area's manufacturing industries, we examine the *"value added"* by such industries. The value added by any industry is just what the expression implies: it is the difference between the value of goods produced by the plants in any industry and the value of the materials, fuel, and power they have bought from others. That difference consists principally of payrolls, profits, and taxes, though some other minor items are also included.[5]

Table 4 summarizes the national growth rates of the New York area's national-market industries, as measured in value-added terms. As the table shows, the New York area's industries have produced changes in value added at rates which have differed little from those of the nation as a whole. Where differences do occur, more often than not they suggest a slower growth rate for New York's industry mix than for the nation's mix. This is a picture quite different from the one based on employment change. When employment change was the measuring stick, it will be remembered, the New York area's industry mix had appeared appreciably stronger than that of the nation; here the picture is one of much less strength.

What do these differences between value-added growth and employment growth imply? They suggest that the mix of manufacturing activity buoyed employment in the New York Metropolitan Region more than

TABLE 4   U. S. Actual Growth Rate and New York Area's[a] "Expected" Growth Rate of Value added by National-Market Manufacturing Industries, 1929–1954

	Percentage change in value added			
	1929–1954[b]	1929–1939	1939–1947	1947–1954
All national-market industries				
U. S. actual	+293.3	−22.0	+227.0	+54.2
New York expected	+254.4	−21.4	+203.0	+48.8
Predominantly consumer goods				
U. S. actual	+189.4	−26.2	+208.0	+27.3
New York expected	+174.2	−25.2	+202.2	+21.3
Others				
U. S. actual	+328.4	−20.0	+233.0	+60.8
New York expected	+313.6	−17.5	+203.5	+65.2

Notes and source, same as Table 3.

it did personal income. And they point to one reason why employment in the Region has shown greater strength relative to the nation than personal income in the Region has shown.*

* The manufacturing mix factor is not the only reason, nor perhaps even the principal one, for the relatively slow growth of personal income in the Region. Another is the shift out of agriculture into manufacturing which has been typical of much of the nation. Compare Richard A. Easterlin, "Interregional Differences in Per Capita Income, Population and Total Income, United States, 1840–1950," *Studies in Income and Wealth*, Vol. 24 (being prepared by the National Bureau of Economic Research).

The value-added characteristics of the Region's industry, while shedding light on one issue, only raise another. Why does the area tend to specialize in industries whose value-added growth is comparatively weak? What is there about the area's history or about its current endowments which generates this emphasis? This is a long story, on which Chapter 5 will throw some light. Meanwhile, however, there is one major issue to be examined here.

EXPECTATIONS AND PERFORMANCE

It was suggested earlier that the actual employment growth of the New York Metropolitan Region's national-market activities since 1929 could be thought of as being the result of two kinds of forces: the strength of the mix of the area's industries, as measured by the national growth rate of employment in those industries, and the ability of the Region to compete with other areas in the nation—to maintain or enlarge its share of employment in each industry where competition with other areas exists.

So far in this chapter, we have looked entirely at the first part of the dichotomy. We have measured the national rates of employment growth in the Region's industries. But we have not yet determined whether, for the period since 1929, the Region has managed to hang onto or enlarge its shares in the various economic sectors in which it specializes.

Outside manufacturing, the evidence is fragmentary. What there is of it suggests that the Region's share of the nation's nonmanufacturing employment serving national markets was on the decline between 1947 and 1956—at least this seems to be true in the home offices of life insurance companies and a few other activities.

In manufacturing, the statistics are much clearer. The predominant tendency for the national-market manufacturing activities is to grow more slowly in the Region than in the nation. This does not mean that *every* such industry followed that course; some showed the opposite tendency. But when all the disparate movements are added up into a single measure of competitive perform-ance, it is clear that the Region's industries, on the average, have been growing more slowly than their na-tional counterparts.

Such an average measure can be seen in Table 5 for the national-market manufacturing industries of the New York area. Here we compare the actual growth of these

TABLE 5   Actual and "Expected" Growth Rates of Employment in National-Market Manufacturing Industries in New York Area,[a] 1929–1954

Percentage change in employment

	1929–1954[b]	1929–1939	1939–1947	1947–1954
All national-market industries				
Actual	+63.4	+3.2	+47.0	+7.7
Expected	+82.8	+6.9	+50.0	+14.0
Transport-sensitive				
Actual	+52.0	−1.0	+55.4	−1.2
Expected	+65.2	−0.3	+62.1	+2.2
External-economy				
Actual	+58.5	+14.6	+29.4	+6.9
Expected	+67.0	+15.9	+28.7	+11.9
Labor-sensitive				
Actual	+27.0	+1.5	+58.5	−21.0
Expected	+56.3	+5.3	+65.0	−10.0
"Footloose"				
Actual	+112.0	−24.1	+58.9	+75.8
Expected	+224.7	+3.3	+68.5	+86.5
Unclassified				
Actual	+66.1	−11.2	+77.2	+5.5
Expected	+93.9	−6.8	+82.8	+13.8

Notes and sources, same as Table 3.

industries in the area with "expected growth" as we defined it earlier—that is, with the growth these industries as a whole would have had if each of them had grown at the national rate.

The table shows up the competitive weakness of the New York area after 1929. At the same time, the table reintroduces some categories first encountered in Chapter 1. Breaking down the national-market industries of the New York area into five groups, it shows that a group of industries we have called "transport-sensitive" and the group labeled "external-economy" industries have performed only a little short of expectation—that the really big differences have appeared in three other groups. Later on, we shall explain why some of these groups performed better than others in the New York area.

The picture of the New York area's competitive performance since 1929, therefore, can be summarized in fairly simple terms. The area entered the period with a mix of economic activity conducive to fast growth—faster growth, on the whole, than the rate of growth in the nation. But this promise was not realized. Instead, competitive forces chiseled away at the area's share in many industries, producing a growth rate which on the whole seems to have been a little less rapid than that of the nation.

We are left, therefore, with two kinds of questions to be answered for the future: granted that the New York Metropolitan Region has heretofore attracted national industries with fast-growing national employment, will this be the pattern of the future? And, whatever the answer may be to that question, will the Region continue to slip in competitive position in the industries comprising its mix? These are the questions to which the next few chapters are addressed.

4

Labor and Freight

The competitive slippage of the New York Metropolitan
Region in one segment of economic activity after another almost invites one to look for some simple all-
pervasive reason for the Region's performance. For example, can we attribute this general slippage in the
Region's employment position to the fact that populations have been moving west and generating new industry and commerce in their localities to serve themselves? Even more broadly, can we simply assume that
"old" areas necessarily expand more slowly than "new"
ones, in accordance with some basic "law of growth"?

These are attractive propositions. But they beg too
many questions and leave too much unexplained. Why
exactly need one assume that "old" areas grow slower
than "new" ones? The New York Metropolitan Region,
though crowded in its central parts, is not "old" in the
sense that land in the whole area has become a scarce
commodity. Only a quarter of its 7,000 square miles
are blanketed with homes and factories. Thousands of
square miles in the Region remain to be developed,
available at prices not much different from land on the
outskirts of Tucson, Colorado Springs, or Houston.

Besides, if one had relied uncritically on the proposition that old areas grow slower than new, or that areas in the East grow slower than those in the West, he would have been misled numerous times in the past in his appraisal of growth prospects in the New York Metropolitan Region. Throughout the latter part of the nineteenth century and the early decades of the twentieth century, the Region managed to keep pace with the nation's growth, long after the eastern seaboard as a whole had settled down to a slower pace of expansion. And, finally, if one were to accept some general propositions about "old" and "new" areas as an explanation of the Region's behavior, he would be at a loss to account for the fact that some splinters of economic activity in the Region have breasted the seemingly general decline and have actually grown in relation to their counterparts elsewhere.

There is no escaping the need, therefore, to take a close look at the Region's position in the nation. And, as an introduction, it will help to recall the figures presented in Table 2, relating to the Region's national-market manufacturing industries. This table showed that industries whose location is dominated by transport-cost considerations are less important in the New York Metropolitan Region than they are in the nation; that industries critically reliant on labor factors have about the same relative importance in the Region as in the nation; and that the lion's share of the Region's manufacturing activity falls in a group of industries reliant on so-called external economies.

But these facts help only slightly in suggesting what forces are likely to affect the future competitive position of the Region. For one thing, they are confined to national-market manufacturing; and though the statistics in our very first table in Chapter 1 dramatized the need to stress manufacturing in our analysis, the locational factors affecting other national-market activities of the Region cannot be safely ignored. A much more basic reason why one must go beyond the intelligence in Table 2, however, is this: An industry concentrated in the Region for external-economy reasons may still trickle steadily outward not because of a relative change in the Region's external economies but because of a labor handicap; and an industry concentrated in the Region because of its need for skilled labor may grow faster elsewhere because of transport considerations. The breakdown in Table 2, therefore, is no substitute for an examination of the competitive factors, one by one. Two of the most critical matters which bear looking into are the Region's position as a labor market and the Region's position with respect to the movement of freight.

THE LABOR MARKET

In most manufacturing plants, the cost of labor bulks larger than any other item except the cost of materials —larger than the amount spent on rent, freight, power, or local taxes. The 1956 wage bill of the nation's manufacturing enterprises as a whole came to 55 per cent of the "value added" by those enterprises. In wholesaling, payrolls made up about 50 per cent of total operating expenses, according to the 1954 federal Census.[1] In most lines of office work—in life insurance companies and in the central offices of large national producers, for instance—the wage and salary bill is even larger in relation to rent, local taxes, and similar costs.

Wages not only are a big element of costs—they also vary greatly from one locality to the next. For some kinds of labor, the differences in wage levels between a metropolitan area in the Northeast and one in the South, for instance, can easily be on the order of 15 or 25 per cent. A heavy *prima facie* case exists for the view that labor costs must be a powerful force deciding where jobs are to be located.

THE FORCE OF HIGH WAGES

For as long as anyone has been able to measure it, the New York area has shown up as a market where labor commanded a relatively high wage. New York's printers were complaining about the high wage levels of the area as early as 1815; more than one hundred years later, in 1919, union rates in key occupations in the printing industry were higher in New York than in any other city except Chicago. Union rates in other industries tell very much the same story. During the first three decades of the twentieth century, in one occupation after another, New York emerges as one of the highest-wage urban centers in the nation. This does not mean, of course, that the wages of every occupation in every industry were higher in New York than elsewhere. Green immigrant labor in the New York area accepted wages which probably were not very different from the lowest prevailing in other parts of the country.

In the mid-1950's, the wage levels prevailing in the New York Metropolitan Region, taken industry for industry and occupation for occupation, were still very high by comparison with those in other parts of the country. There is no very neat way of summarizing the statistics underlying this conclusion; these are developed in considerable detail in one of the volumes of this series.[2] Collectively, the figures show that the *general average* of the Region's wages and salaries is lower than that of a number of other large metropolitan areas, simply because the Region's economy is heavily weighted with industries which, in the nation as a whole, pay low wages relative to other industries. But the significant fact for purposes of locational analysis is that within many individual industries, including the very industries that loom largest in the Region and pull the Region's *general average* down, the Region's employers pay high wages compared with their competitors elsewhere. In important industry after industry, the New York area offers the highest wage level of any large metropolitan area on the eastern seaboard, and a very much higher wage level than that typical of the nation's towns and rural areas. The metropolitan areas of the Midwest outdo the New York area in industries which are a part of the metals complex, and the Pacific Coast's metropolitan areas offer comparatively high wages in various local-market industries such as power laundries. But the relatively high competitive position of the New York wage level is incontestable. When fringe benefits are taken into account—benefits such as paid holidays and vacations, health and welfare benefits, and retirement contributions—New York's high wage level is even more pronounced.

The New York Metropolitan Region's long-term experience with high wage rates suggests a number of propositions. One is that the wage level of the Region has been much more a consequence than a cause of its economic development. The sort of economic activity which was attracted first of all by the Port of New York and later by other unique attributes of the area was prepared to pay higher wages in the Region, if necessary, in order to operate there. Indeed, the high wage level may have been necessary to draw in some of the essential talents from other parts of the nation.

A corollary point is that, with respect to competition with other areas, a considerable segment of any economy like the Region is largely impervious to differences in wage levels. A little reflection will indicate why this is so. In the first place, there are the activities which are anchored to an urban area, willy-nilly, whatever its wage level, simply because they must be close to the market they serve. Consumer trades and services fall in this category; so do local government and some state and federal government activities; so, too, do most construction activities and some local manufacturing operations, like newspapers, bakeries, and bottling works. All told, this group adds up to a considerable part of the labor force, something like three-fifths in the New York Metropolitan Region today.

A number of other groups are anchored to a high wage area like New York because of the area's external economies. In some cases, a single establishment in a complex, by itself, cannot move out of the area unless a much larger group will move with it. Some of these groups are tied together by the fact that they form part of a larger marketplace to which buyers from outside the area are wont to come; we find this situation in some lines of wholesaling, for instance, such as toys, furniture, and dry goods. Some are tied to the area because they rely on common sources of materials or labor or services which no one firm is in a position to provide for itself. Some are tied there because they offer products or services to their customers on specification and on short notice; these have found no way of serving their market thus far except to be located at the customer's doorstep; the makers of braids and buttons, the printers of advertising matter and lawyers' briefs, the testing laboratories for chemicals, metals, paper, and fabrics, the purveyors of legal and management and accounting advice, all of these in one way or another fit the bill. We shall have more to say about all these "clustering" groups in the chapter that follows; here, it is enough to point out that their role in the Region is not inconsiderable, coming to about one-fourth of its labor force.

Then there is the group which has no strong incentive to avail itself of lower wages elsewhere, either because price competition is fairly weak in the industry or because the firms involved cannot afford to abandon the capital they have sunk into their New York area plants, or for both reasons in combination. Take the case of an automobile assembly plant such as Ford maintains at Mahwah, New Jersey, or the Republic aircraft plant at Farmingdale, on Long Island. Companies in industries of this sort, operating a number of plants in various locations throughout the country, typically maintain a fairly uniform wage in all their plants for any given line of work. Partly, this is because such industries, lacking a strong incentive to resist, have accepted a pattern of nationwide wage bargaining. This acceptance has been due in turn to the fact that price competition in the sale of automobiles, aircraft, and similar products does not occupy quite the role in the fortunes of the firm which it does in products whose brand names are a matter of indifference to the consumer. Firms in lines which are not subject to strong price competition, therefore, are much more prone to accept uniform nationwide wage patterns for their plants and to locate those plants without much regard for the going rates in local areas.

There are other types of plants whose management is fairly impervious to such local wage differences as may exist. There are the oil refineries and the producers of pharmaceutical preparations, whose labor costs are so insignificant in relation to other costs that they cannot save very much by searching out locations with low wage levels. And there are some large manufacturers turning out products requiring very high skill, such as special-purpose machinery, who have misgivings about their ability to recruit or train a large, highly skilled labor force in another locality within a reasonable period of time. In all these cases, the firms involved see only limited opportunities to profit from the lower wages of another area, while they see considerable loss involved in the cost of scrapping the physical capital or the or-

ganization which they have created in the New York
Metropolitan Region.

All told, as best we have been able to classify them,
the diverse industries which are indifferent to area wage
differences—apart from those which we have already
referred to in the external-economy group—account for
about 18 per cent of the Region's labor force. One can
think of this miscellaneous group as being somewhat
insulated from the attraction of lower wage areas, with
the insulation laid on quite thickly in some situations
and rather thinly in others. Lower wages alone would
rarely be a sufficient reason for *relocating* any of these
plants. But lower wages might provide a moderate incentive for some—those not inexorably committed to
uniform national wage patterns—to prefer other areas
when locating new facilities. This is one group, therefore, in which the New York Metropolitan Region's high
wage level could be thought of as a potential drag on
expansion, though not one of the first importance.

This brings us at last to a group whose continued
existence in the New York Metropolitan Region hangs
critically on its ability to find wages low enough to
match outside competitors. Almost by definition, this
must be a comparatively tiny group and a continually
changing group, for no large group of this sort could
possibly survive for very long in a high wage area like
the Region.

Time was when the needs of this group had been
nurtured from the boatloads of immigrant labor pour-
ing in a steady stream through New York's harbor.
But, by the second and third decades of the twentieth
century, this supply was already drying up. So it was
that plants in the men's clothing industry and in the
simpler and cheaper lines of women's apparel, faced
with the competition of lower wages from small towns
and agricultural areas, began to leave New York for
these areas. The fact that they chose that particular

period to begin their exodus from the New York area could not be laid solely to the change in immigration, of course. Other conditions emerged to make the change possible. One of these was the truck, which allowed manufacturers to shuttle cloth and garments between New York and the country districts—to cut, finish, and eventually sell the garments in the New York area, while sewing them in the country locations. Another condition, perhaps inseparable from the first, was the ability of the industry to reorganize its production methods; first, to sew garments on a more standardized system, in which unskilled or semiskilled workers replaced the skilled tailor, and second, to perform sewing operations on an assembly-line basis in one kind of establishment while performing the designing, cutting, finishing, and merchandising in another kind of shop in New York. This sort of change freed the industries from their compelling need to keep their entire operation as a part of the New York area complex, a need which had arisen from the problems of communication and from the advantages of sharing in the use of the Region's unique facilities. Thus a large group of industries, once fairly impervious to the competitive wage rates of other areas, became overwhelmingly sensitive to them—at least in the more standardized lines of their production.

At any point in time in the Region's development, one can find a few such industries in the Region's industrial make-up—industries being freed from some previous need to settle in the Region, industries in process of responding to the pull of lower wages in other localities. (At any point in time, too, as we shall see later on, one can find some new industries—indifferent for the time being to lower wages elsewhere—shaping up in the Region to take the place of the old.) At the present time, one can identify splinters of activity in a dozen or so industries in the Region which are under heavy pressure from their competitors in lower wage areas.

Because Census classifications are so crude, some of
these splinters fall in industries classified as being dominated, in a locational sense, by their pervasive and still-
existing need for external economies. Some of the lower-
priced lines in women's apparel; some of the less
exacting or more standardized segments of electronics
production; a few branches of the printing industry,
such as those which turn out standard office forms in
long runs; these and others have a real incentive to
search out new localities where labor costs are lower.
All told, they are estimated to number on the order
of 60,000 to 80,000 jobs in the Region, about 1 per cent
of its labor force. But this number does not stand still.
Next year, technological change in one industry or another may add more plants to the group; and the year
after, still others. This is the process by which wage
rate differences really exert their influence on the Region's growth.

THE IMPLICATION OF CONVERGENCE

Everything changes—not only technology but wage
levels as well. And the businessman who is locating an
enterprise is bound to ask not only how wage levels
stand today but also how they are likely to stand in the
future.

Looking at the history of wages in the New York
Metropolitan Region and the rest of the country, one
may well ask if the New York area's high wage position
will last for many more decades. There is some evidence, for instance, that wage levels in different parts
of the nation have been converging in recent years.
Looking at the southern states as a group, for instance,
one can detect the fact that the wage rates have been
rising there more rapidly than those in the higher wage
regions. What is more, it appears that in a variety of
industries for which a check could be made, the gap

between wages in the New York area and wages in other competing metropolitan areas was being closed somewhat during the period after World War II.

Yet we are disposed to the view that, despite these indications of convergence, very little real change is occurring in the New York area's competitive handicap vis-à-vis low wage areas. And very little added change is likely to occur in the two or three decades ahead.

Why? To answer the question, we must go behind the cold figures and look at some of the processes which have been bringing about the seeming convergence of wage rates in the various areas of the nation. One of these, of course, is the minimum wage laws. There is little evidence to be had regarding the impact of the minimum wage laws on the competitive position of the Region's industries. But what there is suggests that the 75-cents-an-hour minimum established in 1950 and the $1.00 minimum promulgated in 1956 were too low to have much effect on the Region's position. For instance, the 75-cent minimum, as nearly as we can guess, raised the wages of women's dress workers in Dallas, Texas, by only about 3 per cent in 1950; and the $1.00 minimum in 1956 may have increased these wages by another 4.5 per cent. Yet Dallas was then, and still is, one of the lowest wage areas in the industry. In smaller Texas communities the effect may have been a little greater. But this kind of increase would not relieve New York producers to any significant extent from the competitive pressures emanating from such areas. Moreover, as experience in other industries shows, this narrowing is only transitory and tends to disappear as rising wage levels lift all rates above the earlier legal minimums.

Another force pushing up the low wage structure of the nation's underdeveloped hinterlands is the rapid rate of industrialization in these areas. Manufacturing workers have been growing in number in some of the very areas of the nation where wage rates are lowest —in the South Atlantic states and the Gulf Coast states, for instance. For example, as chemical plants have come into these areas, bringing their high wage structure with them from other parts of the country, they have inevitably pulled up the going wage wherever they have appeared. Even textile plants, though their wages may be low by comparison with other kinds of industry, have typically offered opportunities above the going wage in those areas.

Yet the appearance of industry in the agricultural hinterlands has not yet occurred on so large a scale as to mop up the heavy supply of labor overhanging the market in these areas. Part of the supply is the result of the forces we described in Chapter 2—the swift increase in productivity on the farms in recent decades, without a corresponding increase in the demand for farm products. With each generation, the sons of farmers have found themselves idle on the land, with no reason for clinging to the soil and every incentive to find a job in industry. Part of the supply is a product of the high birth rate of farm areas, especially in the Southeast— a noticeably higher rate than that in the nation's larger metropolitan centers including New York. A rough estimate shows that in 1955 the birth rate of rural areas was 16 per cent higher than that of the New York Metropolitan Region.

Nor has the migration of farmers' sons to the cities done much to drain off the surplus rural labor and shift it to the labor-scarce urban areas. It is true that such migration has been going on. For instance, between 1950 and 1955, most of the rural states in the West North Central division and the South showed some net out-migration, while in-migration was evident for the Middle Atlantic states, the East North Central states around the Great Lakes, and especially the Pacific states. But the rate of out-migration of low wage areas has been just about enough to offset the differences in birth rates between urban and nonurban states, hardly more.[3] And it still leaves on tap the large rural "secondary labor force" consisting of wives and daughters who are only waiting for a local opportunity in order to enter the labor force.

The movement of industry to the small towns and countryside and the movement of some farmers' sons to the cities have tended to pull up the *average* wage of many industries in broad sections of the country which are in competition with the New York Metropolitan Region. But these movements have not dried up the large pockets of available labor in numerous localities spread through the country, localities not yet tapped by new industry. Nor have they sopped up the surplus labor appearing in the "distressed areas" of New England and the middle Appalachian range, areas whose labor supply has been released from textiles, coal mining, and pottery production, and has found no alternative employment. For that reason, the convergence of average wage rates between different parts of the country cannot be taken as any indication that the competitive wage handicap of employers in the New York area has been reduced.

Nor has Puerto Rican migration to New York done much to set the area off from other metropolitan areas in respect to labor supply. It is true that in many ways the Puerto Rican has resembled earlier immigrants. Fresh off the boat (more likely, the plane), he has filled the most menial jobs in the labor market at the lowest wages which the market offered. In time, as various studies show, he has made his adjustment to new conditions, set his wage sights higher, added to his skills, and managed to take on a better job, leaving a vacuum to be filled by other newcomers. But Puerto Rican immigration has differed in critical respects from that of the Germans, the Irish, the Italians, and the Jews.

First of all, the Puerto Rican has had far better information about the labor market than his counterparts of earlier eras. Helped by official labor information services, by air mail from the mainland, and by the swift transit offered by the airplane, he has been able to present himself for employment at times roughly corresponding with the existence of employment opportunities. And if the job was not there, or the duties were too onerous, or the climate was too cold, Puerto Ricans have often packed up and gone home. Though earlier migration waves also rose and fell roughly with employment opportunities, there were nothing like the same possibilities for adjusting supply to demand. So the supply of Puerto Rican labor has not overhung the New York labor market in a sodden mass, ready to take on any job at any price. In fact, the 10,000 or 15,000 Puerto Rican immigrants who have been added annually to the New York labor force in recent years have made barely a ripple on the New York wage structure.

There is every reason to suppose that Puerto Ricans will come to the mainland in the future as they have in the past. Though employment opportunities in Puerto Rico are growing, the island's present and prospective birth rates are such that an exportable labor surplus seems inevitable. But this migration is likely to produce even less impact on the wage structure of the New York Metropolitan Region than it has produced in the past. For the Puerto Rican has now begun to establish family links and channels of information with other labor markets—with Philadelphia, Baltimore, Chicago, and other centers. Whereas 95 per cent of the Puerto Rican newcomers settled in New York in the 1940's, the figure is now down to 60 per cent, and should fall lower still. The New York area's shortage of low wage labor is likely to get more acute, rather than easier, compared with competing areas. Only a major change in government policy could alter this outlook.

Another force which might have been expected to produce sectional convergence in wage rates is collective bargaining. But the effect of collective bargaining in narrowing wage differentials between areas can easily be exaggerated. True, the bargains struck by such nationwide entities as the United Steel Workers of America, the United Automobile Workers of America, and the United Rubber, Cork, Linoleum and Plastics Workers of America have probably tended to reduce geographical wage differentials in their industries. But in the industries where it has mattered most for the New York Metropolitan Region, such as apparel and printing, it is doubtful that the existence of collective bargaining has done much to reduce wage differentials.

The limited effectiveness of collective bargaining in this respect stems out of a number of factors. Open-shop competition is one of them. But even in industries where union organization is extensive, the effects of collective bargaining have been limited. In the women's dress industry, for instance, the competition among different producing areas has been so fierce that local labor leaders in low wage areas have commonly been prepared to countenance the continuation of the differential in order to keep the dress plants from moving elsewhere. The differentials have been maintained by various devices, even in lines professedly organized under a uniform wage agreement for all areas.

As a matter of fact, the gradual reduction in the differences in labor-market conditions in different parts of the country, far from helping the New York Metropolitan Region's competitive position, can be said to have added to its competitive difficulties in at least one major respect. It was not many decades ago that only a few urban areas in the country provided a recruiting ground for a large number of skilled workmen, trained to factory methods. To be sure, the rural areas did not usually lack for ingenious craftsmen and tinkers, sufficient for their needs. But few areas could provide a large complement of electricians, machinists, and steamfitters, without straining the inelastic limits of the local labor supply.

One of the effects of World War II was to train men in industrial skills from remote corners of the country. Since then, the situation has continued to change rapidly. The first large plants in any rural area have acted as a training ground, developing a cadre of men skilled in factory requirements. Each succeeding plant has found it a little easier to recruit key men of this sort and has itself contributed to the training process. As a result, plants which once would have settled in the New York Metropolitan Region and other large centers for their unique capacity to provide factory skills, now are in a position to select from a much larger area and, indeed, are doing so.

The results of this changing situation are reflected in the data. The industries in the New York Metropolitan Region which, according to our classification, are heavily reliant on skilled labor have been growing somewhat more slowly in employment than one would have expected on the basis of national growth rates. Though their total employment would have been expected to grow by 18.9 per cent in the New York area between 1947 and 1954 if each industry had emulated its national growth rate, the actual growth was very close to zero. The spread of labor skills was probably not the only force at work in producing these results, but that spread was surely a contribution to the Region's lagging performance.

Looking ahead, we see nothing new to alter the expectation that the New York Metropolitan Region will continue to be a relatively high wage area. In our final chapter, we shall venture the projection that the Region will generate enough labor supply out of its own indigenous population in the next two or three decades to reduce the pressure for in-migration from the low wage areas. But this development, if it occurs, does not presage an easier labor supply situation for industries that pay low wages. An urban labor force, born and reared in the area, is unlikely to accept wages well below the going rate such as the low wage plants in the New York area are forced to pay in order to survive there. More likely, the low wage segments of industry, as they develop, will be forced continually to move outward, looking for an environment in which they can survive.

MOVING THE GOODS

The economic performance of the New York Metropolitan Region, as we pointed out in Chapter 2, has always been sensitive to changes in the movement of goods. From the time, 300 years ago, when Manhattan's tip was a lone Dutch trading post, to the latest expansion of the International Airport at Idlewild, the economic life of the area has been interwoven with the changing technology and currents of trade.

The ties between the Region's development and transportation take several rather different forms. There was a time, for instance, when the Region's ability to perform as a producing and distributing entity was greatly affected by its physical layout. Its rivers, bays, and canals once served as ideal, low-cost highways for shuttling goods from one plant to another within its borders, and added to its competitive advantages over other areas. Conversely, the narrow crowded streets of its cities today are a handicap for the internal movement of goods, and congestion sometimes plays a part in pushing industry out of the Region into other competing areas.

Another tie between the Region's economic course and transportation is created by the fact that for a long time the Region has been selling transportation services to the rest of the nation. But today, only about 200,000 jobs in the Region are tied directly to the Region's port facilities—jobs dependent primarily on the movement of goods which are simply passing through the area. And there are indications that the relative importance of this activity may decline even further.

PORT AND AIRPORT

A number of forces are at work, whittling away at the preeminence of New York as a gateway for foreign trade.

One of them is the continuous westward shift in the distribution of the country's population. This factor, of course, was in evidence long before the "modern era" of the last few decades. In 1840, only 5 per cent of United States population could be found west of the Mississippi River, but by 1900 this had risen to 28 per cent. Today it is 33 per cent and still forging upward. Meanwhile, the Northeast (consisting of New England and the Middle Atlantic states) has been showing a steady long-run decline in its share of the nation's people; and there is every reason to suppose that the decline will continue.

At the same time, there have been shifts in the importance of the various foreign countries trading with the United States. Up to 1900, the European countries accounted for over two-thirds of the foreign commerce of the United States. Since then other countries have gained as trading partners. For instance, the Asian countries increased their share of United States foreign trade from 6 to 24 per cent between the Civil War and World War II. In the same period, Canada almost tripled its share. Geographically speaking, New York cannot be regarded as the national gateway in trading with these countries as it is for European trade.

But, quite apart from the shifts in the location of the nation's population and the shifts in the identity of its trading partners, other changes are occurring adverse to the New York Port's relative position. One of these has been the growing importance—at least in tonnage terms—of the trade in bulk cargoes. Some thirty years ago, bulk cargoes—items such as coal, grain, iron ore, and petroleum, moving in boatloads and loaded and unloaded mechanically—accounted for half the tonnage of United States foreign trade; today they are more than three-fourths. Our projections of the future tonnage composition of United States ocean and foreign trade assume that this trend is likely to go further still.

In the competition for bulk cargoes, the unique advantages of the New York Port have only a limited relevance. It is in the field of general cargo, more than in bulk cargoes, that New York's facilities are of critical importance to the shipper. The general cargo shipper is interested in the frequent sailing schedules of the New York Port because his shipment is commonly too small to justify owning or chartering a whole vessel. He is interested in the special packing facilities of the New York Port because his product, unlike a ton of wheat, is likely to need careful packing. He is anxious for the services of freight forwarders and customs brokers because his shipments are likely to be neither so regular nor so large as to justify maintaining his own personnel at the Port to perform these functions. So New York's facilities for hire—its marine external economies—play a far larger role in the choice of ports by a shipper or consignee of general cargo than by a shipper or consignee of bulk cargo.

In addition to the changing composition of imports and exports, another factor has appeared in recent decades to erode the dominance of the New York Port.

This is the growing role of the truck. When the main railroad lines of America were laid down in the nineteenth century, the Port served as a powerful magnet for them. No other seaport in the country had so many railroads. The proliferation of rail lines and the growth of other parts of the country began to contribute to the erosion of New York's position as the leading port. But the truck has speeded that process considerably. Shippers situated at some point within trucking distance of Philadelphia, New York, and Baltimore—shippers in Cleveland, for instance—now choose among the ports without having to reckon with the fact that most rails still lead to New York. The advent of the truck also has changed the export rate structure, in ways which have made the port nearest the shipper or the consignee, whatever that port might be, more attractive than its distant competitors. Truck rates climb fast with distance; rail rates move up much more slowly.° A shipper once indifferent to the fact that New York was an added 100 miles away from another port, now has to count those added 100 miles as significant. More and more, therefore, shippers who use trucks to haul their products to the water's edge look to the nearest port as the most attractive gateway.

On top of this the position of the lesser ports has been improved by changes in the nation's merchant marine policy. The Merchant Marine Act of 1936, designed to put American flag vessels back in ocean trade, instituted a complex set of building and operation subsidies. Any shipping line is aware that its chances of qualifying for an operating subsidy are increased if it can count on the support of the Congressional representatives from Pennsylvania, Maryland, and other

° For instance, the first-class truck rate from Cleveland to New York is $4.00 a ton higher than that from Cleveland to Baltimore. The differential in first-class rail export rates between the two routes is only 60 cents a ton.

states. The willingness that steamship companies have manifested to list Philadelphia and Baltimore, say, as ports of call probably cannot be explained solely by the volume of business likely to be generated out of these ports. The number of scheduled sailings out of the secondary ports has grown markedly in the last three decades, as illustrated by Baltimore and New Orleans in Table 6. The increase in sailings has been considerably faster than the expansion in the volume of freight passing through these ports.

TABLE 6 Number of Sailings from New York, Baltimore, and New Orleans to Selected Foreign Ports during May 1923 and May 1957

	1923			1957		
Destination	New York	Baltimore	New Orleans	New York	Baltimore	New Orleans
London	19	7	1	11	9	9
Antwerp	10	6	1	35	20	18
Copenhagen ..	9	2	1	24	11	5
Bremen	8	2	1	28	14	17
Marseilles	7	2	4	5	2	2
Naples	8	1	1	32	12	5
Alexandria	9	0	1	10	4	1
Havana	10	5	14	33	12	20
Rio de Janeiro .	10	0	0	28	17	6
Buenos Aires ..	9	0	3	24	15	6
Hong Kong ...	7	2	0	16	14	2
Yokohama	9	2	3	24	13	19

Source: *Shipping Digest,* April 30, 1923; April 29 and May 20, 1957.

Thus, New York is forced to share its port business with other seaside cities. As the process goes on, we can expect these other cities to close the gap somewhat between the unique external economies which the New York Port provides and those which other ports can provide. As in the past, therefore, the process of shift will be self-reinforcing.

Yet, the future of the New York Metropolitan Region as a foreign trade entrepôt is not likely to be a simple extension of what went before. Novel developments are sure to alter past patterns. One of these is the recent opening of the enlarged St. Lawrence Seaway. Ocean-going vessels with considerable capacity and draft now can make their way directly to the Great Lakes area from any point on the globe. Superficially, such a development would seem to offer a major challenge to the New York Port's role in the movement of goods between the Midwest and foreign countries.

Any appraisal of the impact of the Seaway demands a detailed consideration of the interests of the many diverse shippers and consignees involved in the traffic. This subject is explored in another volume in this series.[4] In starkest outline, the analysis comes to this:

The prize at stake in the struggle between the Seaway and the New York Port is a flow of foreign trade which today represents about 25 per cent of the New York Port's exports and about 15 per cent of its imports. Each side has its point of strength in the contest. The Seaway's main point of strength is the fact that it will offer cheaper rates for the trip from some Great Lakes terminus to a foreign port. But the Seaway has drawbacks too. One, of course, is the fact that it will be closed in the winter months. Another is the likelihood that the Seaway will not develop a major port center, but will spread its business among a number of competing ports.

The latter point may prove critical to the competitive power of the Seaway. If one could envisage the development of a single vast port on the Great Lakes, representing the terminus of all Seaway trips, he might foresee the growth at that port of most of the kinds of external economies now indigenous to New York: frequent scheduled runs between that Great Lakes port and all corners of the globe; extensive packing facilities

CHART 7 Major Ports of the Great Lakes and the North Atlantic Coast

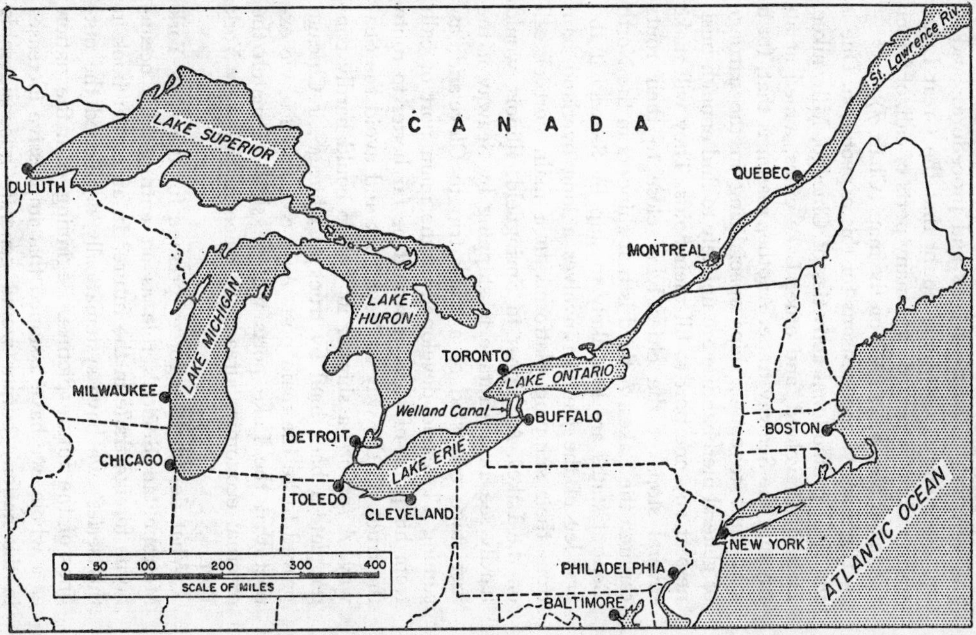

for overseas shipment; a corps of specialists, skilled in
the labyrinth of customs laws and procedures; and so
on. But there is not much doubt that the Great Lakes
trade will be dispersed over many ports of call, of which
the major ones are shown on the map (Chart 7).

There are various reasons for this expectation. One is
the rival promotional activities of Chicago, Milwaukee,
Detroit, Cleveland, and other Lake cities, aimed at attracting the Seaway trade. Another reason is that, for a
long time to come, ships specializing in the carriage
of general merchandise are unlikely to find enough business at any one port to fill their holds. They will make
several stops at the cities lying close to their route
through the Lakes. A third is that shippers in the North
Central states are less likely to ship by Seaway if the
first leg of the journey involves a long overland haul
from their shipping platforms to a main port of call
on the Lakes. A shipper in Springfield, Illinois, would
hardly see an advantage in shipping by Seaway if the
first stage consisted of a truck trip to Cleveland, assuming Cleveland developed as the main port of call;
from his point of view, it would be far better to route
the truck all the way to New York and avoid the Seaway. *A fortiori*, a shipper in Toledo could hardly con-
template a back haul by truck to Chicago, if Chicago
proved to be the main port. As a consequence, we expect that the Lake ports will be slow to match the
external economies already in place in the New York
Port.

What do all these forces presage for the New York
Metropolitan Region's role as an entrepôt for oceanborne foreign trade in the future? In an earlier book in
this series[5] we have systematically developed the outlines of the future picture. Beginning with the nation
as a whole, we have assumed that impressive increases
in the nation's output would generate a considerable
expansion in the nation's oceanborne foreign trade. Ex-

ports and imports of oceanborne general cargo are expected to rise from a 1955 level of 46.1 million long tons to 73.4 million long tons in 1985.

The New York Port's share in this expanding business is seen as declining rather considerably on the export side, from 26.8 per cent to 18.0 per cent of the nation's total. But, on the import side, where the New York Port's competitive position seems better entrenched, the ratio only changes from 28.6 per cent in 1955 to 25.0 per cent in 1985.

The outcome for the New York Port is a modest rise in tonnage, from 12.8 million long tons in 1955 to 16.1 million long tons in 1985. But the rise in tonnage generates no similar rise in employment. Everything points to a continued rapid growth in the mechanization of goods-handling on the waterfront. The containerization of foreign freight so dramatically illustrated by "fishyback"—the carrying of loaded truck trailers on ships built especially for the purpose—may be slower in coming for foreign trade than for domestic commerce. But it is coming, along with other revolutions in the methods of transferring goods between land and water. On balance, therefore, we see a decline in employment directly tied to goods-handling on New York's waterfront despite the increases in projected business.

In any projection of the New York area as a gateway for foreign trade, however, the sea provides only part of the story. Air freight, especially jet-powered air freight, is likely to play a considerable role in bending future growth patterns. Today, New York loads and unloads about one-quarter of the nation's foreign airborne freight, and the proportion is likely to grow further before it declines.

True, foreign air freight passing through New York is unlikely to use manpower on anything like the scale of waterborne traffic. Still, all the observable forces favor New York's growth, not only in an absolute sense but also in relative terms. For the present position of New York in the handling of air freight is analogous in striking ways to the position it held about 1830 in the handling of waterborne commerce.

The air carrier, like the steamship in those days, is going through a technological revolution which is rapidly producing a larger and a swifter vehicle for transport. The increased size of the craft has a number of implications. Larger air fields will be needed, and this will tend to depress the relative growth of secondary terminals for the time being, just as larger steamships choked off the growth of the secondary seaports for a time after the steamships were introduced. This is partly a question of physical facilities, but it is more than that. The jet plane operates most economically by making long hauls and few landings. Hence, a strong tendency will exist at first for the new craft to concentrate their schedules at the largest airports where the chances of taking on a full load will be greatest. For a time, the initial tendency will be self-reinforcing. Maintenance and repair facilities will spring up first in the biggest terminals, making them even more attractive for added jet runs. Specialists in superswift freight delivery will offer their services at these terminals, widening their competitive edge over smaller airports. But eventually, probably at a time beyond the scope of our forecast, other air centers will begin to close the gap afforded by New York's early start.

PLANT AND WAREHOUSE

The swift changes in transportation costs and transportation facilities over the last thirty or forty years have done much more to the New York Metropolitan Region's economic life than to alter its port and airport activity. More significant for the Region's economy has been the effects of these changes on the Region's position as a manufacturing and warehousing center. The effects of recent transportation developments have not been simple. While many segments of the New York area's economy have been losing in their competitive position in the nation's markets because of transport changes, some have actually been gaining.

Scale versus distance. To grasp the full impact of transportation changes in recent decades both for manufacturing and for warehousing, it will help, first of all, to take a brief look at the "transport-sensitive" industries—that is, industries which make their locational decisions primarily on the basis of transport conditions and therefore are especially sensitive to shifts in transport costs and transport facilities. Of course, in one measure or another, locational decisions in all industries are affected by transport considerations. But in this group a second-best location with respect to transportation would handicap a firm much more than would a second-best location with respect to labor costs, or external economies, or communication needs. Steel plants or lumber mills, for instance, would have much less concern with labor-cost differences from one area to another than with the differences in freight bills incurred at different locations. But a manufacturer of high-priced dresses, or a producer of surgical instruments, or a maker of electronic components, when deciding where to locate a plant, is fairly indifferent to the size of his freight bill and much more worried about other types of cost.

The transport-sensitive industries that are important in analyzing the role of the New York Metropolitan Region in the nation's economy are those catering to national markets—to markets broadly dispersed instead of confined to a single metropolitan area or a single section no more than a few hundred miles across. As we saw in Chapter 1, these transport-sensitive national-market industries tend to be underrepresented in the

Region. Whereas they account for 42 per cent of national-market manufacturing employment in the nation, they are only 16 per cent of national-market manufacturing employment in the Region. To put the point in another perspective, the Region has 12 per cent of the nation's manufacturing employment as a whole, but only 5 per cent of the nation's employment in these transport-sensitive national-market industries.

If we peer below the surface, however, it develops that there are many industries in the transport-sensitive group which are heavily concentrated in the Region. For example, in the primary smelting and refining of copper, or in the manufacture of brooms and brushes, or in the processing of vegetable oils, the Region has over 30 per cent of the nation's employment. On the other hand, many transport-sensitive industries of considerable importance in the nation have little representation in the Region, including such activities as steel manufacturing, gray-iron castings, meat packing, paper and paperboard manufacturing, food canning, and lumber sawing and planing.

In each case, what the figures reflect is the outcome of an interplay of two sorts of forces—the advantage of bigness and the advantage of proximity to markets. Up to a point, there are cost advantages to be gained by concentrating production in large plants. But the advantage begins to be dissipated when some of the product has to be shipped for large distances; production costs for such goods may be low, but transport costs are high. The result is that national producers in any location find at some stage in their growth that they would be wise to place branch plants in their more distant markets; otherwise they find themselves unable to meet the local competition in those markets.

This is what lies behind the figures shown in Table 7. Here, it appears that in the transport-sensitive industries highly concentrated in the New York Metropolitan

Region, the plants in the area are large as compared
with their competitors elsewhere in the nation; contrariwise, in the transport-sensitive industries which are
underrepresented in the Region, such plants as the area
contains are comparatively small. The figures suggest
that in the heavily represented industries, producers
have managed to blanket large market territories out of
their plants in the Region. Manufacturers of office and
store machines, organic chemicals, and secondary non-
ferrous metals belong to this category. In the under-

TABLE 7 Size of Plants in Transport-Sensitive
National-Market Industries, New York
Metropolitan Region and U. S., 1954

Industries classified by Region's share of national employment	Average number of employees per establishment	
	Region	U. S.
All industries	107	174
30% and over	276	139
20–30%	232	187
10–20%	106	86
5–10%	89	157
Under 5%	86	214

Sources: U. S. *Census of Manufactures* and New York Metropolitan Region Study estimates.

represented industries, the Region's producers, pressed
by competition from outside the area, have exploited
small corners of the local market; in some cases they
have relied on their savings in transport costs to hold
off outside competitors, while in others they have dif-
ferentiated their product in some way or offered special
services to the customer in order to fend off the outside
competition.[6] Factors such as these explain the presence in the Region of plants for meat packing and
poultry dressing, and for metal stamping, coating, and
engravings.

An equilibrium between transport advantages and the advantages of scale production, however, cannot hold for very long in any industry. In the last three or four decades, the transport-sensitive industries have had to reckon with the fact that transport costs have been rising faster than the general price levels. Between 1947 and 1954, for example, the average level of railroad freight charges rose 41 per cent, while the national wholesale price index increased only 14 per cent. Accordingly, plants in transport-sensitive industries have faced growing difficulties in holding onto customers who were situated farthest from the plant.

The problems of the plants in clinging to customers in distant markets have been exacerbated by another development in transport rates. Though transport rates in general have tended to rise, long-haul rates have climbed faster than those for shorter distances. The reason for this selective pattern of increases is fairly clear, going back to the fact that the economics of trucking are so different from those of railroading. Trucks, in their competition with railroads, do best in short hauls; this is because trucks incur far lower costs than trains at the terminal ends of their journey—in the pick-up and delivery of freight—and higher costs in over-the-road travel. The railroads, to meet the growing competition of the truck, have been obliged to refrain from raising short-haul rates, while concentrating their rate increases on the longer hauls. The result has been that a producer trying to serve his far western customers from a plant in the New York area has faced increasing competition from smaller competitors on the Pacific coast. At the same time, however, a Chicago producer of steel window sash, trying to supply his New York market from his Chicago plant, has also had to face stiffer competition from competitors in the New York area.

Another kind of change in the rate structure has also been pushing plants closer to their customer. In the last

few decades, rail rates on finished products have been
rising faster than those on raw materials. For example,
from 1947 to 1954 the increase in rail revenue per ton
was 43 per cent for manufactures, but only 33 per cent
for raw materials. More and more, the incentive has existed for plants to reduce the shipping distances to their
customers, even if this meant a bigger freight bill in
the assembly of their raw materials.

But, if transportation rates had not undergone these
changes in recent decades, there is a considerable likelihood that plants with far-flung markets in the nation
would still have been under pressure to concentrate
more intensively on smaller market areas, that is, to
"regionalize." Some added factors were pressing in this
direction.

One was the growth of population and income
throughout the country. Such growth meant that, with
each passing decade, the geographical reach of the
market area necessary to keep a plant running at its desired level of output was getting smaller. Plants which
tried to cling to their far-flung markets had to reckon
with the fact that competitors nearer to their customers
might now generate enough volume to operate at efficient levels.

Another factor leading to the regionalization tendency has been the increasing measure of fabrication to
which manufactured products have been subjected. The
chain of processes contributing to a final product has
grown longer and longer. The number of fabricated
units embodied in the final assembly of a product has
multiplied. On top of this, "raw" materials used in
manufacturing have commonly been displaced by fabricated materials, such as artificial fibers and plastic
products.[7] And the increasing complexity of the "inputs"
demanded by most transport-sensitive plants has meant
that being close to the source of any given material has
tended to decline in importance. Locations which might

be unfavorable in the supply of one material are sometimes attractive in the supply of another. In general,
nearness to materials has become less important for the
transport-sensitive industries, and nearness to markets
correspondingly more important.

These national forces have produced a significant
change in the New York Metropolitan Region's transport-sensitive industries. As Table 8 shows, the New

TABLE 8   New York Area's Actual and "Expected"
Growth Rates of National-Market Transport-
Sensitive Industries, Classified by Area's Share
of U. S. Employment, 1929–1954

	Percentage change in employment			
	1929–1954	1929–1939	1939–1947	1947–1954
New York high-share in-dustries[a]				
Actual	+24.3	+3.1	+49.4	−19.3
Expected	+70.5	+12.4	+60.7	−5.6
New York low-share in-dustries[b]				
Actual	+75.2	−3.4	+64.4	+10.3
Expected	+63.1	−7.4	+64.3	+7.2

Note: This table covers the 12-county Industrial Area for
1929–1947 and the 17-county Standard Metropolitan Area
for 1947–1954 (see also our Table 3). The 1929–1954 percentages were obtained by linking the sub-periods. As in
Chapter 3, the "expected" growth rate reflects national growth
rates, since it means the rate at which the group of industries
would have grown in the New York area if each industry had
grown at the national rate.

[a] Industries in which the New York area's share of national
employment was equal to or above its share of U. S. population at the beginning of each period.

[b] Industries in which the New York area's share of national
employment was less than its share of U. S. population at the
beginning of each period.

Source: Same as Table 3.

York area has been losing ground relative to the nation in those that are heavily concentrated in the area.[8] This was true in the period after World War II as well as in the entire period from 1929 to 1954. At the same time, however, the New York area has been improving its relative position in the industries in which its share is conspicuously low. Industries concentrated in the Midwest as part of the metal-working complex of that area, such as the manufacturing of refrigeration machinery and of valves and fittings, have been growing in the New York area at a faster rate than in the nation—a fairly clear indication of the relative weakening of the Midwest complex.[9]

As best we can tell, these trends have a long way to go before they will work themselves out. Relative to the nation, the New York Metropolitan Region stands to lose further in its position in transport-sensitive industries which are overly concentrated in the Region and to gain in those which are underrepresented in the Region. The Region's prospective losses will be augmented a little, and its prospective gains will be curtailed slightly, by the St. Lawrence Seaway's effects on the future location of a few industries. Here and there, one can discern transport-sensitive industries whose affinity to a Midwest location will be enhanced by the Seaway. The ability of the Region's sugar refineries to serve the Ohio market, for instance, could well be undermined by a Great Lakes refinery drawing its raw materials through the Seaway. By the same token, the tendency for automobile assembly plants and steel mills to disperse from the Midwest and to move closer to the coasts could be slowed down by the Seaway: the assembly plants, because they will find it easier to export their trucks overseas from the Great Lakes area; the steel plants, because they will find it easier to import ore and export finished products through the new facility.

Other forces, too, may operate to slow down the regionalization process as it affects the New York Metropolitan Region. One such force is the spectacular growth of piggy-back freight—the hauling of truck trailers on railroad flat cars. Piggy-back combines the most economical features of the truck and the rail; goods are picked up at their origin and delivered at their destination by truck, but the main haul between origin and destination is accomplished by rail. The use of piggy-back makes sense when the trip involves a fairly long haul, justifying a transfer of the load from truck to rail and back again, but not when the trip is so long that the terminal costs are an insignificant part of total freight costs. Trips of a thousand miles or so are likely to be made to an increasing degree by piggy-back. The rise of this kind of freight promises to bring a new rate structure into being, one which pulls down the costs of a thousand-mile trip. If this should materialize, the tendency to regionalization may be slowed a little.

All in all, we expect the regionalization trend to continue in the national-market transport-sensitive industries and in many groups not so classified. But we expect the rate of regionalization to be slower than in the past.

Interaction and movement. Changes in transportation have affected more industries than those which we call transport-sensitive. One has only to recall our earlier account of the garment industry's shift from New York, where transportation changes were seen as an indispensable ingredient in the shift without appearing to be the main cause. In the garment case, it will be remembered, the main reason why many businesses took to the hills was to find a cheaper source of labor. Yet for most firms, the move to Pennsylvania towns like Wilkes-Barre and Pottsville, or to North Carolina locations like Kinston, would have been impracticable without the truck and the high-speed highway to connect these shops with the New York complex.

Similarly, some of the military electronic plants in the New York area which rely on component manufacturers to supply them from low wage areas would have found difficulty using such distant sources of supply without the introduction of air freight. In the words of the logician, transportation changes were a necessary but not a sufficient condition to permit the separation between the users of components and their suppliers.

Transportation innovations will continue to perform this kind of role. As air routes link distant points with greater speed and lower costs, some manufacturing operations heretofore tied to the economy of the New York area may be done in distant workshops. Some of the color and art work performed a few blocks from the office of the advertising agency or publisher by whom it is commissioned, may well be done at distant points on the globe. Conversely, some of the selling and publishing centers surviving in secondary locations in the nation may be sucked into the vortex of the New York area, pulled by the ease and speed of air travel.

But these are developments which are best understood in another context—in an appraisal of the role of "external economies" and of the requirements of speed and communication in the development of the New York Metropolitan Region.[10]

5

External Economies

In some ways, the New York Metropolitan Region offers a paradox for anyone interested in the location of economic activity. Its raw materials are almost nonexistent; its splendid natural harbor, once a major advantage in competition with other areas, is no longer a factor of considerable importance; its location in relation to the nation's markets is hardly of the best; its wage structure is comparatively high. What is more, the Region is not improving its competitive position in any of these respects. Yet its economic performance, measured in terms of employment, has not been much out of line with the growth of the country as a whole. For reasons already hinted at but yet to be spelled out, newly created economic activities seem attracted to the area, and various long-established segments of activity persist in growing in the area at a rate not unlike that of the rest of the nation.

Behind this record, it is evident, lies the attraction of other forces—forces which do not fall under the heading of low wage rates, or proximity to raw materials, or favorable location with respect to national markets. To isolate and understand these forces, it will help first of all to look at the manufacturing sector of the Region's economy, then to turn to various nonmanufacturing pursuits.

PRODUCING THE UNPREDICTABLE

By the time the era of the truck and the airplane had arrived, the New York Metropolitan Region had managed to acquire some extraordinary facilities for manufacturing, unequalled by any other metropolitan area. Within its borders a manufacturer could find an enormous amount of rentable space; an amazingly varied group of suppliers of industrial materials and services; an extremely diversified labor force; and extensive transportation facilities capable of the swift dispatch of any kind of freight in any quantity. These attributes had been the consequence of its earlier growth of a century or so, a growth which depended more than anything else upon the start provided by the Port.

For some of the nation's producers today, these advantages of the New York area are hardly relevant. For some, as we saw earlier, the need to be close to a raw material or to tap a low-wage labor supply simply swamps all other considerations. For others, such as the aluminum producers, cheap power is critical; for still others, including some kinds of chemical and paper plants, the privilege of polluting the air or water without fear of hindrance from neighbors or public authorities is a precious advantage. There is a considerable group, however, whose overriding locational need is to be able to tap a pool of facilities—of space, of skills, of suppliers, or of freight services—such as the New York area is able to provide, and to share these facilities with other producers.

The shops and plants of these industries have certain fairly striking characteristics. In the first place, they are plagued with the fact that their output is unstable in one way or another. It may be unstable because of seasonality. But more important, as a rule, are the instability and uncertainty which come with a swiftly changing product or a highly variable demand. The obvious illustrations come to mind: each run of high-style dresses is a unique creation, demanding different materials, trim, and buttons, and requiring different steps in fabrication. Once created, it may be the proverbial "hit," the dream of every dress manufacturer, or it may be quietly dumped through cut-rate outlets.

Uncertainty of this sort, uncertainty about the product and uncertainty about the demand for it, exists in every line of manufacture that has swiftly changing styles. But there are other lines, too, in which similar uncertainties exist. Military electronics producers, turning out the more exotic types of gadgetry, often battle problems of uncertainty not unlike those involved in the production of a high-style dress. From one month to the next, a producer sometimes has no way of knowing what he may be expected to produce, what materials or processes may be involved, and what volume may be demanded.

So, too, with job printing. Each advertising circular, indeed each printing order except for certain routine jobs like business forms and ruled tablets, is an individual production. It requires type faces, colors, and processes which vary from one job to the next; the printer who holds himself out as a specialist in this field must be prepared for a continually changing product and variations in output.

Publishing is even more surrounded by uncertainty. In publishing a weekly magazine, though one may be able to guess how many copies of the final product will be sold, there is almost no way of telling in advance what resources will have to be brought to bear in order to produce the copy and illustrations of any issue. On short notice, a specialist on the politics of Dahomey and the Voltaic Republic, on the geography of Tibet, or on the properties of strontium 90 may have to be rounded up; library facilities which can disgorge the facts about the paleolithic era may be needed; and so may illustrators who can provide a credible version of the astronaut in flight. Each issue, therefore, is a challenge to the publisher's ingenuity and resources. And so it goes: with toys, tailored to the latest style craze or the most recent scientific breakthrough; with "one-shot" magazines, aimed at catching the latest twist in foreign cars; with greeting cards, tuned to the current slang phrase or the most recent headline.

Businessmen in lines of this sort must suit their methods of operation to such uncertainties. They cannot commit themselves to specialized machinery; for specialized machinery, though well able to turn out long runs at low cost, usually is not easily adapted to swiftly changing products. The dressmakers dare not commit their capital to button-making machinery; the printers dare not stock all kinds of type faces nor all sorts of presses; the electronics producers manufacturing advanced forms of gadgetry cannot accumulate the whole range of testing equipment nor turn out a full assortment of components. Instead, each must rely on outside specialists who can fill his needs as the needs arise. Nor can such firms ordinarily hope to run more than one establishment; there are too many decisions to be made which demand the swift consideration of management. In short, they are committed to single-plant firms; to comparatively small establishments; and to methods generally lacking in the use of heavy capital equipment.

These are the sorts of economic activity which tend to concentrate in the New York Metropolitan Region. If we put the transport-sensitive industries to one side and look at the remaining national-market industries, we find that those in which the Region "specializes" to a marked extent—those in which it has 30 per cent or more of the nation's employment—are typically of the kind in which the one-plant firm predominates. The figures in Table 9 underline the point. In the 66 industries where the prevalence of the one-plant firm is very high, 47 have 30 per cent or more of their national employment in the Region; by contrast, in the 83 industries where the prevalence of the one-plant firm is very low, only 10 have 30 per cent or more of their national employment in the Region.

Industries dominated by single-plant firms are, gen-

TABLE 9   261 Industries Other Than Transport-Sensitive,[a] Classified by Domination by Single-Plant Firms[b] and by Concentration in New York Metropolitan Region, 1954

	Total number of industries	Number of industries in which Region's share of national employment is:			
		30% or more	20–30%	10–20%	Under 10%
Industries grouped by percentage of plants operated by single-plant firms:					
Very high (95% and over)	66	47	8	7	4
High (90–95%)	45	16	12	7	10
Low (80–90%)	67	16	9	20	22
Very low (under 80%)	83	10	9	18	46

[a] This table covers 261 "4-digit" manufacturing industries —all except those classified as transport-sensitive. All 261 are considered to be national-market industries.

[b] Based on data for U. S., not Region.

Sources: For national data, U. S. 1954 Census of Manufactures. For Region's shares and further notes, see Robert M. Lichtenberg, One-Tenth of a Nation (Cambridge: Harvard University Press, 1960)—his Table 9 and appendices there referred to.

erally speaking, industries with small plants, little mechanization, and—at least when they deal in consumer
goods—a comparatively heavy reliance on outside suppliers. This is seen in Table 10, where the industries
with a very high prevalence of single-plant firms are
also seen as the industries with the smallest number of
employees per plant and the lowest horsepower per
employee.

TABLE 10 Characteristics of Industries Other
Than Transport-Sensitive, Classified by Domination
of Single-Plant Firms, United States, 1954

	Average number of employees per establishment	Horsepower per employee
Industries grouped by percentage of plants operated by single-plant firms:		
Very high (95% and over) ...	25	1.45
High (90–95%)	47	2.06
Low (80–90%)	81	3.48
Very low (under 80%)	308	8.44

Note: This table covers the same 261 "4-digit" manufac-
turing industries covered in Table 9. Data are for U. S., not
New York Region.
Source: U. S. *1954 Census of Manufactures.*

The emphasis in most of the lines concentrated in the
New York Metropolitan Region, it will be recognized,
is not only on change but on speedy change. If speed
were not essential to survival, one might envisage some
of the shops and plants in these lines relocating in areas
where labor was cheaper. Indeed, there are producers
of certain one-of-a-kind products who feel no need to
be located in an environment like that of New York.
For instance, producers of made-to-order giant turbines
and generators are not found in the Region, because

they operate on production schedules which call for delivery three or four years after the placement of an order. But a high-style dress is sometimes conceived and executed in a fortnight; an advertising brochure may be only hours or days in the making; a lawyer's brief is often printed between midnight and morning. In businesses producing such things, the entry of new competitors is usually easy; a new firm need not have much in the way of capital because there is no need or opportunity for heavy investment in equipment and because there are no dominant brand names whose lead must be overcome. But exit may be just as easy as entry; the future is precarious and every possible advantage in speed and flexibility must be fully exploited.°

So far we have stressed two factors tending to cause a pronounced clustering of certain industries in the Region—the life-or-death need of the shops and plants to share certain common facilities, and their need to tap these facilities at top speed. But there is still a third point accounting for these clusters, a point closely related to the other two. This is the critical role played by face-to-face contact. Were it not for this third element, the pronounced clustering tendency would not be nearly so much in evidence.

Outside facilities, of course, are used in varying degrees by American industry whether or not it is located in an urban setting. Few plants make or stock all the spare parts they need to keep their machinery running. Few have all the materials on hand to meet every con-

---

° A reflection of the emphasis on speed in these industries can be seen later in Chart 9 (in Chapter 7). The chart shows that the industries which are highly concentrated in the New York Metropolitan Region tend heavily to favor a particular portion of the Region—New York City. Those not heavily concentrated in the Region show a more dispersed pattern of location within the Region, favoring New York City less and the counties outside the City more.

tingency in the production schedule. But when a non-urban plant needs to draw on resources outside its four walls, the probability is fairly high that it can specify its need in a telephone call—that it can impart the specifications of a needed part or material by reference to a catalogue number or in some other unmistakable way.

By contrast, the communication needs of the clustering establishments typically demand face-to-face communication. Consider the advertising agency, judiciously selecting a combination of type faces and colors pleasing to the eye; the dress manufacturer, fingering fabrics and eyeing button shapes for use in his latest creation; the lawyer, checking proof on briefs in the small hours; or the publisher, discussing with prospective authors his conception of a forthcoming article. Neither the letter nor the telephone will be entirely adequate. The effort to reduce the cost of speedy personal communication is an added force pulling the establishments concerned into close proximity.

For all the emphasis on external economies, speed, and contact in the industries classified here as "external-economy industries," many plants in these industries survive outside the main cluster, away from the New York Metropolitan Region. Though the Region contains some 30 per cent of the nation's employment in the external-economy industries, a vigorous 70 per cent appears to supply national markets from locations outside the Region. While there are cases in which these external-economy industries are grouped in subsidiary clusters outside the Region, the typical situation is one in which such outside locations are widely dispersed.

A hint of the reason for the existence of many plants dispersed from the main cluster is offered by the fact that the average establishment outside the Region in these external-economy industries is somewhat larger than the average establishment within it; and this difference shows up whether the industry is heavily concentrated in the Region or not. This is sharply different from the situation which we came upon in the transport-sensitive industries. We saw in Chapter 4 that the Region's establishments in transport-sensitive industries heavily represented in the Region are larger than their outside competitors.

Two reasons come to mind for the smaller size of the external-economy plants in the New York Metropolitan Region, compared with plants in the same industries elsewhere. One is the shortcomings of our figures. What is an industry? Is "women's shoes" an industry, or should we be separating high-priced shoes from all the others? Wherever it has been possible to make the separation, that has been done. There have been numerous cases, however, in which plants under the same Census sobriquet should not have been directly compared, because the industry outside the New York area was really producing a different product.

The other reason is more substantive, however, and begins to provide a lead to future trends. There is more than one way to make the same shoe or dress or toy. One is the way of the New York Metropolitan Region's producers: to accept the handicaps of high labor costs, traffic congestion, urban rents, and urban taxes while exploiting the advantages of speed, flexibility, and external economies. The other is to shed the New York-type handicaps while accepting the disadvantages of remoteness and inflexibility in a larger and more self-contained plant. The fact that both patterns exist side by side in many industries suggests that the triumph of one type of operation over the other is not inevitable.

Still, the historical trends in some of these industries indicate strongly the direction in which the current is running. If we turn back to Table 5, in Chapter 3, it is apparent that the external-economy industries—industry by industry—have been growing more slowly in the New York area than in the nation—not very much more slowly, to be sure, but more slowly. This is not true of all external-economy industries; the New York area has managed to increase its share of the nation's total in some whose product has been shifting from a fairly standardized type of output to one with greater style variations—for example, luggage, handbags, and small leather goods. Similarly, the production of games and toys has grown faster in the Region than elsewhere as the rate of change in the nature of the product has speeded up. On the whole, however, these cases have been exceptional. Much more commonly, one finds the Region's employment in external-economy industries growing more slowly than the national growth rate.

Behind this tendency, our industry studies suggest, lie two kinds of cases. One kind is exemplified by the radio industry. In the 1920's, that industry had all the earmarks of an activity whose establishments were heavily dependent on external economies, speed, and personal contact. Its technology was unsettled and changing rapidly; its production methods were untried; its market was uncertain. Accordingly, at that stage, producers were typically small in size, numerous, agile, nervous, heavily reliant upon subcontractors and suppliers. Mortality in the industry was high. In those circumstances, the attraction of an urban area like the New York Metropolitan Region was especially strong.

A decade or two later, however, the technology of the industry had settled down. Production methods were standardized and sets were being turned out in long runs. Now, the critical competitive questions had become transport and labor costs, rather than product design. The small firm faded from the picture and large assembly plants appeared at lower-wage locations more centrally placed for national markets. An industry which once was in the external-economy category had evidently changed in nature.

The second case is suggested by an illustration already used in our labor and transport discussions—the locational separation of the various stages of the manufacture of women's apparel. In this case, spurred by the development of the truck, the industry has been relocating its sewing in areas of low labor cost, while maintaining much of the designing, cutting, finishing, and selling in the New York area. In other words, those phases of the industry's operations which are not especially reliant on external economies, speed, and contact have been departing from the New York environment, while the phases dependent upon these factors have remained behind.

Anyone concerned with projecting the employment which the external-economy industries are likely to generate in the Region seems inescapably involved in predicting the thoroughly unpredictable. As there arise new industries of the sort which require external economies in their early stages, the chances seem high that the Region will be a favored location at first; then, as maturity sets in, these industries are likely to spread out to lower-cost locations. As new technologies develop which allow existing external-economy industries to "decompose" their processes and to transfer some of them to another area, they too will join in the outward move. But one can only guess at the speed of these processes of birth and maturity and technological shift.

So far we have concentrated on the question of employment, our principal yardstick of growth. But employment is only one measure of the contribution of an enterprise to the Region's economy. Another, as we have seen, is "value added"—a dollar figure made up principally of the payrolls, interest payments, and profits of the firm. In Chapter 3 we promised eventually to consider why the Region's industries showed a greater tendency to expand in employment than in value added. By now, the answer should be evident. The Region's economy is heavily weighted with external-economy industries—with industries producing unstandardized goods, continually changing their process and product, and assiduously avoiding commitments in machinery, buildings, and other fixed capital. These are industries that are the most restricted in opportunities to expand productivity. For such industries, continued growth of demand does not bring much increase in output per worker; it simply means the employment of more workers. This is why some of the major industries of the New York Metropolitan Region have such slow-growing productivity.

The comparatively slow growth in value added by the Region's industries stems out of still another fact—that small-firm industries are industries where entry is easy. Where entry is easy, profit margins and wage levels are constantly under pressure. As a result, even when productivity increases occur in such industries, such increases are not allowed to find their reflection in higher profits or higher wages per unit of output; instead, they are squeezed out of the value-added measure by the onslaught of competition.

This points to a telling conclusion: to the extent that the New York Metropolitan Region's industrial mix continues to be heavily weighted with external-economy industries, as our projections assume it will, the Region will be less able to count on productivity increases to bolster its per capita income than the nation at large. To be sure, the tendency toward the regionalization of industry promises to give the Region a manufacturing mix more like that of the rest of the country. In the course of time, therefore, there should be a reduction in the differential between the Region and the nation in the growth of value added per worker. But for the next two or three decades, the continued differences in industrial mix will continue to generate such a growth differential.

THE NATION'S BUSINESS

Despite the obvious differences between producing goods in a factory and producing data and decisions in an office building, there are some remarkable similarities between the underlying forces in the external-economy manufacturing industries and the forces at work in office activities.

Before we get to those similarities, it must be said that to try to account for the location of the nation's office workers in any conclusive way is an exercise in acute frustration. In manufacturing pursuits, there are hard production facts to deal with. Materials are assembled for processing and sale; labor costs, transportation costs, rent, and other costs are reflected in the price of the products; and these products are offered on a market in which some measure of competition from other producers often exists. The observer is able to draw some reasonable inferences, therefore, about the forces tending to shape industrial location. He is entitled to assume that manufacturers are in a position to distinguish a good location from a poor one; or, where they make no such conscious distinction, that an economic version of the Darwinian principle, feeble and dilute though its effects may be, operates to push industries toward the location which yields the largest return. But in office activities, at least office activities set up in separate establishments outside of plants or stores, the chances of a rational location pattern are not that good.

The central office of a large corporation, for instance, produces no easily defined product, whose costs can be "priced out" at alternative locations. With every intention to approach the location problem "scientifically," no management could say with anything like the assurance that applies in plant location why one city should be preferred to another. No Darwinian principle operates, even in dilute fashion, to destroy a central office which has been located in error; such an office can survive for decades, absorbing the cost of its uneconomic location in the total cost structure of the firm, without anyone the wiser.

For all that, most of the office labor force of the New York Metropolitan Region is located there for reasons which are hardly obscure. In the first place, some 44 per cent of the office workers in office buildings in the Region are engaged in purely "local" activities. There are the government employees serving the Region's populations, the neighborhood banks, insurance field offices, and real estate agents, the wholesalers catering to the retail stores in the Region, and the miscellaneous business offices serving these and other local activities. By and large, these office workers are in the Region in order to be close to their market—in order to minimize the cost of face-to-face contact with the customer.

The remaining 700,000 or so office workers in the Region's office buildings, however, perform much more than a Regionwide function. The wholesalers offering wares to a national market, the central offices of manufacturers, the home offices of life insurance companies, the big commercial banks, and the securities brokers and dealers, together with the advertising agencies, management advisory firms, and other satellite services, cater directly or indirectly to markets well dispersed beyond the Region. For these, an alternative location outside the Region would be a distinct possibility.

The tendency for office entities of national scope to cluster in New York is not as easily documented as one might suppose; but various indications of the tendency do exist. For instance, of the 500 largest industrial companies listed in the *Fortune Directory* of 1958, 156 have their home addresses in New York (and many of the others maintain administrative offices there). Over half the 332 management consulting firms which are members of the American Management Association have headquarters or branches in the Region. The Region accounts for more than 30 per cent of the personnel of the nation's life insurance home offices. Most of the nation's principal underwriters and brokerage firms also maintain New York headquarters.

We have already indicated the historical process by which the great cluster of wholesalers, central offices, banks, and related activities came to be located in the New York Metropolitan Region. The Port begat the wholesalers; these strengthened the pull upon the financial institutions; finance attracted the central offices; the latter drew the advertising agencies and others; and each new accretion reinforced the old, giving it an added reason for its earlier location. In each instance, the factor attracting a new activity to cluster in the Region was its need for face-to-face communication.

Of course New York was not the only city with "national-market" office activities, but there were powerful forces pulling such activities into a few large clusters, and New York has always been by far the largest. As in manufacturing, certain critical activities could not be easily entrusted to letter or telephone—the conferences between banker and customer; the higgling between buyer and seller; the probing for news or gossip, contacts or favors. The subtle by-play of negotiation and consultation demanded central gathering places where the nation's business could be transacted.

The preference for just a few large clusters of activity stems not only from the need for face-to-face communication but also from the uncertainty and changeability that characterize many of the firms. The financial community furnishes good illustrations. It makes little sense for a securities broker or dealer, or a large investing institution such as a casualty insurance company, to staff itself with a full complement of analysts capable of providing expert advice on every type of security. The background and information needed to analyze the prospects of an iron ore producer in Labrador are different from those needed to analyze Australian government bonds or a first mortgage on an office building in Seattle. Yet the interests of many entities in the financial community range from day to day, abruptly and unpredictably, among fields as diverse as these. As a way of serving these interests efficiently, therefore, the tendency of many of the financial community's participants has been to locate close to one another, drawing on the specialists among them to fill their unpredictable needs as they arise. In short, they rely on external economies.

The tendency of large central offices to congregate at a New York location is traceable to much the same forces. The needs of the elite group in the central office of a large company are as variable and unpredictable as those of any "producer." From week to week, their interests vary from some esoteric provision of the Internal Revenue Code to the political situation in Cuba; from the effectiveness of spot television commercials to the efficacy of operations research; from the best place to build a factory to the best time to issue stock. Once again, it is uneconomical for such offices to staff themselves internally to deal with every such problem; the only feasible pattern is to draw upon specialists as the need arises. And the most efficient locational arrangement is one which permits the specialists and those they serve to be congregated at a common point.

The tendency for wholesalers, financial institutions, and the central offices to congregate where facilities can be shared and contact is easy gains additional strength from the other factor in our triad of factors—by the emphasis on speed. In many of these activities, survival depends in part upon the capacity for quick decision-making. The need for speed is least in those offices not troubled with the day-to-day vagaries of a competitive market, and it is greatest where competition is keen, but it exists in some degree for every business decision-maker.

All this explains why New York is the business capital of the United States. Nonetheless, there is considerable evidence, despite the patchy and unsatisfying character of the available statistics, that the office activities in the New York Metropolitan Region have not been growing as fast as those in the rest of the country. The Region's proportion of national employment in business services and in finance declined between 1947 and 1956. The former dropped from 28 per cent to 24 per cent, and the latter from 19 per cent to 16 per cent.[1] In the central administrative offices of manufacturing firms, it is true, the Region's employment seems to hold up, standing at 23 per cent of the national total in 1937—as best we can estimate—and 22 per cent in 1954.[2] But relative decline is noticeable from 1947 to 1956 in the Region's employment in the home offices of life insurance and property insurance companies, and in commercial banking.

Most of this seeming decline of New York, however, is probably due to the relative rise of local, rather than national, office activity in other areas. Commercial banking offers a clear illustration of the difference. Our detailed study of the locational forces at work in the financial community indicates that the preeminent position of the New York Metropolitan Region's great banks as the nation's money-market institutions has been maintained without impairment during the last few decades, even though the Region's employment in commercial banking as a whole has declined substantially in relation to the nation. So, too, with central offices. Though the number of such offices outside of the New York area has no doubt grown, there is no evidence that the tendency of national firms to prefer New York as a central office location has weakened. The outside growth of office work seems to be due to the fact that other sections of the country have been expanding their populations and economies at a faster rate than the Eastern seaboard, generating new companies with interests confined to those sections.

The case of life insurance home offices illustrates a number of the tendencies described above. The New York Metropolitan Region has always been a major center for the home offices of life insurance companies. Between 1947 and 1956, however, employment in life insurance home offices in the Region slipped in relative terms from 37.8 per cent of the national total to 31.3 per cent.

Behind this slippage lay two facts: companies located outside New York tended to concentrate their operations in more limited markets than those located in New York; and the concentration on more limited markets by these outside companies seemed to be paying off in the form of higher growth rates.[3] Indeed, apparently in recognition of the fact that home offices which were nearest the market did best, Prudential Life followed a policy of dispersing its home-office operations out of the New York Region into a series of regional centers.

Just why home offices located close to their markets should do better than those located at a more remote national center is not altogether clear. What is clear is that, as far as life insurance is concerned, some erstwhile advantages of a national center have disappeared. The advantages to life insurance companies of constant communication may well have been great when mortality tables were new and unreliable, when policy terms were changing and untried, when epidemics were not uncommon, and when the coverage of the typical company was small. Today, however, all these elements of uncertainty have been greatly diminished. And as uncertainty has declined, the advantages of frequent and speedy communication among the companies have declined with it.

The same point is worth making with respect to the investment activities of the life insurance companies. Time was, six or eight decades ago, when life insurance companies were free to speculate in the stock market, and did. But state regulations have put an end to such speculation in the last half century, confining the companies to "legal lists" of securities or to highly restrictive investment criteria. Since then, the advantages of being close to the market in order to take account of the latest morsel of information and the latest analysis have declined very substantially. The penalties for moving their head offices out of the New York Metropolitan Region, or of dispersing such offices into a number of sectional centers, as Prudential has done, are no longer so great. And the possibility of operating from new locations outside the financial centers with some chance of success has grown accordingly.

The future role of the great office cluster in New York depends in part on the degree of risk and uncertainty in the nation's economy. A sedate and predictable economy will minimize the need for clusters; a swiftly changing one, with all its uncertainties, will increase it. The reader need not be told that this is one aspect of the future which, critical though it may be, thoroughly defies projection.

There are other future trends, however, that can be foreseen with more confidence. One is the likelihood that air travel will be speedier. Just as the truck and air freight have released some activities, such as the sewing of garments, from their ties to the Region, so it might be argued by analogy that swifter air travel may release some of the Region's office activities to far-flung sections of the country.

Our disposition, however, is to expect the opposite. The increased speed of travel to New York, in our view, is likely to encourage the growth of clusters of office activity in that area, rather than otherwise. The reasons for this expectation are illustrated by the problem of the central office elite. This problem is to maintain two links in the chain of communication: to maintain an easy flow of facts and decisions from headquarters to branch plants, warehouses, and regional sales offices, and to maintain an easy interchange of ideas by the elite headquarters personnel among themselves and with their outside advisers. The advent of the jet airplane offers the elite two possibilities: to spread out more in the field, closer to operations, with the assurance that they can assemble swiftly at some headquarters point as needed; or to congregate in even greater degree at a headquarters point, with the assurance that they can disperse swiftly to any point in the field as needed.

There is not much doubt which of these offsetting pulls will be the more dominant. The most probable outcome of the increased freedom offered by swifter air travel will be the further concentration of the office elite at a few headquarters cities. This tendency will be fortified by the use of high-speed electronic data-processing machines. For these machines will contribute to the centralization of data-processing and decision-making at fewer points in the structure of the giant company. Though it is not a foregone conclusion that the data-processing activities will be located under the same roof as the decision-makers, there is typically a preference for locating them in some degree of proximity.

These expectations will find some measure of reflection in our image of the Region's future.

6

From Jobs to People
to Jobs Again

This is a good point at which to take stock of what we know about the Region's growth in the last few decades. As nearly as we can tell from the incomplete figures, the Region's economic growth has roughly approximated that of the nation, when measured by employment, and has lagged behind the nation, when measured by income. The employment record turns out to be the net result of two kinds of forces: on the one hand, the Region proves to have a mix of activities whose manpower requirements have been growing fast in the nation, faster, apparently, than jobs as a whole; on the other hand, the Region has been growing more slowly than the nation in many industries, the occasional exceptions being found principally in the "first-city" communication-oriented kind of activity.

There is a temptation to rest at this point; to assume that because we know something about the changing opportunities of the Region to sell its goods and services to others, we know all that is needed to understand the Region's development. For it is a common assumption in economic analysis that the overriding force which determines the growth of any area in a nation is the opportunity of that area to sell its goods and services to others; and that the group engaged in these activities supports the area's nonworking populations and the area's "local" jobs such as those in retail trade or local government.

There is no denying that this simple way of looking at the growth of the New York area goes some way toward helping to understand its performance. Yet the approach is too simple. It misses some critical forces which have modified the New York area's growth pattern.

FROM JOBS TO PEOPLE . . .

It will be remembered from Chapter 2 that, for a long time, the area we now know as the New York Metropolitan Region had been growing in population faster than the nation as a whole, and so had most other metropolitan areas. About 1930, however, this relative increase came to an end for many large metropolitan areas in the East, including the New York Region; and thereafter these eastern areas grew more slowly than the nation. The slowdown was not as pronounced for the New York Region as for some others, such as the Boston and Philadelphia areas, but it was unmistakably taking place. Between 1940 and 1956, the Region's population fell from 9.51 per cent of the nation's total to 9.18 per cent.

Despite the old saw that there is no such thing as a native New Yorker, most of the inhabitants of the New York Metropolitan Region probably were born there and most can expect to die there. In looking for the cause of the population changes, therefore, a good place to begin is with births and deaths.

For a long time, the rate of natural increase—the change represented by the excess of births over deaths

—has been lower in urban areas than in rural areas. The New York Metropolitan Region, most of whose people have lived in an urban setting, has reflected the pattern. In 1955, the rate of natural increase in the Region was 11.2 per thousand inhabitants, while in the United States it was 15.6.

The difference in natural increase between the Region and the country as a whole has been shrinking, of course. So much of the rest of the country has become urbanized that any other result would have been surprising. As far back as the record stretches, however, the Region has had to look to currents of migration as an important way of adding to its population. In the decades since 1920, even without the waves of European immigrants that had characterized former times, the Region's population increase arising out of net migration has amounted to between 28 and 60 per cent of its total population increase.

In earlier chapters, we pointed out that the young men and women who had been drawn to the Region in the great migrations of the nineteenth century and early twentieth century came in hopes of a better life. But they came with imperfect knowledge about the job market, sometimes with the firm conviction that New York's streets really were paved with gold. If jobs were not forthcoming at once, they had neither the knowledge nor the funds to move on. Their presence, and the prospects of more to follow, provided the bases for some of the Region's growing industries. Though economic opportunity was the lodestone for migration, the fact of the migration's existence generated some of the opportunity.

More recently, migration has played a lesser role in the Region's growth; but it still retains some significance. Puerto Rican men and women have poured in—and out —in good numbers. On balance, their migration since 1946 has been swelling the New York area's population at a rate of something like 350,000 per decade. Young white women from the continental United States have also appeared in significant numbers—about 60,000 of them between the ages of 20 and 34 during the 1940's. Negroes of both sexes and of practically all ages also have moved into the Region in large numbers; in the job-seeking 20-to-34 age groups in the same decade, the total has been 69,000 men and 76,000 women.

Most of these in-migrants can be thought of as responding to economic opportunity, but not all. Some of the Puerto Rican women, for instance, probably came to the mainland because of their husbands' job opportunities, not their own—then joined the labor force when they discovered that some apparel plants were begging for their services. Some of the white women from other parts of the continental United States surely came with star-struck notions of careers as actresses or models, but remained to wait on tables or pound a typewriter. Some of the Negroes may have been fleeing from Southern rural poverty without much knowledge about alternative opportunities in New York. Still, New York's economic opportunity influenced the responses of all these groups. And it may be expected to influence like groups in the future.

Nonetheless, one major stream of migration—an outward stream—probably has been motivated by forces which hardly go under the head of economic opportunity. From ages 45 and up, ages at which the mobility of people is ordinarily quite low, white men and women can be found leaving the Region in impressive numbers. In the 1940–1950 decade, 102,000 white men and 90,-000 white women over 45 left the Region for parts unknown. A crude check of the 1950–1957 period indicates that this continued at roughly the same pace.

We can guess where these older whites went and why. At age 45, the proportion of the population that is in the labor force starts to decline; by choice or because of disability, some begin to work only sporadically, or retire altogether. By age 60 to 70, of course, retirement becomes general. Our guess is that the act of retirement is the catalyst which accounts for the out-migration, and that many of those involved, with grubstakes provided by their savings or pensions, leave the Region for such areas as Florida and California. The fact that the out-migration is evident among the whites but not the Negroes adds strength to the hypothesis, for the whites are in a better economic position to make the choice. New York, it seems, is a great place to work but no place for retirement.

If this is the reason for the migration of the 45-and-over group out of the New York area, the migration will probably grow in importance during the next two or three decades. The increased coverage of Social Security and the proliferation of private pension schemes will add to the freedom of residential choice for older people. The increased speed and ease of travel by air and road will favor their decision to move, since return visits to children and grandchildren will not be difficult. This stream of out-migration, then, is a factor to be taken into account in any projection of the Region's future, one which would be missed if the projection were based upon changes in job opportunities alone.

While the out-migration of older people has been tending to reduce the Region's population relative to its job opportunities, another force has been pushing in the opposite direction. The Region, like urban areas in general, has always had a comparatively high proportion of its population in the labor force, that is, in the group which is working or looking for work. One reason for this high proportion is that urban populations, having lower birth rates than rural populations, contain a higher proportion of adults. Another reason is that a significant portion of an urban area's labor force consists of people who have come from other places to look for a job. So in the New York Region the steady stream of young women coming into the area for work and the tide of Puerto Rican and Negro males add elements to the work force which do not exist in areas where in-migration is lacking.

One simple measure of the consequences can be seen in Table 11, where the percentage of the Region's population in the labor force is compared with the like percentage for the nation as a whole. The Region's rates of labor-force participation were higher than those of the nation on each of the three dates shown.

TABLE 11   Percentage of Population in the Labor Force, U. S. and New York Metropolitan Region, 1930, 1940, 1950

	1930	1940	1950
Total			
U. S.	39.6	41.6	42.2
Region	45.8	45.3	43.7
Males			
U. S.	60.4	61.9	60.9
Region	67.4	64.5	61.8
Females			
U. S.	18.2	21.2	23.9
Region	24.2	26.5	26.5

Source: Regional Plan Association, *Bulletin* 87 (June 1957), Table 16, p. 24.

But the table shows something else too. The difference between the nation and the Region has been narrowing, partly because male participation rates in the Region have been coming down to the nation's level, and partly because female participation rates in the nation have been coming up to the Region's level. Behind this pattern of convergence lies a story which has already been told in part in earlier chapters. As the country became more urbanized, convergence was inevitable. Even the populations which remained behind in rural areas and small towns became culturally less different from urban populations in the course of time. Nonurban women became readier and abler to take jobs than ever before, and the males in urban and rural environments encountered smaller disparities in educational opportunities and needs. The net effect has been a higher rate of labor-force participation outside the Region and a slight decline in the Region's rate.

If employers outside the Region could not have counted on drawing some of their added labor from the kitchens of the farms and small towns, the Region's development pattern might have been different. It is possible that alternative locations in the South or the Pennsylvania coal country would not have been quite as attractive for producers in some industries represented in the Region and that, accordingly, the Region's growth would have been speeded up. In that case, the Region's share of the nation's employment would have been higher and its share of population might have been higher as well, though not by as much as the employment share.

But other population and employment patterns could also have developed, and we would be wrong to insist too vigorously that the changing pattern of labor-force participation outside the Region did have precisely the results we have suggested. All we can reasonably say is that, for the future, differences in rates of labor-force participation between the Region and the rest of the nation are unlikely to be as important as they have been in the past.

. . . TO JOBS AGAIN

There is always a considerable group in any metropolitan area whose livelihood seems to depend on servicing the needs of the local population, rather than on selling goods or services to the rest of the world. We have indicated that, as nearly as we could tell, these servicing jobs accounted for about 60 per cent of the total employment of the New York Metropolitan Region.

There is a strong temptation, as we said before, to think of these jobs as a "passive" force in the Region's development, as primarily a by-product of the Region's activities in selling its goods and services to the rest of the world. According to this view, stated in its most naive form, one need only know what is happening to the Region's "export" opportunities in order to be able to judge what is happening to its whole economy.

We have resisted succumbing completely to that assumption, for many reasons. It is not only that some population movements seem unrelated to the Region's "export" opportunities and have to be taken into account independently before one can go on to consider the size of local servicing jobs. Besides this, developments in the local sector itself can operate to affect the export sector. For instance, shifts such as that from "local" hand laundries to "local" laundromats could well have improved the Region's competitive position by releasing a labor supply whose existence could have made the position of the apparel industry in the Region more tolerable. We know, too, that the wage structure in the "local" retail trades has influenced the wage structure of such industries as millinery and toys, somewhat impairing their ability to hang on in the Region. Nor are these isolated cases; they underline a general point that there are subtle and sometimes powerful causal flows between "export" industries and "local" activities in the Region, with the causation running sometimes one way, sometimes the other. And the fact that we cannot always measure these flows but can only articulate their existence is no reason for overlooking them altogether.

Still, it cannot be denied that the variations in "local" activity from one decade to the next have moved in close parallel to those of the Region's total population and income, even though the changes in population and income reflect "export" as well as "local" activity. Consumer trade and services are usually thought of as the activities *par excellence* which cater to the local market. Chart 8 shows the close ties between the Region's receipts and employment in these consumer activities, on the one hand, and its personal income on the other.

CHART 8   New York Metropolitan Region's Share of U. S. Personal Income and of U. S. Retail Trade and Consumer Services,[a] 1929–1954

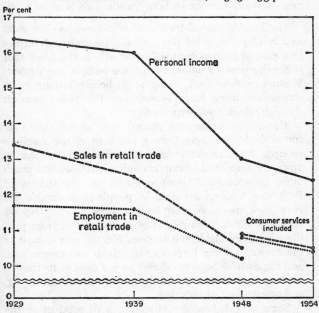

[a] For 1929–1948, data were available for retail trade only. The 1948–1954 data include both retail trade and consumer services.

Sources: U. S. *1929 Census of Distribution;* U. S. *Census of Business* for 1939, 1948, and 1954; *Survey of Current Business;* and New York Metropolitan Region Study estimates.

Though the Region's relative importance in the nation is not the same when measured by the three series in the chart, and though the parallelism in their movement from decade to decade is far from perfect, this parallelism is still the most prominent feature in their performance since 1929. Even so, there are various aspects of the Region's retail trade and consumer services worth exploring, especially if one is concerned with projecting the Region's performance in the next few decades.

THE "EXPORT" OF CONSUMER TRADE AND SERVICES

The Region's retail trade and consumer services exist mainly to provide for the Region's residents; nevertheless, part of their output is "exported"—in the sense that it goes to persons whose homes are outside the Region. Visitors to New York, living at its hotels, buying in its shops, attending its theatres, are the main conduit through which these exports flow.

Though we judge that visitors from outside were responsible for no more than 5 per cent of the Region's receipts from all its consumer trades and services in 1954, the impact of visitors on individual lines was much more pronounced. About one-fifth of the tickets of Broadway theatres are used by people from outside the New York area, according to spot surveys. The Region's hotels, of course, draw most of their revenue from people who live outside the Region. Nearly 10 per cent of the revenue of the Region's nightclubs and restaurants, and somewhere between 6 and 10 per cent of its movies and sports receipts, probably go to the care, feeding, and amusement of outsiders.

Some of this business is simply a by-product of the central offices, sales activities, and financial operations in which New York City specializes; yet about 70 per cent of the visitors to the City are there for vacations or conventions, and therefore the business they bring is not generated automatically out of the other business activities of the area. For our purposes, therefore, it is useful to develop some clues to the future location of the attractions which play a role in bringing visitors to the Region.

In 1958, when the Dodgers and Giants abandoned New York baseball diamonds for points west, their departure seemed to support the view that the metropolis was losing some of its attributes as the nation's first city. But what has actually been happening in the realm of entertainment seems more complicated. Some of the attractions which once were concentrated in the New York area have indeed been spreading out through the country; but others have remained concentrated in the area. And the basis for distinguishing one group from the other invokes familiar locational principles, principles which we encountered earlier in our discussion of manufacturing, wholesale trade, and finance.

The kind of activity in which the New York area has yielded ground relative to the nation is exemplified by horse racing and by bands, orchestras, and entertainers. Between 1948 and 1954, the New York metropolitan area's share of the nation's horse racing receipts fell from 20.5 per cent to 17.3 per cent, a drop of almost one-sixth; and the area's share of the nation's receipts from bands, orchestras, and entertainers fell from 31.0 per cent to 23.6 per cent, nearly one-fourth. In both of these pursuits, a spreading out of the activity across the country could be discerned; bands, orchestras, and entertainers were rising in centers like Chicago and Los Angeles, while horse racing was spreading in a more diffused pattern.

In clear contrast has been the New York area's performance as a center for commercial art galleries and the theatre. Between 1943 and 1957, the number of regularly established art outlets in New York City expanded faster than the number in four other cities for which like data could be had—Chicago, Boston, Philadelphia, and San Francisco; and the general impression in the trade is that New York's position as the nation's art-gallery center is more firmly entrenched today than it has ever been.

The story as regards the legitimate theatre is much the same as that for art. During the 1920's, while America's stock, road, and vaudeville companies were declining, the number of Broadway productions rose almost continuously. After 1930, as sound movies and television successively chopped into the theatre business, Broadway theatres weathered the blows much better than those outside New York. In a recent, eight-year period, from the 1949–50 season to the 1957–58 season, Broadway playing weeks declined by only 6.5 per cent, while road-show playing weeks dropped by 29 per cent. The contrast between New York and other areas is even more pronounced if we take account of the recent mushrooming of New York's "off-Broadway" theatrical activity.

Why the disparity between horse racing and the band and orchestra business, on the one hand, and art and theatre, on the other? The answer, we believe, lies in the fact that the first pair of activities does not experience anything like the advantages from clustering that accrue to the second pair. Art outlets, like high-style dress manufacturers, sell a product which thrives on comparative offerings and which demands comparative shopping; but the race tracks offer a product which does not benefit significantly from having another race track nearby. The theatre draws heavily on a pool of unusual facilities not to be had at more than one or two places in the nation, to recruit its players, design its sets, and stage its productions; but the bands and orchestras of America draw from a much larger pool of talent, sufficient for their needs. So we are back to a familiar set of principles. External economies and unstandardized inputs lead to clustering; and where clustering is demanded, the area with the early lead tends to retain or extend that lead. These are the criteria by which one may identify the consumer "exports" in which the New York Metropolitan Region is likely to lose or gain ground in the future.

FROM SALES TO JOBS

But our discussion of the exports of consumer goods and services is in some respects a digression from the main theme. Possibly 95 per cent of the Region's sales in retail trade and consumer services are "local" sales to the Region's residents. Would one go very far wrong in assuming that the role of local trade in the Region's economy is pretty much determined by variations in the Region's income?

In one of the underlying volumes in this series, the changes in the structure of the Region's retail trade and consumer services are examined in some detail.[1] These changes are extremely complex, and their complexity gives one pause in making simple assumptions about the future role of trade and services. In some service lines, for instance, the Region's sales as a proportion of national sales have been considerably higher than the Region's share of national income would seem to warrant; and in some of these cases, the tendency has been for the Region's sales to decline in relation to the national total, moving toward the level indicated by the Region's share of income.

The Region's behavior in individual lines of trade and services can be attributed in part to basic shifts in living patterns in the Region and the nation. Thirty or forty years ago, a larger proportion of the Region's population lived in crowded cities than is the case today, and a larger proportion of the nation's population lived on farms; accordingly the consumption patterns of Re-

131

gion and nation were considerably different in some ways. But as the crowded cities and the farms have both lost position to the ubiquitous suburbs, the Region's consumption patterns and the nation's consumption patterns have moved closer together.

This result has required one kind of mix change on the part of the Region and a very different one in the nation. The differences could be discerned in the changed position of personal services (such as beauty shops, cleaners, and shoe repair shops) between 1948 and 1954. As the citified portion of the Region's population declined and as the suburban portion grew, the sale of these services in the Region dropped to a level which accorded more closely to the Region's share of national income. Much the same thing happened in the repair and servicing of motor vehicles and in parking facilities. As a larger proportion of the Region's passenger cars were garaged and maintained outside of the Region's cities, expenditures per car in the Region moved down toward the national level.

With developments such as these affecting the Region's mix of trade and services relative to the national mix, it is not in the least surprising that *employment* in the Region's retail trade should have taken a course somewhat different from *sales* in the Region's retail trade. Between 1929 and 1954, the Region's share of the nation's retail trade employment did not drop quite so far as the Region's share of the nation's retail sales. But the disparities in performance between sales and employment were not very great—and they were even less toward the end of the period than in its earlier phases.

In the end, therefore, it is the parallelism—not the divergence—between the Region's performance and the nation's performance which emerges as the dominant characteristic of retail trade and consumer services, after suitable account has been taken of the trends in the

Region's share of national income. In assaying the future, we assume that much, perhaps most, of the Region's convergence towards a consumption pattern more nearly resembling that of the nation at large has already taken place. So parallelism is anticipated, albeit a parallelism which accepts the persistence of the remaining differences in the Region's consumption patterns and which reflects the differences which the Region's declining share of the nation's personal income is expected to produce. These are the expectations that underlie the projections set out in our final chapter.

7

The Distribution of Jobs
within the Region

Inside the New York Metropolitan Region, there is as
much variety as one can find in any American metropolis
—variety in land use, variety in jobs, variety in residents,
variety in governmental structure. The Region contains
the most densely settled neighborhoods to be found anywhere in the nation, with 200,000 or 300,000 residents
packed into a single square mile, as well as many
sparsely settled reaches, embracing seashore, fox-hunt-
ing clubs, and even an Indian reservation. It has clusters of thousands of tiny shops in some districts, and
plants which approach the proportions of River Rouge
in others.

Up to now, our general approach has been to disre-
gard these differences and to look on the New York
Metropolitan Region as if it were a single homogeneous
unit. But the economic performance of the Region,
present and prospective, cannot really be understood
without exploring its internal structure. In this chapter,
therefore, we shall consider how the Region's various
parts are functioning today, observing the role of the
old cities, analyzing the forces at work in the suburbs,

detecting the differences between the New York and Connecticut counties on the east and the New Jersey counties on the west.

As we traced the evolution of the New York Metropolitan Region in Chapter 2, a heavy emphasis was placed on the area surrounding the Port, especially the five counties of New York City. Almost it seemed that the 6,600 square miles of the Region outside New York City, stretching eastward 120 miles to Montauk Light, northward 90 miles to the corner of Massachusetts, and southwestward 50 miles nearly to Princeton, were getting short shrift in the analysis. This emphasis on the center could easily seem overdone to anyone concerned with the Region's future. Yet it is an emphasis easy to understand. For the activities in which the Region specializes, the activities which give the New York area its special characteristics as a "first city," are also the ones which are the most highly concentrated in the center of the Region.

Take the various segments of manufacturing. If we examine the industries serving a national market, as is done in Chart 9, it appears that most of the industries whose national employment was heavily concentrated in the Region (therefore high on the chart) also had an unusually heavy concentration in New York City within the Region. The City had other concentrations of industry, too, some not especially overrepresented in the Region. But, for all that, it was in the City that one found an unusual portion of the activity which gave the Region its distinctive place in the nation.

Nor was this true for manufacturing alone. In the various wholesale trades, in the various segments of the financial community, even in the different lines of consumer trade and service, unusually high concentrations of employment in the New York Metropolitan Region went hand in hand with unusually high concentrations in New York City. For instance, the Region's share of

CHART 9　New York City's Share of Employment in
New York Metropolitan Region, Related to
Region's Share of Employment in Nation, by
117 National-Market Manufacturing Industries

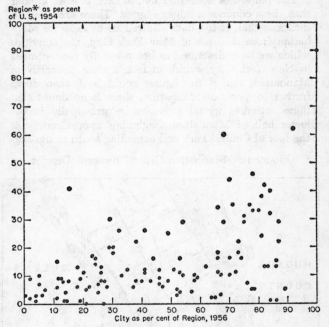

Region* as per cent
of U. S., 1954

City as per cent of Region, 1956

* Here the 22-county Region is represented by the 17-county Standard Metropolitan Area—a statistical necessity which makes very little difference in the positions of the 117 dots.

Sources: State departments of labor and U. S. *1954 Census of Manufactures*.

the nation's employment in merchant wholesaling of dry
goods and apparel, in securities trading, and in theatrical
presentation and services, was 53, 32, and 43 per cent,
respectively, on the most recent available date; and
New York City accounted for 96, 98, and 97 per cent
of the three corresponding activities in the Region.

The pattern of concentration, in fact, is even greater
than these comments might suggest. There are clear indications that, if the data allowed us to separate Manhattan from the rest of New York City, the activities
which we have described as being heavily concentrated
in New York City would, in fact, appear primarily in
Manhattan; and if the figures could be broken down
further by parts of Manhattan, there is no doubt that
these activities would prove to be principally in the
lower half of Manhattan, beginning approximately at
the foot of Central Park and extending south to the Bat-

CHART 10   Manhattan Central Business District

tery—an area we refer to as the "central business district." (See Chart 10.) The facts will not be stretched too much if we say that the unique aspects of the New York Metropolitan Region's economy are concentrated in this minuscule area of nine and one-third square miles.

The figures in Table 12 take on a special interest in the light of the role of Manhattan and the central business district. These figures reflect the extraordinary concentration of jobs in the crowded blocks of Manhattan and the swift tapering off of densities as one moves outward from Manhattan.* The three main zones given in the table, the Core, Inner Ring, and Outer Ring, are mapped in Chart 11.

High job density goes hand-in-hand with the unique functions of the New York Metropolitan Region. And the reason for the tie is not hard to find. In Chapter 5, we stressed the fact that the New York area, adapting itself to its handicaps imposed by a chronically high wage structure and by remoteness from the center of the nation, had come to specialize in activities whose locational needs were primarily of another sort. These were activities which drew heavily on external economies, stressed speed of operations and swift change, and had a compelling need for face-to-face communication. Because such enterprises must have an environment where these needs could be satisfied most readily, they have concentrated in the Region's most congested area.

* The reader who attempts to reconcile the figures shown in this chapter with those presented elsewhere in this book will occasionally find minor differences in magnitudes. Because of the peculiarities and limitations of the available data, we have relied principally on federal sources for comparisons between the Region and the nation, and upon a mixture of state and federal sources for comparisons among parts of the Region. This shift in sources also required the use of different dates—principally 1954 for the federal data and 1956 for the mixed state and federal data.

TABLE 12 Employment by Counties, New York
Metropolitan Region, 1956

	Miles from Manhattan[a]	Thousands	Per cent of Region	Thousands per square mile
Entire Region	—	6,699.8	100.0	0.97
Core	—	4,301.5	64.2	14.08
Manhattan[b]	—	2,717.5	40.6	121.32
Hudson	4	289.1	4.3	6.33
Brooklyn	7	664.9	9.9	8.41
Queens	8	398.4	5.9	3.49
Bronx	8	231.6	3.5	5.26
Inner Ring	—	1,572.3	23.5	1.09
Richmond	11	38.8	0.6	0.64
Essex	11	424.7	6.3	3.35
Bergen	12	222.5	3.4	0.95
Passaic	14	170.1	2.5	0.88
Westchester	19	229.8	3.4	0.53
Union	19	201.5	3.0	1.96
Nassau	20	284.9	4.3	1.00
Outer Ring	—	826.0	12.3	0.16
Middlesex	25	137.2	2.0	0.44
Rockland	25	30.9	0.5	0.18
Morris	25	61.4	0.9	0.13
Monmouth	31	68.8	1.0	0.14
Somerset	33	38.7	0.6	0.13
Fairfield	40	249.4	3.7	0.39
Suffolk	42	112.7	1.7	0.12
Orange	48	58.1	0.9	0.07
Putnam	49	7.1	0.1	0.03
Dutchess	64	61.7	0.9	0.08

[a] These are our rough estimates of the straight-line distance from the Empire State Building to the approximate center of population (not the geographical center) of each county. For convenience, the counties are listed in the order of these distances.

[b] Manhattan's central business district (see Chart 10) had an estimated employment of 2,475,000 or 266,000 per square mile.

Source: Our estimates based on federal and state figures. For details see Edgar M. Hoover and Raymond Vernon, *Anatomy of a Metropolis* (Cambridge: Harvard University Press, 1959; New York: Doubleday, Anchor Books, 1962), Appendix A.

CHART 11   The Three Main Zones of the Region

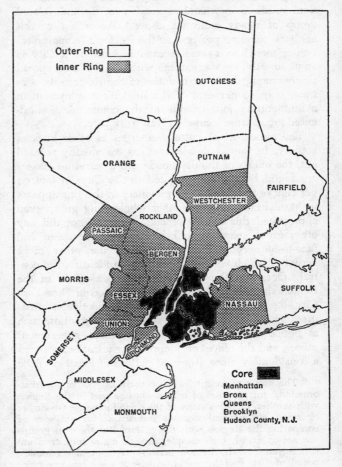

A clear indication of this appears as one analyzes the location of the Region's manufacturing industries, classifying them crudely according to their "communication" needs—a shorthand expression for the interrelated group of needs indicated above.* According to this analysis, some 78 per cent of the Region's "communication-oriented" jobs were located in New York City in 1956, mostly in Manhattan, with the balance spread thinly among the other counties of the Region. By contrast, only 40 per cent of the Region's employment in manufacturing jobs outside of the communication-oriented group were located in New York City.

The same sort of pattern emerges in other lines of activity. In the wholesale lines, as we already pointed out, the offices of the dry goods and apparel merchants are found heavily concentrated in the City; in fact 94 per cent of the Region's employment in this line appears in Manhattan alone. No other wholesaling group even approached this degree of concentration; nor did any other group manifest so heavy a need for speed and face-to-face communication. Among the other office activities which we have been able to identify, the central offices and the radio and television offices of the Region showed the heaviest concentration in New York City—84 per cent and 96 per cent, respectively, measured by employment. More staid office activities, such as public utility offices, real estate offices, government offices, and the offices of nonprofit organizations showed a considerably more dispersed pattern of location in the

* The group of industries we classify as "communication-oriented," for purposes of comparing one part of the Region with another, includes many of the same industries we earlier classified as "external-economy industries" for purposes of comparing the Region with the nation. But the two groups are not identical; for example, though many industries are concentrated in the Region because of external economies, not all of them find the need to cluster at some common point in the Region in order to satisfy communication needs.

Region, partly because of the differences in their communication needs and partly because of their orientation to local markets.

As we move outward from Manhattan to Brooklyn, Queens, and the Bronx, and to Hudson County in New Jersey, the pattern swiftly changes. In these areas, though the jobs are still crowded closely together in the old cities, the densities are a small fraction of those encountered in Manhattan. What is more, the nature of the economic activity in these areas is sharply different from that in Manhattan. To be sure, the proximity of Manhattan is evident in various ways. Numerous apparel shops are found in these areas, often tied in some way to the sales and cutting rooms of the central business district. So are many printing establishments, producing advertising matter and other products on behalf of clients in the central business district.

But much of the industry in these close-in areas has no umbilical tie to Manhattan. In many cases, the existence of a plant in these crowded inlying counties is explained by the fact that the external economies required by its operations are satisfactorily supplied in an environment not so highly specialized as Manhattan's. Rentable space is to be had in considerable quantity, sometimes in industrial loft buildings erected for the purpose, more often in little garage-style buildings or in outmoded plants of an earlier vintage. What is more, the prevailing rental range in these areas is somewhat lower, on the whole, than that in Manhattan—considerably lower than that in Manhattan's specialized loft districts, such as the Garment Center. A survey based on selected "Industrial for Rent" advertisements in 1956 showed industrial rentals in Brooklyn and the Bronx offered at about 32 per cent below those of Manhattan's nonspecialized loft districts, on the average; rentals in the Hudson-Bergen-Essex area were about 20 per cent below those in the Manhattan districts; and rentals in

Queens were about on a par with the Manhattan group.

Apart from rentals, the inlying counties immediately surrounding Manhattan—the other counties classified as "Core counties" in Table 12—offer other external economies. Contractors, suppliers, and maintenance facilities are at hand in considerable variety, ready to supply materials and services on short notice. Power, water and sewage, and police and fire protection offer minimal problems, except for a few industries with unusual requirements.

The Core counties surrounding Manhattan are notable for another important economic activity. For any manufacturer whose market consists principally of the consumers of the New York Metropolitan Region—for bottling works, bakeries, ice cream plants, and the like— these are preferred locations. One of the major locational problems of such a plant is to speed its product through the Region as fast as it can be loaded into trucks. Manhattan might perhaps be a more ideal distribution point, in terms of crow-fly distances to the various outlets of the Region. And so it is for some such plants, notably the big metropolitan daily newspapers. But in most instances, a Manhattan location presents a serious drawback. It requires the trucks to work their way through the heavily congested streets as they shuttle between the plant and the widely dispersed outlets of the Region.

To overcome this difficulty without getting too far from the market's center, most plants tend to locate in the other Core counties just outside Manhattan. At the same time, they tend to avoid location at the outer reaches of the Region. As a consequence, some 63 per cent of the Region's employment in consumer-goods industries catering to the Region was found in New York City in 1956. By contrast, industries producing principally for other manufacturers in the Region had only 42 per cent of their employment in New York City. Still more diffused in location were the "national-market" industries other than those in the communication-oriented group; for these industries, only 34 per cent of the Region's employment was in New York City. (Of course, as already said, the "national-market" industries which most sharply distinguish the New York area from other parts of the country showed an opposite tendency, the tendency to cluster in New York City.)

A related observation about these inlying counties: just as they constitute preferred locations for producers to the local market, so too they offer preferred sites to the truckers and wholesalers whose locational aim is to cut the time and cost of making deliveries and pickups through the Region. This is why wholesalers and distributors of such products as beer, tobacco, and groceries are so heavily represented in these areas, while being underrepresented in Manhattan. This is also why trucking terminals have gravitated in such large numbers to the Jersey meadowlands—one of the few remaining open stretches located close to the Region's center; it is why the Bronx Terminal market, a recently created fruit and vegetable wholesaling center, has thrived at its off-center location; and it is why Queens and Brooklyn have attracted so many depots for distributors.

But the industries found in these inlying areas are not all placed with so obvious a logic. In a few neighborhoods, such as Hunts Point in the Bronx and the Newtown Creek area of Brooklyn, one still finds fairly considerable clusters of heavy industry prone to give off noxious odors, generate dense smoke, or otherwise perform in ways which seem incompatible with the heavy residential use of the surrounding areas.

These plants are, of course, a reminder of the days when Hunts Point and Newtown Creek were remote from the center of the City and when "nuisance" industries could reasonably expect to operate without harassment in such areas. Today, though their location may seem anomalous because of the neighborhoods that surround them, these plants have nonetheless found a certain adjustment with their nearby neighbors. The residential areas surrounding the plants, built up originally for comparatively inexpensive use, have now deteriorated sufficiently that the pressures upon these plants to move elsewhere or modify their operations seem to have declined.

As one travels outward toward the more thinly populated counties of the Inner and Outer Rings of the Region, the nature of jobs changes quite dramatically. The teeming activities of office and loft, organized for speed, for change, and for personal contact, fall away. In their place, one finds the less hectic pace of the suburban commercial centers and the suburban plants. The transition is not all that regular, of course. A few Inner Ring cities, notably Newark in Essex County, breathe a little of the stir and bustle of New York City's central business district. Each of these cities offers a subregional center where the communication-oriented activities associated with some part of the Region tend to congregate: lawyers with a local clientele, local government offices, real estate offices handling local property, and so on. Here and there—but quite exceptionally—one finds a large national institution with substantial needs for communication headquartered away from the main concentration in Manhattan. General Foods in White Plains and Mutual Benefit Life in Newark are notable cases. At one point or another, too, especially in the older Inner Ring cities, little loft enterprises are to be found quartered in rented space and managing well enough on the external economies that are available in the environment.

But the differences in economic activity are more striking than the similarities. They are evident, for instance, in the very much larger size of the average manufacturing plant. This difference in size is not just due to the fact that the counties surrounding the Core areas harbor fewer communication-oriented industries, organized in clusters of little firms. If the communication-oriented industries and other special groups such as the nuisance industries are excluded, there is still clear evidence of the tendency for the larger plants to prefer a location outside the Core counties. In 1956, out of 101 industries in which the comparison could be made, some 83 showed a higher average plant size in the Region's counties outside New York City than in the City —size in this case being measured by number of employees. Looking at the phenomenon another way, we find that industries typically organized in larger plants were much more heavily concentrated in the counties outside the Core, especially in the Inner Ring counties, than industries organized in small plants. This tendency shows up sharply in the figures in Table 13.

TABLE 13   Distribution of Manufacturing Jobs in Zones of New York Metropolitan Region by Size of Plants, 1956

	Number of employees (thousands)	Percentage shares of Region's employment (NYMR = 100)		
		Core[a]	Inner Ring[a]	Outer Ring
All industries covered by table[b]	1,310.4	49.6	32.0	18.4
Industries with average establishments of:				
60 or less employees	734.6	61.2	24.7	14.1
61 to 240 employees	435.3	43.3	37.2	19.5
More than 240 employees	140.5	7.7	54.1	38.2

[a] In this case Richmond is included in Core instead of Inner Ring.

[b] Excludes communication-oriented industries and certain other special categories; also excludes establishments with less than 4 employees.

Source: Our estimates, based on data collected by state departments of labor under unemployment insurance programs.

Of course, the Region's counties outside the Core are different not only from the City but also from one another. Nor do the differences among them simply arise out of the fact that some of the counties embrace fairly good-sized cities, with their characteristically intensive blanketing of the land and their aging structures. There are other differences as well. The Outer Ring counties, such as Suffolk, Dutchess, and Orange, still contain huge stretches of undeveloped countryside, quite different from the more intensively developed suburban stretches of the Inner Ring. The counties on the New York State side of the Region have managed to develop an economy with little reliance on the use of the railroad net, while New Jersey's industry is heavily oriented to rail use. Besides, there is the related fact that some counties show a strong commitment to heavy, noisome industry, whereas others tend to attract activities with a more genteel appearance—activities which, in the words of one planner, "look like a college campus and smell like Chanel No. 5."

Some of the reasons for these differences are rooted in obscure history. But some are evident enough. Take, for instance, the distribution of the noisome industries —industries which offer a fire hazard to their neighbors, or give off unpleasant stench or dense smoke, or betray other antisocial characteristics. A certain proportion of these, as pointed out earlier, are in a few blighted industrial enclaves in the Core, such as the Newtown Creek area of Brooklyn and the Hunts Point area of the Bronx. But larger concentrations of such industry are found in the mosquito-ridden estuary areas of the Hackensack and Raritan Rivers and the waterways connecting them. The affinity of such industries for those areas is explained by topography. These marshy expanses, spotted here and there with outcroppings of rock, cannot easily be developed for residential use and do not raise the problems of residential propinquity that exist almost everywhere else in the Region.

Besides, the estuary areas of New Jersey contain good dumping areas for chemical waste, provide splendid opportunities for water-borne transport, and above all afford some of the most extensive rail facilities in the nation. Since the noisome industries tend also to be processors or users of bulky products, such as coal, petroleum, and metal ores, the transportation facilities of these areas are especially attractive.

The advantages of the New Jersey side of the Region over the New York side with regard to rail facilities are manifested in various ways. A 1956 survey of some 476 plants in the Region, nearly all of them outside New York City, showed that 55 per cent of the plants on the New Jersey side were equipped with rail facilities, while only 40 per cent in the rest of the Region had such facilities. In the same year, industries offering products of low value to national markets tended to be more heavily concentrated on the New Jersey side of the Region than those shipping high-value products.[1] Without much doubt, the difference reflected the greater concern of the producers having low-value products to minimize the costs of their shipments to national markets.

But the Region has not always had the same pattern of economic activity within it, and a few decades hence, more change will have occurred. Our next step is to see what these currents of intraregional change may be.

8

Jobs in Motion

"New York will be a great city," an English traveler once observed, "when it gets built." New York, of course, is still being built and rebuilt, and today the same thing can be said for some thousands of square miles in the New York Metropolitan Region.

Behind this rebuilding lies a process by which each area of the Region is forever being tested and retested for its most efficient economic use. The old wholesaling areas of downtown Manhattan, once so accessible to Port traffic, have faded out as the railroad and the truck have suggested a new pattern of location. The chemical plants and refineries of Newtown Creek, faced with the need for more waste-disposal space and for a deep-draft channel and docking areas to accommodate modern vessels, have transferred some of their facilities to the Jersey meadows. The big bakeries of the Region, confronted with the need to serve a growing suburban population and to avoid the congestion bottlenecks of the Core, have shifted eastward to Queens or westward across the Hudson. Apart from the relocation of firms, the pattern has been changed by the decline or death of old firms in outmoded locations and the rise of new firms in more favorable sites.

Some of the shifts in the Region's economic activities, of course, stem directly out of the shifts in its populations. Jobs in most retail trades, in neighborhood banking, and in a number of other "consumer-oriented" activities, for example, are best explained by these population shifts. But the shifts in other economic activities in the Region do not depend importantly on population shifts; and these are the activities on which this chapter focuses.

A BIRD'S-EYE VIEW

Table 14 shows what has been happening to manufacturing and wholesale employment in New York City, in the six next largest cities of the Region, and in the rest of the Region. The big pattern is plainly evident: growth has been slower in the cities than outside. In-

TABLE 14 Manufacturing and Wholesale Trade Employment in New York City, Other Major Cities of New York Metropolitan Region, and Rest of Region, 1929–1954

(in thousands)

	Manufacturing[a]				Wholesale			
	1929	1939	1947	1954	1929	1939	1948	1954
New York City	563.2	507.6	741.0	743.9	237.3	241.4	314.9	287.4
Six next largest cities of Region[b]	183.9	157.5	198.5	187.8	17.9	22.3	34.6	35.2
Rest of Region	275.0	285.4	458.6	525.1	14.1	19.6	37.0	58.8

a Production workers only.

b Newark, Jersey City, Bridgeport, Yonkers, Paterson, and Elizabeth.

Sources: U. S. Censuses of Manufactures and Business.

deed, absolute declines have sometimes taken place in the cities. In New York City, wholesale employment fell off in recent years, while manufacturing employment was just about unchanged. In the six other large cities, wholesale employment increased somewhat, but manufacturing employment declined.

Another way of looking at the trends is presented in Chart 12. Here, the distribution of certain kinds of jobs among the three main zones of the Region is traced through the last quarter-century. The Core (Manhattan, the Bronx, Brooklyn, Queens, and Hudson County) has seen its share consistently decline. The Inner Ring and Outer Ring have consistently increased their shares.

In some ways, of course, these patterns are too simple, even a little deceptive. New York City is no homogeneous mass. The Manhattan central business district, if it could be shown separately, would evidence an even greater retardation in the growth of manufacturing and wholesaling than the City as a whole. And some of the outermost areas of the Bronx, Brooklyn, and Queens would show the kind of sprightly increase which is typical of suburban territory. What is more, the record is incomplete: figures on central office employment, for instance, so critical in describing what has been happening to the central business district, are not available for any length of time and could not be included in the "business services" item in the chart. These are all rather significant qualifiers of the first impressions offered in Table 14 and Chart 12. And we shall have occasion to return to some of these matters as we carry our story further.

SEARCHING FOR SPACE

Despite all the qualifications, however, it is fairly evident, in manufacturing at least, why the oldest sections of New York City have slowed up in growth and

CHART 12 Employment Distribution by the Three Main Zones[a] of New York Metropolitan Region, in Four Selected Activities,[b] 1929–1956

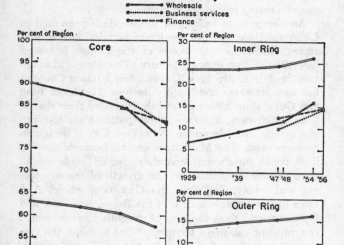

Legend:
- Manufacturing
- Wholesale
- Business services
- Finance

[a] For map of zones, see Chart 11. For total employment by zones, see Table 12.

[b] "Manufacturing" means production workers only. "Business services" consists of a large number of activities including advertising, accounting, credit agencies, duplication and stenographic services, news syndicates, radio-television, and legal services. The coverage differs somewhat as between 1947 and 1956.

Sources: For manufacturing and wholesale, U. S. Censuses of Manufactures and Business, 1947 and 1956; for finance and business services, *County Business Patterns*.

even declined, and why a similar phenomenon is to be discovered in the other old cities of the Region. As numerous field investigations have suggested and as our studies once more confirm, the search for efficient space lies behind much of the tendency.

What is "efficient space"? Seventy-five years ago, it might have been a mill-style building of five or six stories perched on a water-front location where it could exploit the advantages of river transport while sitting close to the labor pool of the cities. But the railroad and more especially the truck have changed all that. Today, goods can be hauled to and from a suburban location where more land is available; and labor can be assembled by private car or bus. In recent years, manufacturers in the New York Metropolitan Region have dramatically increased their use of land. Our surveys indicate that the amount of plot space per worker in the postwar suburban plants of the Region is over four times as great as in suburban plants built before 1922. In the new plants more than an acre of land is used for every ten workers.

The attractiveness of big sites might not have been so great, however, were it not for the technological changes going on inside many plants. The extensive use of continuous-material-flow systems and automatic controls, commonly calling for straight-line runs of several hundred feet, makes the typical city block an obsolescent site on which to set up a large modern plant. Today, the usual practice is first to design the production process, then to "wrap" the building around it. For some chemical processes, in fact, no building is erected and the production equipment sprawls naked on the land.

Still, the outmovement of plants from the cities of the New York Metropolitan Region, particularly the outmovement of large plants, might not have been so rapid were it not for the formidable hurdles to expansion at their existing sites. In neighborhoods like the west side of Manhattan, the Ironbound district of Newark, Long Island City in Queens, and the industrial districts of Passaic and Jersey City, one finds plants jammed among schools, churches, playgrounds, and homes, unable to break through in any direction. The acquisition of more site space is only one of their problems; the rezoning of such space is another.

So manufacturing has been favoring the open spaces of the Region. To gain a clear view of the ways in which the tendency has been manifested, it is helpful to exclude a few groups of industries—the communication-oriented group and others—because of the special locational forces that operate in those groups. In the remaining manufacturing industries, having more than two-thirds of the Region's manufacturing employment, our data show two significant facts about the outward tendency. First, industries with growing employment in the Region have been registering a much speedier outward shift from New York City than industries whose employment has stagnated or declined; indeed, the latter do not seem to have shared in the shift at all. Second, industries characterized by large plants have been shifting outward faster than industries characterized by small plants.[1]

Concerning this last point, it is important to note that both the large-plant industries and the small-plant industries have been participating in the suburban movement. Indeed, small plants have often ridden on the coattails of large ones, in the following manner. Many of the large firms that have vacated obsolescent structures to occupy new suburban or rural plants were already somewhat removed from the Region's very center. Their departure has thrown rentable space on the market at points which were less centralized than the old industrial loft districts. Thus, areas like Long Island City, Yonkers, and Jersey City have become rivals of the Manhattan central business district in the provision of rentable space to small enterprises. And the process promises to continue. Nonetheless, the rate at which small-plant industries shift outward has been slower than that for large-plant industries. The principal reason for the difference in rate, we suspect, is the reliance of small plants on external economies. Though external economies too are spreading in the Region, they still are more abundant in the densely packed central areas.

There are signs here and there in the Region that the old cities may not be altogether quiescent in the face of the inroads made on their manufacturing employment. Serious efforts may well be made by New York City and other municipalities to provide industrial space on attractive terms. They may use devices similar to those now used in urban renewal projects—that is, by acquiring sites through condemnation procedures on behalf of private users, by selling acquired sites at a discount from the acquisition price, by giving special tax treatment to industry on such sites, or by a combination of these and other devices. But it would not be realistic to assume that measures of this sort could change the picture drastically. Most plants in a position to build are now sufficiently uninhibited in their choice of land that acreage offered in city areas would have to come close to the price of undeveloped sites in the Inner and Outer Ring counties. (Some firms, newspaper companies for example, would of course pay more for city land; but such firms do not add up to a large proportion of all manufacturing.) This means that land acquired at a price of, say, $200,000 per acre in built-up city areas would have to be marked down to about $20,000 or $30,000.

For even more compelling reasons, there is little cause to anticipate any large-scale public program of new loft construction for industrial renters. Such a program would have to provide space at prices not much above those offered in the obsolescent factory buildings of the Region. According to our calculations, any new loft structure would have to be leased at an annual rental of about $3 per square foot in order for the developer to obtain a satisfactory yield, even if the developer received his land free of cost; this is three or four times as much rent as the small plant now has to pay for loft space in the Region.

So far, however, we have been considering only manufacturing space. Though much of the analysis applies as well to warehousing and distributing space, it does not apply at all to the space required for offices. If some office establishment had an incentive for leaving the office district of Manhattan (the incentive, as we shall shortly point out, is not very strong in most cases), it would not expect to save much in space costs by virtue of the move. Two comparisons are helpful in illustrating the point.

Take the position of a large central office anxious to occupy modern airconditioned "prestige" space. Its annual rental for such space in Manhattan's central business district would run in the neighborhood of $7 per square foot, or about $1,300 per employee. In a prime suburban location, after taking into account the increased space required for the installation of parking facilities and lawns outside the building, and cafeterias and other consumer services within, the cost of space per employee would be roughly the same as in Manhattan's central business district.

The user of run-of-the-mill modern office space would be faced with a somewhat similar outcome. In Manhattan's central business district, his space costs would be in the vicinity of $4.75 to $5.50 per square foot. In Newark, his costs would be roughly the same, and in Brooklyn just a trifle lower.

Manhattan's competitive disadvantage in providing plant and warehouse space, therefore, does not apply to office space. The office district's external economies, such as its shopping facilities and mass transit lines, help to overcome the disadvantage of high land costs. The fact that office space can be piled up layer on layer over a costly building site without any loss in efficiency— indeed, with some gains—contributes to the same end.

THE NEED FOR COMMUNICATION

We suggested earlier that the location of a considerable part of the economic activity of the New York Metropolitan Region was dominated by a need for swift and easy communication and by a need to share common facilities external to the firm. Indeed, some 600,-000 of the Region's 1,900,000 manufacturing jobs, according to our classification, were thought to be in establishments of this sort. The same is true of a considerable proportion of the 1,200,000 office workers in office buildings in the Region; a minor segment of the workers in wholesaling activities; and even a few "consumer" activities such as art galleries and high-style dress shops. If our reasoning is right, these have nothing like the same freedom nor the same incentive to search out added space that other activities in the Region have.

Still, certain locational questions do arise for activities of this sort. It is true that the communication-oriented branches of the apparel industry have an overwhelming need to cluster, but they have no need to cluster at exactly the same point from one generation to the next. Nor have they done so. Clusters such as those created by the apparel industry, the wholesaling groups, the central offices, and the "unstandardized" consumer outlets have gradually been moving northward from their early locations near the southern tip of Manhattan. More than anything else, the northward move has been a consequence of the way in which residences have spread to the north, east, and west (but not south), and the way in which mass transit facilities have been developed to accommodate that growth. Time after time, in the course of our studies, the location of the Grand Central Station and the Pennsylvania Station and the paths of the New York subway system have been assigned a major role in explaining why these clusters came north. The latest manifestation of that northward crawl is the new Lincoln Center for the Performing Arts, on the west side, most of it just north of the central business district as ordinarily delineated. Here, the new Metropolitan Opera House, the new concert hall, and other such facilities promise to attract added developments of the sort commonly associated with the central business district.

For all that, we do not anticipate much further northward movement of the communication-oriented clusters on Manhattan Island, at least not during the next twenty or thirty years. Some of the basis for this conclusion will be found in later chapters. Borrowing a little from the later discussions, however, we do anticipate considerable net growth in the total number of jobs housed in the present central business district. More important in magnitude than the growth, however, will be the shifts from manufacturing, wholesale, retail, and goods-handling jobs to many kinds of office jobs. Those economic sectors which are expanding will find ample opportunity to accommodate their needs by rebuilding inside the present limits of the central business district at somewhat higher densities on sites previously devoted to other uses. Thoroughfares not previously used very much for office buildings, such as Second, Sixth, and Eighth Avenues, will gradually acquire such structures, just as Third and Park Avenues have been doing in recent years.

Part of the reason for anticipating little further northward crawl of central business district activities is the sustained dominance of mass transit facilities as a means for bringing workers into Manhattan. Even today, with the use of the subway falling off and the use of the private car and bus at new heights, some two-thirds of the travel to Manhattan's central business district is done by subway and suburban train. This proportion will surely decline in the next decade or two but not sufficiently, according to our best guess, to overcome the drawing power of the Grand Central and Pennsylvania Station areas as focal points for Manhattan's midtown clusters.

The rivalry between the old Wall Street financial district and the midtown area of Manhattan is another matter. The giant commercial banks of New York City, long anchored to a tiny area around Wall Street and Broadway, have been going through a period of soul-searching about the wisdom of a northward move. Two factors have been adding to the attractiveness of midtown: (1) the entrenchment there of the central offices of large corporations, which are among the banks' principal customers; and (2) the spread of the banks' work force farther and farther from the tip of the island. The die seems pretty well cast for downtown, however, at least for the next twenty years or so. While midtown may grow somewhat faster in total financial employment, we are guessing that Wall Street will still be the unchallenged financial headquarters of the City. Heavy investments by the major banks in new office facilities in the old financial district and determined efforts to get rid of the archaic goods-handling functions of the area, such as the Fulton Street fish market and the Washington Street produce market, promise to make the area livable as an office headquarters for another generation. Added parking areas will probably blossom in the area; even some high-rent dwelling units promise to become available, providing an apartment-in-the-city for a few busy executives. Still, if the midtown area should continue to widen its advantage in mass transit facilities —especially in suburban facilities—the pressure for a northward move can be expected gradually to reassert itself.

Though we anticipate a rise in the total employment of the central business district, due to the vitality of the office sector, it should not be assumed that communication-oriented activities will be as closely concentrated in the central business district as heretofore. For all their need to cluster, one can expect some of these activities to grow more rapidly in the counties outside New York City than in the City itself. On the basis of the figures in Table 15, in fact, it appears that between 1947 and 1956 there was a decline of employment in communication-oriented manufacturing industries in New York City—not simply a relative decline but an absolute decline as well. Other kinds of employment classified in the communication-oriented category also showed comparatively slow growth or actual decline in the central portions of the Region during this period. For a miscellaneous group of business services, the Core counties' share of the Region's employment fell from 87 per cent to 81 per cent; for nonprofit organizations, the ratio fell from 82 to 65 per cent. Even the wholesaling of goods and apparel and the wholesaling of furniture showed a relative decline in Manhattan, though the other boroughs of New York City expanded to absorb some of the loss.

These shifts could mean that some of the establishments involved were breaking away from the clusters and learning how to operate away from the mass. But our field work suggests a very different explanation. As nearly as we can tell, something more subtle was going on—an internal division of functions in many firms, and a splitting away of that portion of the firm's activity which had little need for direct contact with the cluster. Much earlier in this account, we suggested that this internal reorganization of firms and industries was taking place; that the apparel industry had been reorganizing to separate the designing and selling functions from the sewing; that the publishing and printing industry had been separating the publishing from the printing; and so on. In each case, the communication-oriented functions have remained behind in the urban cluster, while the standardized, repetitive functions have

TABLE 15 Distribution of Communication-Oriented Manufacturing in New York Metropolitan Region, 1947 and 1956

	Number of employees (thousands)	Percentage shares of Region's employment (NYMR = 100)			
		New York City	Hudson	Essex	Rest of Region
Communication-oriented industries, total					
1947	418.6	82.6	3.9	2.9	10.6
1956	415.0	77.5	4.6	3.5	14.4
Segments of the apparel industries					
1947	259.5	84.2	3.8	2.1	9.9
1956	234.6	80.7	5.0	2.0	12.3
Segments of the printing and publishing industries					
1947	89.5	82.2	3.1	2.0	12.7
1956	101.3	73.8	4.1	2.4	19.7
Others					
1947	69.6	77.2	5.5	7.0	10.3
1956	79.1	72.7	4.1	9.0	14.2

Source: Our estimates. For definitions and details, see Edgar M. Hoover and Raymond Vernon, *Anatomy of a Metropolis* (Cambridge: Harvard University Press, 1959; New York: Doubleday, Anchor Books, 1962), Table 13.

sought advantages, such as transportation and labor advantages, in distant areas.

This amoeba-like behavior is encountered here again in our comparison of the Region's parts, for some of the operations being peeled off have not left the Region; they have come to rest inside the Region but outside its main communication-oriented cluster. For example, sewing plants for women's dresses (but not designing and selling offices) have grown in the suburban counties of the Region; these plants typically process garments of sufficiently high style that there is no strong need to seek out the more distant low wage areas of eastern Pennsylvania. Dry goods and apparel wholesalers also have expanded in these outside counties—but the expansion, as nearly as we can tell, has been in the storing and shipping of the goods, not in the selling. Central offices also have shown some expansion of employment in the suburban counties. But once again, apart from a maverick or two like General Foods, it has been the repetitive, internally self-contained office which has been located there rather than the externally-oriented activities of the elite executives.

Our views on this score are buttressed by the results of our questioning 22 headquarters offices that had moved a portion of their New York City activities to other parts of the Region. The firms indicated that the functions typically transferred had not been the elite functions—the decision-making activities, requiring intimate consultation with outside specialists. Instead, typically, they were repetitive data-processing, such as accounting, billing, tabulating, keeping Social Security records, preparing division payrolls, and handling sales orders.

Another kind of factor also lies behind the record of more rapid growth in outside counties of the activities labeled communication-oriented. For all the refinements of the analysis, the underlying statistics are very crude.

The employment in "nonprofit organizations" may cover the staff of the United States Council of the International Chamber of Commerce, but it also includes the part-time secretary of the Millburn (New Jersey) Boosters Club. Life insurance employment may include the home office of Metropolitan Life, but it also covers the Bergen County field office of such an organization. In short, some of the employment of these groups is directed to a small local market and its principal communication need is to be close to the "customers" it serves.

The activities which we have dubbed communication-oriented, therefore, very likely will continue to show considerable growth at localities away from their main clusters in Manhattan. Of all the possible causes of such growth, however, the one of largest potential significance is the relocation of the repetitive function of the central offices at points in the Region distant from the elite group. Those employed in routine activities in the office community probably outnumber the elite group 50 or 100 to one. There are good reasons for anticipating moves on the part of some of them. Though the cost of space, as we saw, is not one of these reasons, the changing nature of the labor market may well be.

Symptomatic of the possibilities of change is the fact that in 1910 the Metropolitan Life Insurance Company drew 46 per cent of its office force from Manhattan homes, but in 1946 drew only 15 per cent, and probably draws even less today. The extraordinary advantage of Manhattan over any other place in the Region for the collection of large aggregations of office workers is being watered down by the dispersion of the labor supply. Of course, Manhattan's advantage of centrality is still there; scarcely another place exists in the Region, except perhaps downtown Newark, that is effective enough as an assembly point to keep an office with a complement of 500 or 1,000 young women workers fully staffed. But the advantage is shrinking; and unless the disposition to hire young Negro and Puerto Rican women for office work increases swiftly, Manhattan's advantage will shrink even more.

The introduction of electronic data-processing equipment, a development which will gain momentum in the next decade or two, may also speed the separation of routine office functions from the elite activities. Today, many members of the elite group assume two types of duties; supervision of routine office functions and participation in management decisions. The first of these functions promises to become more highly specialized and more remote from management as automatic processes take over. This could speed the locational separation of routine functions. Indeed, many of the separations noted in the survey mentioned earlier took place in connection with the adoption of data-processing machinery.

Of course, many important segments of the office community have shown no disposition to disperse their routine activities to suburban locations, not even when automatic processes were widely adopted—a fact which accounts in part for our expectations of growing office employment in the central business district. Commercial banks, for instance, have typically installed such equipment in their central offices or in buildings nearby; so have life insurance companies. The routine operations of the large commercial banks depend on the swift movement of so much paper generated in the central business district that another location for their routine functions may be infeasible. And the home offices of life insurance companies, our analysis suggests, have so few compelling face-to-face communication needs that their elite group can afford to be wherever the routine functions are best performed, rather than the other way around. The existence of such situations suggests the unwisdom of projecting too rapid or too extensive a physical separation of routine from elite functions.

FREIGHT, LABOR, TAXES

Nothing accounts for the movement of jobs within the New York Metropolitan Region quite as much as the changing needs for space and the changing needs of various communication-oriented activities. Those changing "needs," of course, have not been simple; they have been intertwined with transport innovations, with considerations of labor supply, and with many other things. Transport and labor considerations, however, have had other effects on location as well, some of them not yet touched upon.

While the truck has offered manufacturers and wholesalers the freedom to look for locations well removed from the crowded old cities, it has also changed the attractiveness of the different sections of the Region in other ways. Time was when an enterprise distributing its product through the New York Metropolitan Region from some central point tended to favor a location on the New York side of the Hudson River. The river crossing was such a formidable barrier at times, as crowded ferries or inclement weather tied up traffic, that prudence demanded a location on the easterly side of the river where the bulk of the market lay. But the tunnels and bridges completed during the first half of the twentieth century whittled down the barrier and today the inlying New Jersey counties offer as good a vantage point for distribution in the Region as those to the east. This was evidently one of the factors which accounted for the shift between 1947 and 1956; during this period, the New Jersey counties increased their share of the Region's employment in local-market industries producing for consumers, from 23.1 per cent to 27.9 per cent.

At the same time, however, the bridging of the river barrier also has reduced Long Island's isolation from national markets. Producers located in Long Island no longer feel so remote from their customers in the South and West. True, Middlesex County, New Jersey, situated at the southwesterly edge of the Region, still offers somewhat better vantage points than Long Island for distribution to the rest of the country, with savings of about two hours in truck travel time and savings of fractions of a cent per pound in freight rates. But on balance the truck has tended to reduce Long Island's hurdle in attracting transport-sensitive industry serving national markets, for the difference in rail time is far more than two hours.

The increased use of air freight for intercity shipments will reduce the disadvantage further. So will the more widespread use of piggy-back freight, allowing Long Island plants to tap New Jersey's rail facilities without facing the time-consuming operation of floating rail cars across New York harbor. So, too, will an effective system of circumferential highways, skirting the worst of the congestion in the Region's Core. (Indeed, the circumferential highway system in general will give a boost to many heretofore peripheral locations including those in Somerset, Morris, Passaic, and Rockland Counties, at the expense of existing distribution centers such as Middlesex County.) The Narrows Bridge linking Long Island to the mainland by way of Staten Island promises to be a major part of such a circumferential system; this can be seen in Chart 13 which shows the major expressways of the Region, present and contemplated. Long Island's geographical disadvantage, therefore, will be gradually reduced, but it will not be fully surmounted.

Turning to labor, we find in some ways a similar story. Here, too, the differences which once existed among parts of the Region are being reduced. We saw

CHART 13   Major Expressways of New York Metropolitan Region

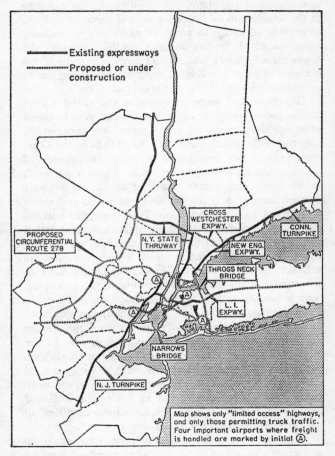

- **————** Existing expressways
- **··············** Proposed or under construction

PROPOSED CIRCUMFERENTIAL ROUTE 278

N. Y. STATE THRUWAY

CROSS WESTCHESTER EXPWY.

CONN. TURNPIKE

NEW ENG. EXPWY.

THROGS NECK BRIDGE

L. I. EXPWY.

NARROWS BRIDGE

N. J. TURNPIKE

Map shows only "limited access" highways, and only those permitting truck traffic. Four important airports where freight is handled are marked by initial Ⓐ.

some evidence of this in our earlier discussion: because of the rise of the automobile and the changing distribution of populations in the Region, the capacity of the Manhattan and Newark central business districts to provide an adequate supply of office help is gradually being matched by the suburbs. In like manner, the lower manufacturing wage scales existing in some of the outlying areas of the Region are gradually being pulled up to the scales prevailing in the central cities.

This process of wage convergence was still going on in the period 1947 to 1955. Hourly earnings in breweries, which in 1947 had been 12 per cent lower in the counties of the Inner and Outer Rings than in the Core, were only 2 per cent lower in 1955. In commercial printing, the difference narrowed from 5 to 1 per cent; in handbags and purses, from 33 to 18; in women's dresses, from 16 to 7; in women's underwear and nightwear, from 19 to 9; and so on. To be sure, the narrowing was not perfectly uniform; and some differentials still remain. But it is fairly clear that we are drawing to the close of the period in which lower wage rates are a factor attracting industry outward from the Core to other parts of the Region. Henceforward, if a manufacturer is pressed to look for lower wages, he will have to leave the Region altogether, just as many firms have already done. Nor will a move just beyond the Region do, in most cases. Though a few pockets of cheap labor may perhaps still be found on the edges of the Region in northwestern New Jersey, these will be easily sopped up. Industries in search of lower wage costs will ordinarily have no alternative but to follow the well-trod path to the South or to the "stranded communities" of the Pennsylvania coal fields and New England.

When we turn to the subject of taxes, once again we encounter similarities in the course of events—a leveling out of the differences among the various areas of the Region. Not that the tax systems or tax levels encountered by industry in the various localities in the Region are uniform; far from it. As for the tax structure, that of New Jersey puts more emphasis on property taxes and less on income taxes than is the case in New York. What is more, New Jersey localities commonly levy not only on the land and building of any business but also on its "personal property," including machinery and inventories. And New York City distinguishes itself from other localities in the Region by imposing a tax on the gross receipts of business. These differences are important because businessmen place a certain emphasis on the *form* of a tax, quite apart from its level. Our field work suggests that they have particular aversions to the paperwork associated with the New York City gross receipts tax and to the arbitrariness of valuation practices involved in New Jersey's personal property tax.

As for tax *level*, the variation from one locality to another is enormous. A comparative analysis of state and local taxes paid by manufacturing firms, as of 1955, shows that the levels at three city localities in the Region (Jersey City, Union City, and Newark) were three times as high as those in the locality with lowest taxes (Teterboro, New Jersey).

Of course, any generalization about relative tax levels is replete with conceptual pitfalls. A given tax structure hits different types of business with different force. Our generalizations were based upon a sample of 25 manufacturing firms actually operating in the Region. For each of these firms, we calculated what the state and local taxes would have been at each of 64 selected localities in the Region; and from these calculations we constructed an index reflecting the "typical" tax level for manufacturing plants at each of the 64 locations.[2]

A summary of the resulting figures, given in Table 16, establishes that there is little difference in the average level of taxes as between the New Jersey locations and the New York locations. However, tax levels at the large city locations in the Region tend, on the whole, to be significantly higher than those in other portions of the Region.

TABLE 16   Local and State Tax Levels of Manufacturers in Various Parts of New York Metropolitan Region, 1955

(Average for 25 selected firms, placed hypothetically at 64 locations, equals 100 per cent)

Average at 29 New York State locations ...	103.3%
Manhattan	129.6
Bronx, Brooklyn, Queens	122.3
Other 25 locations	99.9
Average at 31 New Jersey locations	96.2
Newark	140.6
Jersey City	160.1
Other 29 locations	92.5
Average at 4 Connecticut locations	119.5
Bridgeport	133.8
Other 3 locations	114.7

Source: Survey by New York Metropolitan Region Study. For details, see Edgar M. Hoover and Raymond Vernon, *Anatomy of a Metropolis* (Cambridge: Harvard University Press, 1959), pp. 55–60, 277–287. New York: Doubleday, Anchor Books, 1962, pp. 51–56, 262–271.

If this kind of measure could have been constructed over long periods of time, there is some doubt what the trends would show. There are various indications that a growing population in any area raises the level of local expenditures in that area and generates an increase in local tax levels.[3] In general, municipalities with a larger population tend to broaden the scope of their services, adding hospitals, libraries, and recreational services to the basic police and fire departments. This tendency raises the relative level of taxes in municipalities undergoing growth. We shall discuss in the next chapter how populations are growing fastest in the "newer" areas of the Region and slowest in the high-tax jurisdictions, a trend which may reduce existing differences in tax levels.

On the other hand, we cannot be sure whether the increasing use of state and federal funds by municipalities will contribute to the convergence trend or whether it will bring the opposite result. True, the enclaves where extremely low tax levels exist, such as Teterboro, are likely to be pulled up more closely to other areas by the growing importance of state taxes relative to local taxes. But the leveling tendency may not be universal. In the past, many localities—not necessarily the ones with the highest tax levels—have managed to use state and federal subsidies for education, roads and other facilities to lighten the local tax burden. It may well be, despite the larger role of state and federal programs, that local tax differences will persist, creating a modest outward push for industry.

SYNTHESIS

Any effort to synthesize all these various tendencies in some general statement about the locational pulls on enterprises in the Region is conceptually dangerous. Each enterprise is unique, laying a different emphasis on space, transport, labor, and taxes in its locational decisions.

Accordingly, if these factors had been working at cross-purposes, some pulling enterprises in one direction, some in another, an attempt at a synthesis would have faced major difficulties indeed. But the locational forces have tended to operate in just a few main directions, generally reinforcing one another rather than otherwise.

In the area encompassed by Manhattan's central business district, for instance, we observe a growing tendency toward office specialization. Manufacturing and wholesaling jobs are leaving the area, not only in relative terms but also in absolute numbers. Even the communication-oriented segments of these activities show an absolute decline (although this may be a statistical mirage induced by classification problems). Besides, even office work appears to be growing more slowly in Manhattan's central business district than in the Inner and Outer Rings. But office work in the central business district is growing at a sprightly rate, nonetheless, and promises to continue its growth, particularly in finance and business services. As for other specialized communication-oriented functions such as legitimate theatres, art galleries, and art museums, these will remain concentrated in or near the central business district even if they do not expand much in employment.

Beyond the central business district, stretching outward for many miles, the pattern is very different. In the close-in portions of Brooklyn, Queens, and the Bronx, and in most of Hudson County, some feeble expansion in wholesaling and distribution activities may be taking place. But this growth, if it is occurring, tends to be offset by the absolute decline in nearly every other branch of economic activity. And the picture is not much different in the oldest portions of such long-established industrial centers as Yonkers, Bridgeport, Newark, Paterson, and Elizabeth.

At the edges of these aging areas, the pattern changes. Extending outward from the outer parts of the Core counties, skirting the centers of the old suburban cities, areas of rapid employment growth extend in all directions. As one approaches the Outer Ring, the centers of growth are spottier, interspersed with large tracts of open land.

All the signs point to a continuation of the decline where it now is occurring and a continuation of growth in most of the remaining parts of the Region. The expansion of communication-oriented activities in the offices of Manhattan's central business district can reasonably be anticipated, subject to various qualifications which we shall develop in the next chapter. But in most of the land in the Core counties outside the central business district, the consequences of obsolescence apparently will go on unchecked. The prospects in these "gray areas" are for a continuation of the decline in jobs and for a creeping enlargement of the neighborhoods subject to such decline. The same prospect seems in store for most of the land embraced by the old cities in the outlying counties. The Region's job growth, apart from the heightening of its communication-oriented office activities, will center principally in the sparsely settled land of the Inner Ring and Outer Ring.

Even so, there are grounds for supposing that the difference in job growth as between the inlying areas of the Region and the newer areas, so evident in the ten-year period following World War II, may be reduced a little in future years. The inexorable abandonment of obsolescent quarters will surely continue. But the added incentives to move outward, heretofore provided by wage-rate differentials and by lower taxes, will not be so strong; at least, establishments anxious to find such savings are less likely to shift from the Core counties to the Rings, though they may well leave the Region altogether in their search.

These are the assumptions to be embodied in the projections presented in the final part of this volume. What will not be reflected in those projections is the possibility that the tendencies suggested here will engender some massive reaction on the part of governments and enterprises, aimed at arresting or reversing the trends. This is the kind of contingency with which no projection can expect to cope.

9

From Tenement to Split Level

The vast shift in urban populations from the cities to the suburbs over the past few decades has been chronicled and dissected about as thoroughly as any major development in contemporary America. The character and dimensions of the shift are well enough known. Since 1940, the suburbs of the nation's metropolitan areas have been growing several times as fast as the cities and towns they surround. Between 1950 and 1959, over 99 per cent of the 16.1 million population increase in the nation's metropolitan areas was reported outside of the central cities. Indeed, the central cities of a number of major metropolitan areas have reached the point of absolute declines.

At the same time, some have professed to see the beginnings of a countertide. Here and there, especially in the largest metropolitan areas including New York, it has been claimed that the weary commuter is returning from his ranch house in Suburbia to an apartment closer to his job in the central city. It has been suggested also that the exodus to the suburbs, whether or not already arrested, is likely to be halted in the future by a prospective increase in the number of America's older citizens.

These are issues of critical importance in any projection of future developments inside the New York Metropolitan Region. To assess the likely pattern of future developments, we can begin by taking a closer look at what has happened to population growth during recent decades.

THE CHANGING NEIGHBORHOODS

Few neighborhoods of the New York Metropolitan Region have remained stable in population for very long. In periods as brief as a decade or two, some have experienced explosive increases in population, some significant declines. Numerous forces have contributed to these population changes. Typically, increases have gone hand in hand with building booms; but they also have occurred through widespread "conversions" of old structures, through the doubling-up of families and the opening of rooming houses. Neighborhood declines have sometimes come about through the wholesale wrecking of old structures or the encroachment of business uses; but more commonly the population has simply "thinned out" in the existing structures, leaving smaller family groups in the same old dwelling units.

The net result of the various processes of population change may be seen in Chart 5, which traces the number of residents in various parts of the Region since 1900. In the period after 1920, the chart is dominated by the contrast between the swift growth in population outside of the Region's major cities and the stability or decline in population within the cities.*

---

* This chapter—indeed, almost the whole book—was in type before any results of the 1960 Census of Population were known. Preliminary figures released in June 1960 do not affect the validity of our discussion of past trends, for they clearly show the strong tendency of the old cities to become less crowded. The tendency is even stronger, in fact, than we envisioned in some of our 1965 projections—a fact which we shall mention again in footnotes to the final chapter.

The fact that populations could decline in some neighborhoods of old cities is hardly news. Manhattan's East Side had begun to register declines by 1910, and the island as a whole had begun decreasing in population by 1920. In one decade or another after 1920, Jersey City, Newark, and Paterson also registered net population declines. But the extensiveness of the declines occurring in some neighborhoods of these old city areas was obscured by the fact that growth was taking place in other neighborhoods at the same time; the city totals, therefore, often showed a bland stability, compounded from growth in some areas and decline in others.

By 1957, however, population declines had become endemic to large portions of the old cities, areas so large as to dominate the city totals. For the four principal boroughs of New York City, the pervasiveness of the decline can be seen in Chart 14. All Statistical Districts in Manhattan, almost all of them in Brooklyn, most of the Bronx, and portions of Queens show a drop in population.*

So much for first impressions. What lay behind these changes in population totals? Considerable light is shed on the shifts by getting down into the neighborhoods of the Region and observing the various phases through which they have passed. This kind of analysis involves a lot of risks, of course, mostly risks of oversimplification and over-easy generalization. No two neighborhoods are exactly alike; no two mature and decay in quite the same way. Still, we are not altogether foreclosed from generalization: there are common stages in the evolution of many neighborhoods, stages whose existence

---

* Chart 14 is based on 1950 and 1957 population figures which the Department of City Planning, New York City, developed from Census data. In Richmond (Staten Island), the only borough not shown on the map, the two northernmost districts decreased by about 4 per cent and the other four districts experienced gains ranging from 12 to 46 per cent.

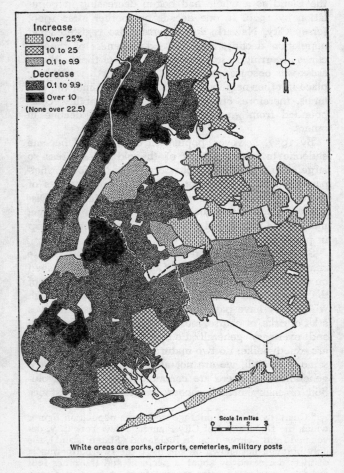

CHART 14 Population Change in Four Boroughs
of New York City, by Statistical Districts,
1950–1957

Increase
Over 25%
10 to 25
0.1 to 9.9
Decrease
0.1 to 9.9
Over 10
(None over 22.5)

Scale In miles
0 1 2 3

White areas are parks, airports, cemeteries, military posts

seems to explain what we see in the population trends.

Stage 1 in the evolution is the transformation from undeveloped rural land to residential neighborhood. Thirty or forty years ago, during the building boom of the 1920's, that change was taking place in a great arc not very far from Manhattan and in lesser arcs on the outer edges of Newark and the other old cities of the Region. In portions of Essex and Bergen Counties, and in wide areas of the Bronx, Queens, southern Westchester, and western Nassau, one can still recognize the neighborhoods created in that period. The housing there was responsive to the wants of that era—high-rise apartments crowding small sites near mass transit facilities; two-family houses shoulder to shoulder on shaded streets, sometimes with their single-car garages, sometimes without; more elaborate suburban dwellings in a few neighborhoods, on sites spacious by the standards of the 1920's but undersized by those of persons with analogous income status today.

Depression and war slowed down the growth of new neighborhoods for fifteen years or so after 1929. When building was resumed in the late 1940's, the arc of swiftest growth had shifted farther outward from the old city centers. Now one could see the new neighborhoods springing up just beyond the earlier ring. Bergen and Essex Counties still were growing swiftly, but they were growing at points farther from the Core and on a style different from that of the 1920's—with more spacious use of the land and with much less regard for the location of suburban railroad lines, trolleys, and buses. The Bronx and Queens still had their growing edges, but the swiftest changes were to be found farther out, in middle Westchester, middle and eastern Nassau, and Rockland. By the late 1950's the arc of swiftest growth had moved still farther outward touching Monmouth, Middlesex, Somerset, and Morris Counties, swinging through undeveloped parts of Rockland and northern

Westchester Counties, and biting a big portion out of Suffolk County on Long Island.

In the last few years, the pattern of development characterizing Stage 1 has changed further. Stage 1 is now almost exclusively a stage of single-family construction. In fact, in the counties of the Region now passing through that stage, such as Suffolk and Monmouth, over 95 per cent of the new dwelling units are in single-family houses. What is more, development now is more diffused; colonies of homes have been rising in cow pastures and potato fields, with considerable open space between colonies. Inside the colonies, too, land is being used with a more profligate hand. In Passaic County, for instance, though the average lot in new subdivisions had been only a little more than one-quarter of an acre in 1950, it rose to nearly half an acre by 1957. In Westchester County, roughly the same sort of increase took place during the same period.

Some neighborhoods, after arriving at Stage 1, have settled back to a long period of quiescence. Others, however, have not allowed many years to pass before beginning to show signs of Stage 2. In this phase, another rash of building takes place—only this time apartment houses dominate more than before. In the 1950's, this pattern was appearing very strongly on the outermost edges of some of the Core counties, in a few sizable Inner Ring cities (Elizabeth and Paterson), and in some commuter settlements with exceptionally good access to New York City, such as the commuter stops on the Hudson Division of the New York Central and on the Long Island Railroad.

The increased emphasis on apartment houses during this second stage is not hard to understand. The cost of land sites acquired in the course of Stage 2 is usually much too high for single-family development. Some of the sites acquired in Stage 2 are patches of open space, by-passed in the first building wave because of the pitch of the land or because of rocky outcroppings, or simply because they were not for sale at a reasonable price. Other sites are developed in Stage 2 by buying up and demolishing the oldest single-family structures in the neighborhood. In any of these circumstances, the cost of acquiring and preparing the site for building has been high.

Some years after the completion of Stage 2, the neighborhood is sometimes ripe for Stage 3—for downgrading and conversion. At this juncture, there is little new construction but there is population and density growth through the crowding of the existing structures. In some neighborhoods, Stage 3 may never happen or may be delayed so long that its theoretical possibility does not matter. The stretch of Fifth Avenue facing Central Park, for instance, went through Stage 2 some fifty years ago, but still clings to its high-income character. The Riverdale area in the northwest corner of the Bronx, more recently converted to apartment structures, promises to hold its quality for some time to come.

But much of Manhattan's upper West Side, sections of the middle Bronx and Brooklyn, and neighborhoods in New Jersey's older cities have lately seen the shift. It is in Stage 3 that the old structures in the aging neighborhoods begin to be offered to the newest in-migrants in the Region—today to Puerto Ricans and Negroes, yesterday to the Italians and Jews, before that to the Germans and Irish. Ignorant of the housing market, strapped by lack of income, anxious to be part of a large labor pool, these groups take what they can get in the crowded central areas of the Region; and what they can get is usually the structures just giving up the ghost as middle-income habitation. For the most part, the newcomers are young—at the time of life at which they are building a family. Shortly after settling into their new quarters, therefore, they are likely to add further to the population of the newly "invaded" neighborhoods.

After the in-migrant couples have settled down, however, the pattern is ready for change again. Now we come to Stage 4, the "thinning-out" stage characteristic of slum areas a few decades after they have been turned over to slum use. This is the stage at which, today, we find large areas of Manhattan, including Harlem and the lower West Side, and considerable portions of the Bronx and Brooklyn, as well as the inner sections of Jersey City, Newark, and Paterson.

There is a temptation to suppose that this thinning-out process comes about because families enveloped by these unsavory surroundings flee the slum areas as soon as they can, leaving unfilled vacancies or boarded-up structures in their wake. Without doubt, this sometimes occurs. But more of the population decline is accounted for by another process. Families in the run-down neighborhoods of the Region move infrequently, less often than those in the newer neighborhoods. The 1950 Census showed, for instance, that only about 8 per cent of the population of the Bronx, Brooklyn, and Hudson County had moved in a prior twelve-month period, whereas the proportion in counties like Richmond, Passaic, and Fairfield was between 13 and 16 per cent. Once settled, the heads of families tend to stay put; it is their children and their boarders who move out, for the most part, leaving their elders behind to enjoy more space in their deteriorating structures. So it is that some neighborhoods in the lower East Side today are heavily dominated by aging immigrants, remnants of the wave of Jewish migration of the early twentieth century and of the early Puerto Rican wave of the 1920's.

We come at last to Stage 5, the renewal stage. This stage is no more inevitable than the ones that preceded.

Where Stage 5 occurs, it usually takes two contrasting forms.

One of these is luxury apartments, either built on the sites of decayed tenements painstakingly assembled by private developers, or created by the expensive remodeling of old brownstones and other structures of felicitous design. So far, this kind of renewal has been confined to only a few areas in the Region. The East Side in Manhattan is laced through with renewals of this sort. Greenwich Village has begun to show a good deal of such activity. And here and there, in cities of the Inner Ring, one sees a high-priced apartment structure that could be said to represent the private recapture of slum-blighted sites.

The other type of neighborhood renewal is much more dependent upon the action of public authorities and the availability of public funds. Sometimes there are subsidies to private developers, aimed at bringing down the site costs or reducing the cost of borrowed money to levels at which medium-priced rentals can be charged; and sometimes there are continuing operating subsidies to bring rentals within reach of low-income families.

In New York City itself, renewal projects of heroic proportions have been developed during the past twenty years, involving public funds in various ways. The programs have affected a considerable number of people; over 85,000 dwelling units were built between 1946 and 1957, and nearly 500,000 people are housed in these structures. Yet, all told, the effects of these programs on land use in the City have been astonishingly small. The land area these projects occupy is not much over two square miles. In Manhattan, Brooklyn, and the Bronx, where renewal has made the greatest progress, only 1.4 per cent of the total land area has been involved. Even when we add private building to public renewal, we find that in these three boroughs, in the twelve years from 1946 to 1957 inclusive, only a fraction of 1 per cent of the dwellings were replaced per year.

THE UNDERLYING FORCES

The ferment of the Region's neighborhoods has produced a distribution of the Region's populations clearly responsive to a few basic demands. One way to detect these demands is to trace the residential patterns of groups of breadwinners at different levels of the income ladder.

Consider those at the top. Such people are drawn, to a disproportionate extent, from managerial and professional occupations.[1] Therefore, if access to the job were the only consideration in selecting a residence, this group would be expected to have a considerable affinity for the center of the Region—mostly for Manhattan and secondarily for Newark. At the same time, however, the income level of this group gives its members considerable freedom to choose a home wherever their desires lead. If they prefer a short trip to the office and spur-of-the-moment access to the bright lights and cultural diversions of Manhattan, the high cost of tolerable living quarters in Manhattan need not act as a bar. Contrariwise, if they prefer spacious country living, even though it involves two or three cars for the family and an expensive commuting bill, they are in a position to pay the price.

In point of fact, this group has exercised its freedom of choice by selecting every combination of access and spaciousness. Some have settled in a fifty-block stretch of Manhattan's East Side where a three-and-a-half room "cooperative" apartment can be had with an initial payment of $15,000 or so, and something like $175 monthly as maintenance charges. Others have preferred a little less access and a little less congestion, choosing equally costly housing in attractive and convenient areas like Riverdale and Brooklyn Heights. Still others have clung to old, relatively exclusive inner-suburban communities that grew up around rail commuter stations in the days when only the well-to-do commuted from such distances at all: Westchester communities like White Plains, Scarsdale, Bronxville, and Pelham Manor, and New Jersey suburbs like Short Hills.

But these communities, though they have managed to retain some of their pristine exclusiveness by restrictive zoning, still have not satisfied the wants of some of the higher-income group for spaciousness and semi-isolated luxury. So another segment with jobs in Manhattan and Newark has accepted the long and expensive daily trip from remote places like Pound Ridge, New York; Wilton, Connecticut; and Red Bank, New Jersey. As a result of this variety of choices, we find professional workers making up a disproportionately large part of the population of Rockland, Morris, Nassau, and Westchester Counties, as well as of Manhattan; and the managerial group shows up strongly in Nassau and Westchester. (Notice the omission of such counties as Bronx, Brooklyn, Queens, and Essex; we shall return to them later.)

Wherever they have settled in suburban areas, the upper-income groups have bought comparative spaciousness—that is to say, they have tended to select communities where living densities were low, as compared with other communities having a similar degree of access to Manhattan. This tendency can be seen in Table 17, which presents some figures based upon a survey of 200-odd communities in the Region as of the mid-1950's; the communities are located in a belt made up of five whole counties and parts of two others, a belt predominantly suburban in character and predominantly in the Inner Ring. In this table, the municipalities are classified by family income and also by access zones according to the length of commuting time to midtown Manhattan; access zone 1 is closest, access zone 2 is fifteen minutes beyond, and so on. Here, we see that in any given access zone the communities whose families had the highest median incomes were also communities with comparatively low residential densities. Other things equal (such as access), it is evident that people in the New York Metropolitan Region who can afford it will use their income to buy spacious living.

TABLE 17   Dwelling Units per Acre of Residentially Developed Land[a] in Selected Municipalities Classified by Median Income and by Access to Manhattan

Ranking of municipality based on median income per family[b]	Access Zone				
	1	2	3	4	5
Top fifth	—	3.82	3.86	3.26	—
2nd fifth	—	5.69	5.29	4.05	3.21
3rd fifth	—	8.90	6.22	6.52	3.28
4th fifth	7.80	9.61	8.48	5.39	4.31
Bottom fifth	27.79	7.86	9.29	2.23	3.83

[a] In 1954–55.
[b] In 1949.
Source: Edgar M. Hoover and Raymond Vernon, *Anatomy of a Metropolis* (Cambridge: Harvard University Press, 1959), p. 170. New York: Doubleday, Anchor Books, 1962, p. 161. Income data were from U. S. *Census of Population*.

As we descend the income scale, the pattern changes. One major reason for the change is that building costs, coupled with zoning regulations and building codes, rule out the choice of new construction for a substantial portion of the Region's population.

A major group, therefore, is limited in its choice of housing to the existing stock or to subsidized housing, wherever the housing may be. Just how each segment among the users of second-hand dwellings has made its choice is described in one of the underlying reports in this series.[2] Here, it will be enough to look at two or three segments of particular interest.

One is the group defined by the Census as clerical workers. In terms of income, these workers rank below the professionals and the managers but well above the laborers and service workers. As we saw in earlier chapters, the main job market of the clerical workers is Manhattan, with a lesser concentration in Newark. The principal concentrations of their homes are in the boroughs just outside Manhattan—in Brooklyn, the Bronx, Queens, Richmond, and Hudson County. These, therefore, make up a considerable proportion of the subway riders who daily fill the trains into Manhattan's central business district. Given their inability to command precious high-priced space in the lower half of Manhattan and their unwillingness to occupy slum space in that area, their compromise between access and spaciousness is found in the "bedroomy" boroughs just beyond Manhattan, lending a solid middle-class stamp to these areas.

Further down on the income ladder, we come to the least affluent of the Region's inhabitants, most of them confined to the oldest and most obsolescent structures of the Region (and, of course, to the low-cost public housing units). For many of these people, it is not income alone that confines them to the oldest housing of the Region, but also color or ethnic origin. Negroes and Puerto Ricans—but especially Negroes—still encounter difficulty in breaking out of the oldest neighborhoods. This problem is becoming less acute in the Region, but it is still one of considerable importance in shaping residential patterns.

The lowest income groups in the Region, therefore, are largely confined to Manhattan and Hudson County, to large portions of Brooklyn and the Bronx, to parts of Queens, and to the more central districts of cities like Newark, Paterson, Passaic, Elizabeth, and Bridgeport

—districts which were fully built up long ago. Some low-income families, too, are found in small dilapidated enclaves in well-to-do suburban neighborhoods; still others are found in shanty towns in the Ramapo Mountains and other "rural slums" scattered through the Region's outer reaches; but these groups outside of the old cities are not important numerically.

For the bulk of the lowest income groups, the run-down housing in the Region's oldest areas provides reasonably good access to the major job markets. For their livelihood, these groups rely heavily on unskilled service and factory jobs and goods-handling jobs. Various sources help us to pinpoint the counties where these types of jobs are most commonly found. As best we can tell, the jobs of "laborers" are found in greatest number in the Region's heavy industrial belts: one on the New Jersey side of the Hudson River from the Amboys up to Weehawken; another on the New York side from Hunts Point and Long Island City down to Brooklyn's Red Hook. The jobs of "service workers"—a mixture of occupations, including such callings as barbers, domestics, watchmen, and elevator operators—are strongly concentrated in Manhattan. But the importance of domestic help in high-income counties of the Inner and Outer Rings, such as Westchester and Suffolk, gives "service workers" some importance in the mix of occupations in those areas.

Though the job market and the residential areas of the lowest income groups coincide reasonably well, they are a little out of kilter in one respect. On the whole, the residences are more tightly confined to the center of the Region than the jobs. These groups, therefore, account for a considerable part of the "reverse commuting" that goes on every day in the Region—commuting outward from the center each morning, rather than the other way around. As a matter of fact, some streams of "reverse commuting" represent the fastest-growing elements in the changing commuting pattern. Groups of Negro and Puerto Rican men, traveling by car pool from Harlem and the Bronx to the New Jersey industrial belt each morning, have swelled the daily outbound flow over the George Washington Bridge. Groups of Negro women, traveling daily from upper Manhattan and the Bronx to Westchester communities, also contribute heavily to the reverse flow. This is a factor to be reckoned with in projecting the future distribution of population in the Region.

When the whole picture of residential location in the Region is totted up, it confirms some very old saws. As Chart 15 shows, Manhattan proves indeed to be a borough of the very poor and the very rich. In the Core counties surrounding Manhattan, though pockets of low-rent housing are important and growing more so, the general pattern is of a heavy commitment to the middle-income groups. Beyond these counties, in the Inner Ring, the high-income professionals and managers place their dominant stamp on the income distribution. And in the remote counties of the Outer Ring, the net impact of wealthy exurbanites, middle-income craftsmen and factory workers, and low-income domestics is to produce an income distribution little different from that of the Region as a whole.

Apart from job access and income, however, there is another characteristic that accounts for the Region's population distribution; this is the prevalence of children in the family. The higher the proportion of children in the household, the stronger is the incentive for a family to seek lower-density single-family housing with agreeable neighborhood conditions and good schools. This drive seems to permeate every income level and every racial group in the Region. All appear to have an eye to the advantages of an environment which will boost the children's chances, educationally and socially. But each family has to satisfy that drive

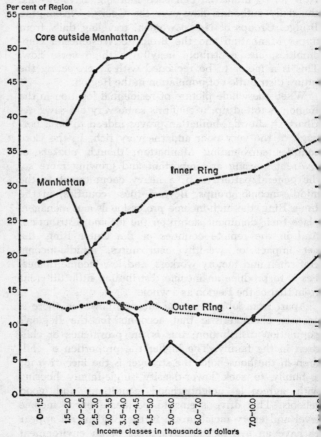

CHART 15 Geographic Distribution of Income Recipients by Income Classes, New York Metropolitan Region, 1949

Per cent of Region

Core outside Manhattan

Inner Ring

Manhattan

Outer Ring

Income classes in thousands of dollars

Note: "Income recipients" means families and unrelated individuals reporting income.
Source: U. S. 1950 *Census of Population.*

within the limitations imposed by its income level and by its general preference for living among people of its own kind.

The results of these preferences are seen in Table 18, which presents an analysis based on the 200-odd Inner Ring communities previously covered in Table 17. Though the table looks complicated on first glance, it makes a number of simple points. In each of the five income classes shown, the communities with a low proportion of children tend to be those in which there is good access to Manhattan but high living densities; and where the proportion of children is high, the access-density position is reversed. What is more, the communities with a low proportion of children are those with more multifamily dwellings and with little building activity.

This preference of all income groups to find less congested living whenever children are involved, at least to the extent that their means allow, is seen in the distribution of age groups in different parts of the Region. Though 22 per cent of the Region's population was under 15 years in 1950, the comparable ratio in Manhattan was only 16.7 per cent. In the other Core counties it was 22.1 per cent; in the Inner Ring, 23.7 per cent; and in the Outer Ring, 23.4 per cent.

There is a method, therefore, in the evolving patterns of the Region's neighborhoods—a method which reflects the choice between job access and spacious living for each income level and which mirrors the preference of each for more spaciousness as children appear on the scene. But the location of jobs has been changing, and so have the modes of travel to and from jobs. Income levels also have been changing, and so have the age make-up and family composition of the Region. All these changes must be taken into account when one projects the Region's future.

TABLE 18   Characteristics of Selected Municipalities in the Region, According to Income and Proportion of Children[a]

Ranking of municipality based on median income per family, 1949	Dwelling units per acre of residentially developed land, 1954–55	Per cent of dwelling units in multifamily structures, 1950	Average access rating[b]	Per cent increase in dwelling units, 1950–1954
Municipalities with LOW proportion of population under 15 (less than 22.5%)				
Total	11.9	32%	2.12	6.2%
Top fifth	6.8	40	2.25	11.5
2nd fifth	5.6	19	2.00	10.4
3rd fifth	10.6	33	2.25	4.9
4th fifth	8.8	30	2.22	6.6
Bottom fifth ..	16.0	39	2.00	5.7
Municipalities with MEDIUM proportion of population under 15 (22.5 to 24.5%)				
Total	7.8	18%	3.03	11.8%
Top fifth	3.4	11	3.33	17.3
2nd fifth	4.4	18	3.40	18.5
3rd fifth	8.0	18	2.70	14.7
4th fifth	7.8	23	3.09	11.2
Bottom fifth ..	16.2	26	2.83	6.8
Municipalities with HIGH proportion of population under 15 (over 24.5%)				
Total	4.6	12%	3.19	19.0%
Top fifth	3.5	10	2.94	21.9
2nd fifth	5.1	12	3.24	18.4
3rd fifth	5.2	6	3.09	21.8
4th fifth	8.7	16	3.40	5.0
Bottom fifth ..	4.1	21	3.80	23.5

[a] Age data from U. S. 1950 *Census of Population*.
[b] Average of access zone numbers as in Table 17.
Source: Edgar M. Hoover and Raymond Vernon, *Anatomy of a Metropolis* (Cambridge: Harvard University Press, 1959), p. 180. New York: Doubleday, Anchor Books, 1962, p. 171.

THE FORCES IN MOTION

The largest single force leading to the redistribution of the Region's populations is the changing location of the Region's jobs. As we have seen, jobs are not located in the Region altogether independently of where the work force lives. Some manufacturing plants are obliged to settle close to low-income neighborhoods in order to recruit workers at rock-bottom wages. Large research laboratories are prepared to indulge the suburban preferences of their scientific work force by locating outside the central areas of the Region. And of course the location of most jobs in the retail trades and many in commercial banking faithfully reacts to shifts in the Region's population. Nonetheless, most jobs in manufacturing and wholesaling, and jobs in some lines of office work, can shift and have shifted their location from one part of the Region to another without much need to consider how the population itself was shifting.

Given the importance of job access and given the relative independence of so many establishments in locating their plants in the Region, the residences can be expected to follow the jobs more than the other way around. It is not enough, however, to speak of all jobs as if they were a homogeneous mass. Office jobs, we observed—elite office jobs in particular—were holding up in the central business district of Manhattan better than other types. Even though Manhattan's growth in office jobs was comparatively slow, it *was* growth, not decline. And since this absolute growth is likely to continue, the need of high-income people for access to the central business district will almost certainly increase.

This possibility has to be considered alongside another. Spacious suburban living—living which combines exclusiveness with at least tolerable access—will be more and more difficult to attain as the years go by. The upper income groups, fleeing from contact with the outward spread of the speculator's subdivision, are already having to settle in areas which strain the limits of the commuter's endurance. Unless there is a greatly accelerated growth in the use of helicopters, the upper income groups may be forced to resort rather more to luxury apartment living in the City. The numbers involved cannot be large, of course; the price of space for luxury apartments is too high for more than a tiny minority of those who work in the central business district. But their total demand could make a measurable impact on the use of land in and close by the central business district.

Changes in the distribution of jobs inside the New York Metropolitan Region in the decades just ahead are also likely to affect the residential preferences of the lowest income groups, to the extent that they can exercise any choice in the matter. The lowest-income jobs are concentrated in manufacturing, wholesaling, and personal services. Manufacturing and wholesaling activities are showing declines in employment in Manhattan and are evidencing only slight growing power in the other Core counties. The service jobs may still grow a little in the central business district of Manhattan, but the prospect in the areas just beyond that district is one of decline—until one reaches the newer suburbs of the Inner Ring and beyond, where rapid growth is likely. Accordingly, on balance, the need for job access is likely to pull the low income groups outward from New York City toward the Inner Ring.

This likelihood is enhanced by various factors. One is that the Puerto Rican, by any yardstick that can be found, seems to be following the same patterns of adjustment as those of other immigrant groups before him. Allowing for the fact that no two such groups have experienced exactly the same adjustment process, the Puerto Rican's adjustment seems very much like those

of groups with somewhat similar cultures in the past—
a little like the pattern of the Southern Italian, for instance. In general, field studies show that his job skills
have increased, his job opportunities have expanded,
and his aspirations or those of his children have risen.
The trek of the German from the East Side to Yorkville
and Brooklyn, and of the Jew from Rivington Street to
the Bronx and White Plains, promises to be repeated
once again by the Puerto Rican.

The position of the Negro, too, is showing signs of
change, though at another pace. The social and con-
tractual bars which have excluded the Negro from suburban neighborhoods in the Region, even when he was
in a position to pay for space in those neighborhoods,
seem to be weakening a little. It is hard to demonstrate
this sort of conclusion by objective means. But there are
various straws in the wind. The recent rate of increase
in the Negro populations of Inner Ring cities has been
phenomenal. In Newark, the "nonwhite" population
rose 109 per cent between 1950 and 1958. In Mount
Vernon, New Rochelle, East Orange, Montclair, and
Englewood, the rise appears to have taken place at
about the same rate. And all this at a time when populations in Harlem have been declining. True, most of
these increases were simply due to the development of
new black ghettoes in suburban areas, but some represented the diffusion of the Negro's living patterns.

The Negro's desire for less congested living is a force
which will continue to push him outward from the Region's center. An analysis of contemporary Negro peri-
odicals suggests that there has been a rapid adoption by
the Negro of all the status symbols and aspirations of
the whites, including the aspiration for spacious living.
A study of some 82 Negro families which had moved
from a privately owned housing project in Harlem between 1952 and 1956 pointed in the same direction.
Questioned about their move, 72 named "desire to own

a home" as one of their reasons for moving, just as any white group would do. The same study suggests the extent to which Negroes now get help in finding new quarters. Among this group, 35 were led to their new quarters by real estate agents and 33 by friends already in the area. The fact that so many could arrange to buy a house means, of course, that they were not among the lowest income groups in the Region. But their willingness to leave the Negro ghetto and their ability to find homes outside of Harlem through real estate agents and friends point the way which other Negroes will follow to the extent that their means allow.

With their job opportunities moving outward, the chances are very strong that low income groups will grow in the suburban areas as speedily as housing opportunities permit. Large-scale public housing projects in New York City may slow down the move, but it is doubtful that such projects could stem or reverse the flow.

Will housing opportunities in the Region exist to accommodate the flow? The housing which will become obsolescent and ripe for down-grading over the next twenty years will be drawn largely from stock built between 1910 and 1930, during a period when the Region's population increased by about 4,000,000. Much of this housing will be turned over for low-income use; and much of it is located in outlying parts of the Core counties and in the Inner Ring. The obsolescence rate of the block of housing built before 1930 promises to be especially high because most of it was built without much regard for the existence of the automobile. At the same time, no projection which we would consider realistic contemplates an increase in the demand for such housing in the Region anywhere near as great as the prospective increase in supply. The net result, therefore, is likely to be a continued—perhaps an accelerated —thinning out of populations in existing slum housing in the Region. The pressures which generate doubling-up, conversions, and crowded rooming houses in the "new" slums may well be reduced. It is certain that the densities generated in the newly down-graded neighborhoods will be lower than those in the old slums, extending a trend toward declining slum densities which has been apparent in the Region for thirty or forty years.

Developments in passenger transportation facilities in the Region—not only in subways and suburban commuting systems but also in roads, river crossings, and parking facilities—can condition the responses of all groups in the Region to future changes in the location of their jobs. No complex analysis is needed to understand what has been happening in the Region in the interplay between passenger facilities and population shifts. The urge for outward movement came from forces which were partly independent of the passenger facilities. But the speed and extent of this outward movement depended critically on the kind of passenger facilities laid down. New York City's construction of a subway system capable of the speedy mass movement of commuters improved the opportunities for the development of the Manhattan central business district and helped lay an economic basis for cramming nearly 8,000,000 people within its five boroughs. The lower traffic potentials of the transportation system provided by the New Jersey municipalities were a factor in the more diffused growth of that part of the Region.

The overriding force in transportation in recent decades, of course, has been the automobile. Some of its effects have been almost too obvious for comment: it has dispersed population by opening up new territory far from the subway lines and suburban trains; and it has made possible a more lavish use of the land by adding so much to the urban supply. Some of the automobile's effects have been subtle and devious. For example, it has lapped off the cream of the subways' and suburban railways' business by taking over much of their off-peak and week-end volume. Just in the brief period between 1948 and 1956, the number of subway passengers entering the Manhattan central business district outside the hours of 7 to 10 in the morning fell by 20.8 per cent, though the number during those peak hours fell only 11.7 per cent. The impact of the new competition on the subways and the suburban lines, therefore, has been double-barreled: the competition has meant not only a loss of business but a loss of the kind of business which the rails could service without adding much to their capacity and their costs. In the circumstances, the pressure for rate increases on the mass transit lines was inevitable. But to achieve a rate increase was only to be mired a little deeper; for with each rate increase, the off-peak travelers and the commuters—but especially the off-peak travelers—shifted even more strongly to the use of the automobile.

The figures in Table 19 mirror the shift from mass transit to the automobile in trips to the central business district. The thirty-year growth of automobile and taxi travel into the Manhattan central business district is phenomenal; and so is the dip in the use of rapid transit and suburban railroad after 1948.

Figures from another source disclose added aspects of the shifting patterns of travel inside the Region. An analysis of Hudson River crossings, made by the Port of New York Authority, shows some striking changes between 1948 and 1958. Trips from New Jersey homes to Manhattan's central business district declined considerably—the net consequence of a big drop in rail and ferry travel, offset in part by a rise in auto and bus travel. The big growth in river crossings (other than truck crossings) has come from two sources: from New Jerseyites bound for New York locations *outside* of Manhattan's central business district; and from New Yorkers

TABLE 19 Number of Persons Entering Manhattan Central Business District[a] in Vehicles on a Typical Business Day, by Mode of Travel, Selected Years, 1924–1956

| | Thousands of persons | | | | | | Percentage of total number | | | | | |
	1924	1932	1940	1948	1956		1924	1932	1940	1948	1956
Total	2,343	2,697	3,271	3,691	3,316		100.0	100.0	100.0	100.0	100.0
Auto and taxi	249	430	503	577	736		10.6	15.9	15.4	15.7	22.2
Bus	—	40	150	290	246		—	1.5	4.6	7.8	7.4
Truck	82	86	116	80	92		3.5	3.2	3.5	2.2	2.8
Trolley	161	88	59	24	3		6.9	3.2	1.8	0.6	0.1
Rapid transit	1,531	1,752	2,169	2,389	1,970		65.3	65.0	66.3	64.8	59.4
Railroad (commuter)	217	216	206	283	233		9.3	8.0	6.3	7.6	7.0
Ferry (pedestrians)[b]	103	85	68	48	36		4.4	3.2	2.1	1.3	1.1

[a] Here defined as Manhattan south of 61st Street.

[b] Pedestrians are not counted unless they entered by ferry.

Source: Regional Plan Association, Bulletin 91, *Hub-Bound Travel in the Tri-State Metropolitan Region: Persons and Vehicles Entering Manhattan South of 61st Street, 1924–1956* (New York, 1959).

headed for New Jersey points, most of these no doubt being the "reverse commuters" to whom we referred earlier. All told, therefore, the figures confirm the general picture of a dispersion in commuter travel: a breaking up of the simple old pattern of convergence in the central business district; and a shift from rails to rubber.

In view of the way in which jobs and residences seem to be redistributing themselves in the Region, some new difficulties seem in store for the mass transit facilities. Our projections imply that the number of commuters demanding daily access to the central business district, whether by automobile, bus, or suburban train, will show a considerable increase over the next few decades, the increase being due principally to the rise of office work. At the same time, as manufacturing and whole-sale jobs decline in the central business district, the short-haul business of the subways will further decline. The aspiration for the split-level-with-garage in the suburbs which permeates all income levels except perhaps the very highest (where it has already been realized to the extent desired), will surely continue to redistribute the remaining subway riders outward from the center of the Region. Many former subway riders will move beyond the subway's range. Some of them will continue to use the subway for the final stage of the inbound trip to the office; others will make the whole trip by suburban railroad, at the very time when some of the railroad companies will be bending every effort to avoid expanding their facilities to supply a service which they consider profitless; and still others will travel exclusively on rubber tires.

Public subsidies will probably slow the deterioration in the quantity and quality of suburban rail service, but not enough, we suspect, to stem some continued shift from railroads to the automobile. Accordingly, we project an increased use of the automobile for commuting. The bottleneck to the growth of the central business district, therefore, may prove to be the facilities afforded to the automobile commuter—not only the approach roads but the parking areas as well. This is a generalization which applies even more patently to the downtown financial district of Manhattan than to the midtown area.

Outside the central business district, the impact of the automobile promises to be more of what it already has been. The high-speed expressways lacing their way through the Region are continually opening up new stretches of undeveloped territory. Shortly, new roads extending westward from the Hudson River will open up stretches of Morris County and even bring Sussex County, lying just outside the limits of the Region, within commuting range of Manhattan. New circumferential links, such as the Cross Westchester Expressway and Route 278 (see Chart 13 in the previous chapter) will tie the expressways together in a complex which will accommodate travel from one point on the periphery of the Region to another. The pattern will loosen the ties of the residential suburbs to the Region's cities even further, and will give an added impetus for the leapfrogging of residential developments into localities far removed from Manhattan and Newark.

If one adds rising incomes explicitly to the list of variables affecting residential shifts, as we have already done implicitly in our earlier discussion of the Puerto Rican and the Negro, the addition only serves to reinforce the generalizations broached earlier. In 1939, Manhattan residents recorded the highest per capita income of all the counties of the Region, fully 63 per cent above the Region average. At that time, some of the counties which were destined soon thereafter to grow with particular rapidity were reporting a comparatively low per capita income: Bergen and Union were each 15 per cent below the Region average, Queens 21 per cent below, Nassau 26 per cent below, and even Westchester 7 per cent below. By 1956, however, Manhattan's per capita income no longer was the highest in the Region and the fast-growing counties mentioned above had all swung from levels below the Region average to levels above; by that date the Manhattan figure was only 14 per cent above the Region, while Bergen and Union were each 9 per cent above, Queens 6 per cent above, Nassau 25 per cent above, and Westchester 24 per cent above.

What was happening seems apparent enough. In the redistribution of populations in the Region, families at the upper end of the income scale were shifting outward faster than the others. This was the overriding tendency notwithstanding the fact that Negroes and Puerto Ricans—most of them with comparatively low incomes—seem to have had a part in the outward move, and notwithstanding the fact that the demand for high-rent luxury apartments grew considerably in Manhattan. Despite these eddies in the current, one could still describe the current itself as an outward movement of those who could best afford it. And there is little to suggest that the future will differ in this respect from the past.

One other factor needs close examination for its future implications, namely, the changing age distribution and household composition of the Region's populations. It takes no special act of clairvoyance to project, with fair precision, the number of adults, by age groups, likely to be residing in the Region in the next two or three decades; most of these prospective residents are already present in the Region. Our best estimates indicate that between now and 1985, the fraction over 65 years of age will expand the fastest. The group between ages 35 and 64 will be very slow to increase in number, partly because the new arrivals in this group will include the lean crop of depression babies and partly because there will be continued out-migration by those of more advanced years within the group. But the increase in the group aged 15 to 34 will be very rapid.

This pattern would seem to imply, among other things, another upsurge in family formation and another wave of construction in single-family suburban developments, with the emphasis on economy appropriate to the age of the young parents. The increase in the number of older inhabitants may also suggest a rise in the demand for small-household housing, conveniently located. But a "convenient" location for this group need not be the central city. For every one in the group whose income and social ties suggest a central-city location, there are likely to be several whose income or social preferences will rule out such a choice. To the extent that these persons give up their single-family homes in the suburbs, they are likely to settle for apartment-house living in the same neighborhoods, close to friends, children, and other social ties.

These comments add up to a comparatively simple picture. Close by the central business district, we shall see more demand for high-income housing. Just beyond, for miles in every direction, we are likely to see a continued thinning out and aging of populations—a thinning out which may be modified but surely will not be reversed by public housing programs; and a similar trend will probably prevail in the old cities of the Region's outlying counties. Everywhere else in the Region there will be population increase. Some of it will arise from the added building of multiple dwellings. But most of it will be single-family housing, spread out spottily on the landscape, eating up land at new high rates.

PURSUING THE CONSUMER

We have reached the stage in our analysis of the Region's changing structure in which an earlier promise can be redeemed. In the last chapter we said that the locations of employees who are engaged in serving the consumer could best be discussed in conjunction with population trends.

The obvious point that retail trade and consumer services tend to grow in close parallel with population and income was already made in Chapter 6. The related point that the ascendancy of suburban living has changed the "mix" of these consumer activities also was discussed. Our problem here, however, is one of identifying the shifts inside the Region in the location of this changing group of consumer activities.

The dominant fact, of course, is that as residences have redistributed themselves outward from the Region's center, the trades and services which cater to the consumer have followed close in their wake. Chart 16 shows the main trends in retail trade (the selling of goods rather than services). As population grew faster in the Inner and Outer Rings than in the Core, employment in the retail trades did likewise. Retail sales were redistributed outward even faster than population, probably because the personal income of the Region also was shifting faster than population. If we divide the Region up along different lines from those in the Chart, comparing the old cities of the Region with all the rest, the pattern so familiar in other contexts appears once more. Retail trade was growing much more slowly in the old cities than in the rest of the Region. In fact, measured by employment, retail trade was actually declining in those cities in the period from 1948 to 1954, and there are various indications that the decline has continued since.

But there is more to the story. If consumer activities have followed the shift of residences, it is also true that some kinds of retail trade and consumer services have followed residences more faithfully than others. Specifically, some lines have clung more tenaciously to

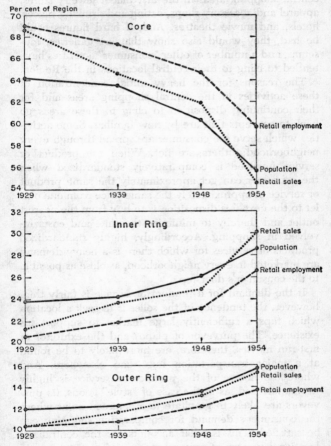

CHART 16 Retail Trade and Population Trends in Main Zones of New York Metropolitan Region, 1929–1954

Per cent of Region

Core

Retail employment
Population
Retail sales

1929   1939   1948   1954

Inner Ring

Retail sales
Population
Retail employment

1929   1939   1948   1954

Outer Ring

Population
Retail sales
Retail employment

1929   1939   1948   1954

Source: Population estimates are our own, based on U. S. *Census of Population.* Other data based on U. S. *Census of Business* for years shown.

the central shopping areas in the hearts of Manhattan, Newark, and Brooklyn. By and large, these have been activities which were more highly concentrated in the central shopping areas in the first place: jewelry stores, apparel and accessory shops, eating and drinking places, hotels, and movie theatres. And, if hard figures could be had, they would also show that art galleries, museums, and a number of other "consumer" activities have tended to cling to their central locations in the Region.

The reasons for the heavy initial concentration of these activities in the central shopping areas and for their continuing disposition to cling to these areas go back to concepts that are by now familiar. Some activities which serve the consumer are spread through every neighborhood; others are not. When the product or service involved is comparatively standardized—when the consumer can get approximately the same product or service at approximately the same price from one outlet to the next—his disposition is to buy from the nearest outlet and thereby to minimize the time and costs involved in shopping. Accordingly, highly standardized products or services for which there is a heavy demand are marketed in every neighborhood, as close as possible to the consumer's doorstep.

If the demand for a product or service is fairly thin, however, the tendency of the seller is to seek a location which taps a sufficiently large market to support his existence. The purveyor of pianos and the exhibitor of first-run movies, therefore, are more likely to be found at a major transportation hub than elsewhere. And where the nature of the product or service is highly unstandardized, as in the case of "style" goods, its purveyors are likely to gravitate to a common point where the consumer's demand for comparative shopping can be satisfied. This is what accounts for the centralized locational pattern of apparel stores, jewelry stores, and art galleries. And some of the unstandardized lines are centralized for still another reason: they serve not only a local market but also a market of out-of-towners brought to the metropolis by business or pleasure.

Table 20 illustrates the shift in sales between the three main central shopping areas of the Region and the rest of the Region for the center-oriented lines from 1948 to 1954. Of the individual trades and services shown in the table, only department stores exhibit a pronounced tendency to shift outward from the central shopping areas. The trek of department stores toward

TABLE 20 Sales in Central Shopping Areas[a] of Manhattan, Newark, and Brooklyn as Percentage of Sales in New York Metropolitan Region, by Selected Consumer Trades and Services, 1948 and 1954

	1948	1954
All retail trade, plus hotels, motels, movie theatres	21.1	17.4
Retail trade		
Department stores	71.5	61.9
Furniture, furnishings, appliances ..	19.3	18.4
Jewelry stores	47.1	44.8
Apparel and accessories	38.6	36.9
Eating, drinking places	25.8	24.8
All other retail trade[b]	8.2	6.3
Consumer services		
Hotels and motels	65.0	63.9
Movie theatres	26.6	29.2

[a] "Central business districts" as defined by U. S. Census Bureau. For Manhattan, this is an area much smaller than the central business district as referred to elsewhere in this volume; the smaller Census area falls approximately between Third and Tenth Avenues and between Central Park and Canal Street.

[b] For example, food stores, auto dealers, gasoline stations, and liquor stores.

Sources: U. S. *1954 Census of Business,* series on "Retail Trade," "Selected Services," and "Central Business District Statistics," supplemented by our estimates.

the suburbs has been in evidence for several decades, and especially in the years after World War II. Some of the old "downtown" stores have gone out of business; others, like Macy's and Gimbel's, have opened branches in the suburbs. The shift in the period since World War II, however, has been more rapid than concurrent population changes and more rapid, in our view, than one might have reason to expect in the future. Department stores, unlike retail lines organized in smaller units, probably make their adjustments to population shifts by fits and starts, not as a gradual or continuous process. These stores are so large in scale that it takes a considerable move in population to engender a locational shift. When the shift occurs, however, a move by any one store has a substantial impact, not only because each store is so large but also because of the response of competitors in trying to match the move. The postwar shifts appear to us to represent a catching-up operation, a massive adjustment to a shift in population which has been going on for some time.

Outside of the three counties in the Region containing major central shopping areas, most consumer trade and service activities have mirrored the shift in employment and jobs from one county to the next with astonishing consistency. In each consumer line covered by the federal Census of Business, a simple formula is capable of expressing with considerable precision the relation between the population or jobs of the county in any year and the number of employees engaged in the particular line.[3] For counties without major central shopping areas, therefore, once we know where the population and other jobs are likely to be, we can predict with a certain assurance the likely location of consumer-serving jobs.

The close tie to population or job changes appears not only in the activities bearing the Census designations "retail trade" and "consumer services" but also in a variety of other activities whose patronage comes from consumers close to their homes or places of business. Commercial banking services are one such activity. Though one tends to think of the banks in the New York area as national institutions, a major part of their jobs is related to such local activities as consumer loans. Besides, the national function is confined to only a few major banks in New York City, most of the others being geared to serve a local clientele. The same can be said for numerous other activities, including life insurance field offices, with their eye to the selling and servicing of local customers; neighborhood real estate offices, managing and selling local properties; local government offices; and most lawyers, doctors, and accountants.

These pursuits—these consumer-oriented segments of banking, law, insurance, and the like—are not distributed in the Region exactly in proportion to residences. They tend to centralize somewhat because of the need to be near clients at their places at work as well as near their residences, and the need for communication with others —lawyers with accountants and with other lawyers, insurance agents with real estate brokers, all of them with government officials, and so on. Hence they compromise between a thoroughly centralized location in the Region and a thoroughly diffused one. But there is not much doubt that the shift of populations has been pulling these consumer-oriented services outward. This is why Nassau and Suffolk Counties saw a 132 per cent increase in commercial bank employment between 1947 and 1956, and why such counties saw spectacular increases in pursuits like life insurance, law offices, and real estate.

As one surveys the outward shift of the populations in the New York Metropolitan Region and of the consumer activities tied to them, the forces behind the shift seem near-inexorable. Basic technological developments in transportation and deep-seated changes in consumer wants appear to lie behind the phenomenon. Here and there one sees evidence of preferences which breast the main tide; the occasional reappearance of a disillusioned exurbanite in his former city haunts, the gradual growth of apartments-in-the-city for the very rich—these are phenomena whose impact cannot be overlooked. The bigger risk, however, is that their implications for the future will be exaggerated rather than overlooked. Short of some fundamental alteration in consumer outlook or in urban environment, the trends for the future seem likely to represent a continuation—even a speed-up— of the dispersive tendencies of the past.

10

City Hall and Town Hall

We have come a long way in our explanation of the development of the New York Metropolitan Region without saying much about one of the major forces in its environment—its local governments. Over 1,400 entities exist in the Region, each with the capacity to raise and spend money and to provide services. Some are general governments of counties, cities, towns, and villages; some are boards administering school districts or other special districts with a statutory existence independent of the towns and villages. A few entities, like the Port of New York Authority, operate across state lines. All told, these governments provide jobs for about 400,000 persons and manage to spend a sum each year which runs at about 9 per cent of the personal income of the Region's inhabitants.

The local governments not only provide jobs directly but also are customers for goods and services. No less important, they themselves provide services—for example, most of the Region's schools, most of its water supply, much of its transportation, its police, fire protection, sewers, and the like. Finally, they exercise regulatory powers, affecting the Region's development through a multitude of zoning, building, and licensing ordinances. Despite the obvious impact of local governments, however, we would mislead the reader if we suggested that their behavior could be integrated into our explanation of the Region's course in quite the same way as labor, transportation, or space. It is not hard to explain some of the differences in political behavior between, say, Jersey City and White Plains, but that is not the same as evaluating the role of political decision-making in the economic and social history of a metropolitan area.

The need to understand such forces, however, is less important in interpreting history than in projecting the future. In the nineteenth century and the early decades of the twentieth, local government occupied a smaller place in economic affairs than it does today. Even then it performed some vital local functions, but also—more commonly than today—it was viewed as an exploitative device for the benefit of people who had managed to gain political power. They distributed Christmas baskets, and sometimes died millionaires. In general, local government was fairly impotent to govern the manner of the Region's growth. And local businesses and local inhabitants, before the day of the truck and the automobile, were fairly impotent to move away from an unfavorable governmental environment.

There were, of course, certain majestic acts of local government. The feats of New York City in creating a water supply system and in bridging the East River to Brooklyn were achieved before the turn of the century. Without them, the shape of the New York area's development would have been different. There were also exceptions to the sluggishness of the people's response to governmental inadequacies; the well-to-do could flee a jurisdiction and often did. Even a century ago Brooklyn Heights was a fashionable residence for commuters to New York. Fifty years ago, Llewellyn Park in West

Orange was a country retreat for the wealthy whose economic existence centered on Newark and New York. At about the same time, places like Scarsdale and Great Neck harbored exclusive communities of a like sort. By one device or another—whether by restrictive covenants or control of the sewage lines—many of these communities controlled the entry of new inhabitants where the cities could not.

There were still other early indications that the behavior of local governments might be affecting the internal development of the Region. Long before the first zoning law was enacted in New York City in 1916, the City was reacting to the disagreeable manifestations of some of its nuisance industries; the location of slaughtering houses, for instance, was being controlled as early as 1898. The shift of some of these industries from Manhattan and Brooklyn toward the wider and opener spaces of New Jersey was probably motivated in part by the assumption that the New Jersey authorities would be more tolerant of their waste and odors.

Still, these were exceptions. Certainly until 1910, possibly until much later, one would not have been far wrong in assuming that local governments were largely a passive force in the environment; that households and establishments lived with local governments as they found them; and that the local governments, though providing some essential services, exerted little impact on the locational choices of business establishments and households in the Region.

LOCAL EXPENDITURE PATTERNS

What can we say about the likely future impact of local governments? One way to come to grips with the question is by observing their expenditure patterns. Such patterns begin to tell us two things about the role of local governments: they give some indication of the services which people are demanding of their local governments, and so offer some clues to the kind of public environment that is wanted most; and they start us on the process of identifying where the stresses and strains are developing—where in the Region local governments may find themselves unable to supply the services that are demanded.

First, a word or two about the over-all totals of local government expenditure in different parts of the Region. Table 21 affords evidence of the fact that there are some real differences in the levels of such expenditures in different parts of the Region, when compared with the personal income of the inhabitants of those parts. In New York City, for instance, local government expenditures in 1955 were a somewhat higher proportion of personal income than in the other New York State counties in the Region,* and the other New York State counties showed considerably higher expenditures, when measured by this yardstick, than did the New Jersey counties of the Region. The same ranking for these three segments of the Region is seen in 1950; but in 1945, the picture was markedly different, with New York City showing a lower relative expenditure level than the other two segments. Since three points in time hardly afford a reliable trend, one dare not jump to hasty conclusions about New York City's comparative performance over time; but the figures do suggest that New York City's high expenditures of the 1950's may be the

* This must be interpreted in light of the fact that the income of New York City's *enterprises* is not taken into account in the comparison, and such income seems to have held up better than the income of New York City's inhabitants. Conceptually, it might have been better to compare local government expenditures with a measure such as the net income of businesses and individuals in the Region, since taxes are paid not only by individuals but by businesses as well. But personal income is the most comprehensive measure for which historical data exist.

consequence of a faster rise relative to personal income than in the other areas.

What lay behind the differences in expenditure levels

TABLE 21   Total Expenditures of Local Governments Compared with Personal Income of Population, New York Metropolitan Region, 1945–1955

	Personal income (millions)	Local government expenditure (millions)	Expenditure as percentage of income
Region[a]			
1955	$35,766	$3,219	9.0
1950	27,876	2,309	8.3
1945	20,287	1,207	5.9
New York City			
1955	18,663	1,919	10.3
1950	16,247	1,464	9.0
1945	13,124	759	5.7
Other New York counties			
1955	6,814	636	9.3
1950	4,328	360	8.3
1945	2,412	168	7.0
New Jersey counties			
1955	10,289	663	6.4
1950	7,301	485	6.6
1945	4,751	280	5.9

Note: Local government expenditures include current and capital outlays for general government as well as municipally owned utilities of all units of government in the Region, from cities to special districts. Direct state outlays are excluded, as well as expenditures of the Port of New York Authority. Personal income figures for 1945 and 1950 were interpolated from New York Metropolitan Region Study estimates for 1939, 1947, and 1955. For further details, see Robert C. Wood, *1400 Governments*.

[a] Excludes Fairfield County, Connecticut, for which figures are not available. For 1957, expenditures in that county are estimated at 5.4 per cent of its personal income.

which we observe in the middle 1950's? We shall probably never have a complete answer to the question. But some understanding of the differences is afforded by Chart 17. The chart shows that New York City stands out in its share of the Region's operating expenditures on public welfare, health, and certain sanitation programs. To be sure, operating expenditures on sewers, highways, and schools are less heavily emphasized in the City than in the Inner and Outer Rings. But, though Chart 17 shows that these offsets exist, we are still brought back to the basic fact of Table 21 that New York City generates a higher level of total expenditures than the other areas, at least when measured against the yardstick of personal income.

In order to develop added clues to the causes of the differences in government expenditure from one local jurisdiction to the next, an analysis in considerable depth was done of expenditure patterns of some 64 communities in the Region. These communities, all located in the five innermost New Jersey counties, covered a wide span in size and condition, ranging from places as old as East Orange to places as young as Saddle Brook. The question we put to ourselves was this: For each major category of local expenditure, what were the community characteristics which seemed to generate differences in the expenditure level from one community to the next?

The reader who is interested in a definitive description of the results will have to turn to another book in this series.[1] The statistical techniques which had to be devised in order to draw dependable conclusions from the data were so complex as to defy any accurate presentation in short compass.

In essence, however, the analysis indicates, to nobody's surprise, that the sheer size of the community almost fully determines the level of its *total* operating expenditures. Size also helps to explain a considerable

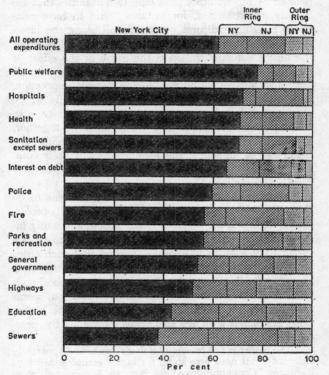

CHART 17 Local Governments' Major Operating
Expenditures,[a] Distributed by Zones[b] of New
York Metropolitan Region, 1957

(Region total = 100 per cent)

[a] The chart excludes capital outlays for highways, schools,
sewers, and hospitals, but small capital outlays of other kinds
did creep into the "operating" figures and could not be separated. Expenditures of Port of New York Authority are not
included.

[b] Inner Ring in this chart includes the Core county of Hudson, and does not include the New York City county of Richmond. For the present purpose, New York City is a more
meaningful concept than the Core. In the Outer Ring, the
New York segment includes Fairfield County, Connecticut.

part of the community differences in levels of expenditure for most individual items in the budget.* But among the individual items a good deal is left to be explained by factors other than size. Communities that are heavily industrialized, for instance, tend to have relatively high expenditures practically all along the line— heavier than size alone might have indicated. (Whether the heavy industrialization is the cause or the effect of the high expenditures is a very neat question, with no very neat answer.) Contrary to the general impression, high expenditures in many items seem the rule where oldsters are heavily represented in a community—possibly because old people and old facilities go together. Finally, when the residents of a community exhibit the hallmarks of affluence, the expenditures of their community tend to be low, particularly in the categories of health and welfare.**

The sum and substance of the analysis seems to be this: The older cities, bearing the stamps of obsolescence, high density, high industrialization, and aging inhabitants, generate higher expenses than their size alone might have led one to expect. The fact that such cities are spared some of the costs of newer communities, such as the get-going costs in opening new neighborhoods and the costs of a large school-going population, seems not to have produced a sufficient offset to the higher costs associated with age and obsolescence. So the pres-

* The reader is put on warning that some of the apparently innocent terms used here stand for highly complex statistical measures. "Community size," for instance, is measured by an index derived from the intercorrelation between population, the property tax base, the total number of pupils enrolled in schools, and still other characteristics.

** Indications of the pressure felt by new and rapidly growing communities are provided by some supplementary tests based on per capita school expenditures, which showed that the communities with a low level of land saturation had comparatively high per capita school outlays.

sure for high expenditures, visible in many communities, seems to be especially pronounced in the older cities. Our next step is to see how these pressures are met.

THE RESPONSE TO PRESSURES FOR LOCAL EXPENDITURE

Localities vary considerably in their responses to the pressure for increased expenditure, and these variations must have significantly influenced the Region's development. In some cases, the main response has been to try to hold down the influx of populations through zoning, in order to reduce the costs which go with opening up new neighborhoods. In others, the chief reaction of local governments has been to find a way of increasing revenues while trying to fend off the political consequences of the act; accordingly they have supported the creation of "independent" special districts with spending and taxing powers to provide schools, water, sewers, and other services, or they have managed to tap state tax revenues through state aid programs. In still other cases, where these avenues of response have been cut off, local governments have simply had to face the discordant music generated by undisguised increases in old taxes and the imposition of new ones.

THE OLDER CITIES

By and large, the older, more densely settled communities of the Region have had the least room for maneuver. They have had fewer opportunities to use their zoning powers as a tool for holding down government costs and maintaining government revenues; they have had less freedom under state laws to generate special districts to relieve them of the taxing and servicing burden; and they have been more limited in their access to state aid. As a group, these communities have had to face up less equivocally than other communities to increases in local taxes.

Though New York City can hardly be said to be "representative" of anything but itself, it does exhibit these limitations on maneuverability that are characteristic of densely settled communities. First of all, land-use controls are a much weaker tool for influencing New York City's development than for influencing the development of some embryo community in the rural reaches of Putnam County. There is so little open space suitable for development left in the City—only 17.4 per cent of its land surface and most of that in Richmond —that even the wisest control of that land would have only a slight effect on the City's total growth. Furthermore, the die is largely cast for most of the land that is left. The kind of development that surrounds such land already determines to a large extent how the remaining open land may be developed. To zone the undeveloped portions of Queens in two-acre lots for one-family structures, for instance, would be almost out of the question; such zoning could not stand up for long under the economic and political pressure to cut the land up in much smaller parcels or to allow apartment-house development.

Since the zoning tool has a limited applicability to the objective of expanding local revenue or holding down local expenditure by channeling private development, we are likely to see New York City leading the way in improvising other tools. More extensive use of public condemnation powers and of public subsidy in the recapture of encumbered land for manufacturing purposes may well be in the cards, as we suggested earlier. Landlords may be compelled to maintain their properties more adequately, a step which would probably generate higher rents and squeeze out some of the inhabitants with welfare needs. The type and volume of transportation may be affected by new controls over parking facilities and parking rates—controls whose effect on the budget would be hard to predict. But we are assuming, for projection purposes, that none of these measures will be revolutionary in its impact.

While New York City's room for maneuver in altering its environment seems limited, the City also is limited in its recourse to other ways of dealing with its expenditure problems. New York State subsidies to local governments might conceivably afford an avenue of relief. But, while state aid formulas have been tailored to reflect such unsubtle facts as the daily enrollment of school children, they have not taken account of such subtle characteristics as the age and economic status of the inhabitants of a community, the obsolescence of public and private structures in the community, and the momentum of its long-established welfare services.

In 1957, therefore, state aid was 19.9 per cent of the New York City government's revenue but 23.5 per cent of the combined revenues of local governments in the other New York State counties of the Region. Per capita state aid to the City amounted to $42.63, while the comparable figure in the surrounding New York counties was $47.70. And between 1953 and 1957, per capita state aid to the City increased 37 per cent while increasing 42 per cent in the state's suburban counties in the Region.

With its alternatives apparently blocked, New York City has had to face up to higher levels of local taxation. Part of its needs have been met by increasing the City's tax rate on the assessed value of real property. From 1945 to 1957, for instance, the rate rose from 2.73 per cent to 4.08 per cent. As a result, the City's levy on "full value" rose from 2.54 per cent to 3.62 per cent.

Like its other lines of response, however, New York City's resort to higher property taxation has definite limits. Apart from the finite tolerance of its citizenry for bearing real property taxes, the City has been hemmed in by a constitutional restraint which places a ceiling on the City's tax rates. The effect of the complex provision is that New York City's rate ceiling is lower than the ceiling applicable to most suburban communities.

New York City's last resort, therefore, has been to rely far more heavily on nonproperty taxes than most other local governments in the Region. Nearly a fifth of its revenue today comes from such taxes, including a retail sales tax and a gross receipts tax.

The incentive for New York City to shift from real property to nonproperty taxes might have existed in any case, even if the state's restrictions had not forced the shift. The strategy of local taxation demands that any locality concentrate its taxes on those entities which are in the poorest position to flee the jurisdiction. We have already seen that manufacturing establishments with large amounts of real property typically rank among those with the weakest ties to the city environment— though there are occasional exceptions like breweries and newspaper plants. At the same time, the business that goes on in offices, salesrooms, and retail stores has less freedom, on the whole, in its locational response to tax increases.[*] It may well be, therefore, that New York City's tendency to rely increasingly on nonproperty taxes stems not only from political forces but from "economic" ones as well.

In any case, New York City's political responses to its fiscal pressures, as nearly as we can tell, will not be drastic enough to require us to modify the general impressions suggested by earlier chapters. For the City

[*] This would argue for levying heavier real property taxes on office structures than on manufacturing plants. In fact, New York City does just that by using assessed valuations which are closer to "full value" in Manhattan than in other boroughs of the City.

government is severely limited in its opportunities to influence locational trends.

The other old cities of the Region manifest many of the strains and limitations seen in New York City. In the five or six years after 1950, Jersey City, Newark, Elizabeth, Hoboken, Union City, and North Bergen all registered increases in their average property tax rates, calculated on the basis of the "full value" of the property. To be sure, as the market prices of real property rose during this period, assessed valuations lagged behind; but tax rates were pushed briskly upward, more than making up for the lag in valuations.

Here and there, old cities in the Region resolutely bucked the trend to higher property taxes. Bayonne in New Jersey and Yonkers in New York State, for instance, both showed declines in their full tax rates during this period. But the price of this policy was evident. In both instances the localities were racked with bitter complaints over service inadequacies.

In trying to appraise the implications of these stresses and strains for the future, it helps to recognize a distinction between New York City and the old cities of New Jersey. In some respects the position of the New Jersey cities is the more difficult. The state aid programs of New Jersey are so much smaller and more rudimentary than those of New York State that they do not offer as much of an escape valve for localities in distress. New Jersey's state aid programs may well be enlarged under the mounting pressure from its urban areas, but it is probably wise to assume that these programs will not catch up with those of New York State in the years ahead.

In addition, the New Jersey cities, even more than New York City, must be wary of the possibility that their measures may drive enterprises and homes out of the jurisdiction. We observed earlier that many activities in New York City's central business district are pinned down in that location for compelling reasons; but this cannot be said for so large a proportion of the activities found in the central business districts of Newark, Jersey City, and Hoboken. In the choice between imposing tax increases or limiting public services, therefore, New Jersey's older municipalities are more likely than New York City to take the latter course.

THE NEWER SUBURBS

Once we leave the older cities for the newer and less crowded suburban communities, the patterns are so numerous that generalization becomes more difficult and more dangerous. Yet, there are two points to be made. The obvious point is that some communities are having severe growing pains. The not-so-obvious point is that a great many communities are experiencing no visible fiscal difficulties at all.

Among the localities laboring under fiscal problems are those which are undergoing or have just undergone a very rapid expansion in population. All at once, communities in the potato fields of Long Island and the undeveloped stretches of Monmouth County are being called on to install streets, sewers, schools, fire-fighting equipment, and police stations, all the trappings of urban living. Their problems in meeting these demands are harder, in many ways, than the problems of the more congested cities as they open new neighborhoods. The sheer size of the old cities means, and for a long time has meant, that though their edges might be growing, the city as a whole consists for the most part of settled neighborhoods; the settled neighborhoods, therefore, help bear the costs of the capital equipment required by the growing sections. In the newer communities, on the other hand, growth commonly occurs all at once through a considerable part of the community's area. Besides, the lower residential density of these newer communities means larger per capita expenditures in some categories; it requires more paved streets and sewers to service a given number of households.

A faint indication of the impact of growth on the need for revenue is provided by our 64 New Jersey municipalities whose expenditures were analyzed earlier. On the average, they registered a decline of 4.9 per cent in full tax rates between 1951 and 1955. Among the 64 communities, however, there were decided differences in experience, depending in part on population growth rates. The 21 municipalities with the highest population growth, for instance, showed a drop of only 1.3 per cent in full tax rates; the 22 with moderate growth dropped 4.8 per cent; and the 21 with either the lowest growth or actual population decline dropped 8.6 per cent.

The fact that swift growth generates fiscal pressure is perhaps nowhere more evident in the Region than in Nassau County, which underwent an enormous increase in population in the years after World War II. In 1945, land-use controls in the central and southern portions of Nassau were primitive. Developers were under little pressure from local governments to provide any but the most rudimentary facilities to the community. As children grew up to school age, as flimsy street paving broke down, and as the spread of septic tanks began to threaten water supplies from shallow wells, the demands on local government piled up fast. As a result, the expenditures of local government in Nassau grew faster than in most counties of the Region, from $94.24 per capita in 1945 to $348.23 per capita in 1957.

Nonetheless, some room for maneuver still existed among the governments of Nassau's underdeveloped suburbs. One response was to proliferate special districts with separate powers to tax and spend in order to provide some of the necessary local services; this maneuver buffered local government officials from the political odium associated with a more direct increase of the tax rate. From 1945 to 1955, the number of special districts in Nassau County which provided local services apart from schooling rose from 173 to 268.

Finally, Nassau's communities helped to bridge the difference between expenditure and revenue by the growing use of state aid. Per capita state aid in Nassau increased by 387 per cent between 1945 and 1957 while in New York City it was increasing 268 per cent. Not counting the revenues from public utility operations, state aid in 1957 represented 22.3 per cent of the total revenue of governments in Nassau as compared with 19.9 per cent for New York City.

All told, the municipalities of Nassau County do not appear to be coming to the end of their respective fiscal ropes, at least not when measured by the seeming capacity of their citizens to pay. By 1957, Nassau had joined Westchester at the head of the list of the Region's counties in per capita income. It is true that Nassau's taxes on real property were 5.0 per cent of its population's personal income, placing it fourth among the Region's counties in that respect. The comparable ratio for New York City was 4.2 per cent, and for the Region as a whole, 4.5 per cent. It is a fact, too, that nerves have been frayed and tempers made ragged as a result of the swift and no doubt unexpected rise in taxes laid on its young home-owning inhabitants. Still, the county's local tax situation does not appear to represent a factor so large as to suggest that future homeowners would try to avoid the "pitfalls" of suburban living by locating in the City and accepting their real property taxes sugarcoated in the form of rent.

The Nassau experience is particularly valuable as a guide to the future because Nassau, in some ways, has been one of the more vulnerable areas of the Region in its exposure to the risks of rapid growth. Its sandy terrain and porous soil make it an especially attractive prize for the mass developer's methods; only Suffolk

County and portions of Monmouth County match it in this respect. Suffolk, though lacking comprehensive land-use controls in some of its eastern reaches, still seems somewhat more alert to its prospective problems than Nassau was ten or fifteen years ago. In the next decade or two, more and more of Suffolk will be caught up in the growth which Nassau and western Suffolk are experiencing today. The same will be true for other areas on the New York State side of the Region—upper Westchester, lower Putnam, and Rockland. But these areas, on the whole, seem a bit more prepared in their responses than Nassau was. On the whole, they seem more ready to impose restraints through zoning and subdivision regulation.

Of course, many suburban areas will experience a much more sedate rate of growth than Nassau has experienced or Suffolk is likely to experience over the next few decades. Suburban areas whose growth rate is held in check by extensive land-use regulations are particularly likely to avoid fiscal difficulties in the process of growth. Historically, one may think of the municipalities of southern Westchester County as exemplifying this group, and it is instructive to take a closer look at their experiences. On the whole, these communities came of age early in the *Drang nach Suburbia;* many were well established, with a well-to-do population, as early as World War I. Even then, Westchester communities were thought of as "quality" neighborhoods with a high level of public services. And, by 1955, one could see a reflection of this "quality" both in professional appraisals of the county's schools and other public services and in the high level of local expenditures on such services.

From an early date, however, many of these Westchester communities were dedicated to the proposition that homes for lower income groups must be excluded from their jurisdiction. A rugged topography contributed to the objective by making the area expensive for the mass developer. Zoning, tailored to the objective, was widely and effectively used. The result was that Westchester managed to avoid most of the fiscal growing pains which Nassau was experiencing in the postwar period. True, Westchester's tax levels were not low; in 1945, in fact, its property taxes were the highest in the Region on a per capita basis. But between 1945 and 1955 it declined to third place, for its increase in per capita property taxes during that period was the lowest of all the Region's counties. Meanwhile, though its revenue from other sources was growing, the growth was not as fast as that of the average suburban county in the Region. The total fiscal and service picture in Westchester was that of a well-oiled mechanism, performing at high pitch under little strain.

THE RESPONSES SUMMARIZED

Generalization comes hard out of so mixed and fragmentary a story. Still, it cannot be avoided if some framework for projection is to be erected. The lessons we derive from the pictures just portrayed and from the demographic and economic analyses summarized in earlier chapters run on the following lines. The fiscal strain under which the older cities of the Region have labored will continue and may get somewhat worse. These cities are faced with revenue needs of a magnitude which their own property tax base is likely to be increasingly inadequate to meet. As the gap grows, a variety of devices will be created to fill it: new nonproperty taxes, larger state and federal grants, and so on. The older cities of New Jersey will be in a less advantageous position than New York City in this difficult game, partly because of the nature of the New Jersey state government and state budget, and partly because these cities are exposed to a greater danger of driving out business and residents when they raise their local taxes.

In the suburbs, the communities in fiscal trouble will not collapse and shrivel away; their local tax demands, on the whole, do not appear so overwhelming in the cold statistics as to suggest that they are unassimilable into the budgets of their inhabitants. Resentment and protest, we assume, will continue to be the order of the day in such communities, but not arrested growth. As for the communities which have avoided fiscal trouble by their land-use controls or other devices, one can see no reason why their unruffled existence should not continue. True, the growing importance of the state taxes, on both the New York and New Jersey sides of the Region, may have some leveling effect on taxes and services. So may the expanded use of special districts, whenever a single district embraces communities of different types. But these seem to us to be fairly slow-moving and dilute levelers.

Still, there will be shifts in the problems and responses of local governments. Some semirural communities will pass over from the somnolescent serviceless state to bursting growth, with all its attendant problems. Some of the older, seemingly well-protected localities of Westchester, northern Long Island, and Essex, Bergen, and Passaic will find that their embattled precincts have been penetrated by low income groups after all. Some will change their zoning laws and building ordinances under inexorable pressures, as old estates are broken up. Others will find that, despite zoning laws and building ordinances, lower-income families have managed to take over the older residences, subdividing the structures as need be to find the means of paying for them. So new social problems will appear and new social services will be required. The typical problems and pressures of the old cities, therefore, will spread a little wider. And, insofar as the developments have any effect on the location of industry and population in the Region, they should tend to further a little the outward shift suggested by the analysis of earlier chapters.

PASSENGER TRANSPORTATION AND WATER SUPPLY

In some ways, the analysis we have just presented is a little too neat. It recognizes that there may be times when the response of local government is so unsatisfying to its constituency that subsequent growth patterns may be slightly altered. But it takes no direct account of the possibility that a great initiative on the part of government, something more than a short-run response to environment pressures, may be generated which would have a much larger impact on the environment, nor of the possibility that there may be a total breakdown in some critical service, distorting the Region's development.

When we begin to consider the possibility of developments which represent a really sharp break with the past, we are at sea almost at once. The number of possibilities of this kind seems infinite; the basis for assigning orders of probability to them seems feeble.

Still, it helps in our understanding of the Region's future development to consider where these great new initiatives or critical breakdowns might develop and to explore some of the forces at work in these areas. Of the various fields in which some such development could conceivably occur, the field of passenger transportation is an outstanding candidate.

THE MOVEMENT OF PEOPLE

In earlier chapters we touched on some of the basic shifts in passenger transport in the Region. For instance, the New York City subways, though charging a flat 15-

cent fare for most trips in the system, each year are obliged to carry the average rush-hour rider to the central business district from a more remote point in the City, offering more mileage for the money and adding to the system's costs. Besides, business on the subways is undergoing a long-run decline; off-hour traffic is declining most, but even rush-hour business has shown some long-run shrinkage.

The trends for suburban railroads have been more mixed. Presumably these carriers have been picking up some rush-hour traffic from ex-city-dwellers-turned-suburbanites. But they, too, have shown heavy declines in the comparatively lucrative off-peak traffic and some have shown a decline in rush-hour customers as well. In a few cases, in fact, suburban passenger lines have given up the ghost. The shifts in population and jobs have, of course, been partly responsible for these trends. The average suburban home is no longer a short walk from the station, and the first stage of any journey commonly demands the use of an automobile. In these circumstances the suburbanite often deems it sensible to make the whole journey by car. The dispersal of manufacturing plants and other employment centers to locations off the main lines of travel has added to the use of the automobile. The development of "reverse commuting" has swelled car travel still further. If our expectations about the future movement of homes and jobs are solidly based, these trends in passenger transport should continue.

We dare not overlook the possibility, however, that some massive changes in passenger transport policy or in transport facilities might intervene to alter the expectations. The analysis in earlier chapters makes it clear that any such innovations would have to buck powerful economic forces in order to exert a significant impact on the Region. Still, various possibilities of this sort have been suggested. For instance, measures have been proposed for making mass transit more attractive (or for making automobile travel less attractive) in trips to the central business district.

Our task here, of course, is not to appraise the desirability of any such measures, but simply to try to decide whether they are likely to occur and whether their effects have to be taken into account in our projection. In judging whether any such scheme might come off in the next few decades, one has to take into account the incredibly fractionized structure of the Region's transportation system. First, there is the separation between mass transit and automobile, a political gulf which seems scarcely bridgeable.

Tunnel, bridge, and parking facilities in the Region are typically provided by a group of semiautonomous public authorities, sustaining themselves through user charges and employing their independent credit facilities to finance their capital expansion. Outstanding in this group are the Port of New York Authority, which operates the interstate Hudson River crossings; the Triborough Bridge and Tunnel Authority, which operates five bridges, two tunnels, and three parking facilities; and numerous lesser organizations of a like type. Less publicized but just as potent are the state highway departments, planning and constructing the highway network in response to state and federal policies.

The ownership of the mass transit facilities, on the other hand, is vested in other groups. The New York City government owns its extensive subway system. Ownership of the suburban rails is spread among numerous private companies. And private and public bus lines abound through the Region.

The sheer diversity of ownership and of jurisdiction presents a paramount obstacle in consciously making important alterations in the Region's public transport policy. But there are more explicit problems as well. Since the semiautonomous public authorities typically finance their operations on the basis of their own credit status, a cardinal principle of management is to build up revenues and maintain solvency. So proposals to stem automobile traffic by prohibitive tolls or proposals to subsidize mass transit from the income generated by the automobile bridges and tunnels are not enthusiastically embraced.

No one can say that the effective resistance of the Port Authority and similar entities to proposals of this sort will continue forever. Still, the independence of the Port Authority is considerable, and the safest assumption for the future appears to be that its operating methods and basis of financing will remain unaltered.

The possibility that mass transit might be placed on a more favored footing relative to the highway is reduced also by the political fragmentation of the Region. Except for proposals to improve the New York City subway system out of City resources, almost any proposal demands the concurrence of a number of jurisdictions. Such concurrence is not impossible. Conceivably, the New York State government could impose some common formula on its local jurisdictions while the New Jersey government could do the same thing. And there is no reason to rule out agreement between the states. In appraising the scope and character of any such agreement, however, one has to recognize that each major mass transit proposal is gauged by any locality partly in competitive terms. Will swifter access from the Essex County suburbs to the New York City central business district divert some of Newark's downtown shopping business? If it may, can Newark's political representatives afford to brush this fact aside? Questions of this sort by one locality or another have bedeviled most proposals for the improvement of mass transit, and they very likely will continue to do so.

It is our assumption that competitive considerations also will stop most jurisdictions from independently imposing restraints on the use of the automobile, such as exorbitant meter charges or outright prohibitions on access and parking. If they could be reasonably sure that hurdles of this kind would shift their traffic back to the mass transit lines, some jurisdictions might be tempted to try such measures. But haunting them all is the partial recognition that potent forces lie behind the decline of the mass transit facilities and the fear that measures to discourage automobile traffic will simply drive business away. And we assume that this fear will constitute a powerful restraint on action.

We do not assume that government agencies in the New York Metropolitan Region will be altogether inactive in the face of rising deficits and declining services in the mass transit field. When facilities deteriorate close to the breaking point, their defenders have often managed to force through some sort of palliative action. For instance, a 1953 reorganization of New York City's subway system, though it did not end the system's operating deficits, did make possible an increase in fares. The separation of capital and operating funds also allowed the City system to tap new sources of revenue and institute some improvements in service. When it became evident that rail service on Long Island was in jeopardy, ways and means were devised to continue service; at least until 1966, the Long Island railroad will operate by state law substantially as a tax-free public authority. The New York State legislature also has extended a hand to the hard-pressed suburban railroads by establishing credit for the purchase of new equipment. On the other hand, when the New Jersey governor sought to move too far and too fast by trying to meet suburban rail deficits with the profits of the New Jersey toll roads, an unsympathetic electorate killed the proposal.

We assume that mass transit operators will manage to stay afloat, even if they cannot improve their lot very much. Their efforts in the end may require them to look for new subsidies, including funds from federal sources, but *in extremis,* such support is likely to appear.

WATER IN SHORT SUPPLY

The list of possibilities in which great governmental initiatives or marked governmental failures might conceivably occur is distressingly long. Unprecedented urban renewal programs—vast in scope and in financial commitment beyond anything so far seriously considered—could set our expectations about future developments on their ear, by making the older areas of the Region more attractive to homes and industry than we have assumed. Extensive air pollution could choke the congested portions of the Region and force swifter dispersal of homes and industry. (Extensive air pollution *control* could have something like the same effect on a few branches of industry.)

One more possibility demands a little closer look here, that relating to water. There are many things about the water supply that are complex or obscure. One is the nature of the governmental structure involved in decisions on the Region's water supply. Another is the economic consequences of the water shortages which appear from time to time in some sections of the Region, especially in some of the New Jersey counties.

What is perfectly clear, however, is that, in the normal course, the demand for water will skyrocket in the Region during the next few decades. For New York City no serious water problems are in prospect. The City's billion-dollar investment in waterworks provides a supply estimated to be adequate to the needs of its population until the year 2000. And in the suburban counties of New York State, though water consumption will rise sharply, the presence of the City is reassuring. A solicitous New York State legislature has authorized suburban communities to tap the City's supplies when appropriate, and these communities appear adequately supplied for the next twenty-five years at least.

It is the New Jersey part of the Region that appears more likely to experience short-run water shortages and ensuing obstacles to economic development. In a group of New Jersey counties whose coverage differed only a little from the New Jersey portion of the New York Region, actual water consumption in 1953 was 420 million gallons daily, compared to what the engineers call a "safe yield" of 415 million at that time. Engineering estimates reported to the New Jersey legislature at that time projected steadily rising requirements for the future: over 500 million gallons per day in most of the 1960's; 620 million in 1980; and 750 million in the year 2000. A more recent United States Army Corps of Engineers survey foresees difficulty for the New Jersey areas in meeting their expanding needs unless added sources are tapped.[2]

The problem for New Jersey is not the lack of developable resources. It is rather the incapacity of the New Jersey governing system to respond with reasonable alacrity and firmness to a predictable increase in consumption. As a consequence, no integrated water supply system was developed for the northern Jersey counties as they grew. Whereas New York City began the selection of upstate sites as early as 1842 and its suburban neighbors gradually came to integrate their systems with the City, Jersey communities have by and large maintained a pattern of "going it alone." Some 36 systems, some private, some public, span the northern counties of the state. As the countryside has been developed and population densities have risen, these small independent enterprises have found increasing difficulty in developing reserves to make up an adequate total supply.

Today, reservoir sites need to be selected and construction authorized to provide an integrated supply for the entire Jersey segment of the New York Metropolitan Region. If the process of urbanization had not gone so far, each locality could still leapfrog over the country-side to find its own supply. If some sort of effective plan existed for allocating the water of the Delaware River Basin among the bordering states, then no difficulty would arise. But the small, separate systems are increasingly constrained and there are no institutions in being that have the power to react to the problem effectively; consequently the task of providing water falls perforce to the state, as the only public agent available. And so far, the state has been unable to act decisively.

One of the underlying volumes in this series recounts the dreary history of the state government's past efforts to develop an adequate water supply for its communities.[3] Every locality, it appears, wanted the water but no locality wanted the reservoir site. The state government was indecisive. The major political parties were highly sectional in their orientation. The result for a long time was no action. Eventually, in 1958, a season of drought prodded the legislature and the public to adopt a plan which will ease the crisis for a time.

The critical barrier to action has not been any sheer physical impediment, such as scarce rainfall; it has been the inability of the legislative process in New Jersey to produce decision. Nevertheless, we would be reluctant to assume that the New Jersey communities will accept a prolonged crisis in water supplies in the future without some counteraction to ease the situation. True, the counteraction may come so late as to court avoidable short-run disasters in some areas. And if the responses are late enough and inadequate enough, water problems could stunt the residential growth of the New Jersey side relative to that of New York, especially the newer suburban portions of New Jersey. But once again, we assume enough response on the part of local government to continue deferring the problem in its gravest form.

Indeed, that is the basic assumption which emerges from the present chapter. By one short-run measure or another, the local governments will muddle through, allowing the Region's households and enterprises to follow their own proclivities—that is, to grow more swiftly in the newer suburbs than in the older cities. Even as we make the assumption, however, we are aware of the thin ice underfoot. Political decision-making is not always rational; and the form of its irrationality is not always predictable. Our assumption that local governments will muddle through but not much more does not reflect some naive notion of economic determinism. It reflects the total absence of a basis for assuming anything else. Besides, a projection based on this assumption is likely to have wider utility to those concerned with the future development of the Region than a projection based on any one of the scores of alternative assumptions which would involve some marked change in future political behavior.

11
Metropolis 1985

We move now from analysis to forecast, from an effort at understanding to an effort at projection. Our task is to portray the people and the jobs of the New York Metropolitan Region in quantitative terms for the years 1965, 1975, and 1985. Some readers, eager for the seemingly solid numbers which would embody all our conceptions of the future, may see this chapter as the culmination of the New York Metropolitan Region Study. Others, however, will recognize that the chapter is an epilogue—an excursion beyond the limits of reason into the realm of faith.

INTRODUCTION TO AN EPILOGUE

THE GRAND SCHEME

Any rational projection of an area like the New York Metropolitan Region presupposes the existence of some sort of "model," some sort of articulated conception of how a complex mechanism like the New York area grows and changes over time. The glimmerings of such a model were evident in earlier chapters, as we traced through the forces affecting the Region's growth. At this point, however, it will help to recapitulate the main elements in the structure.

The take-off point for any projection of the Region's future is a projection of the nation. Though the Region is hardly a microcosm of the United States, it is exposed to most of the cultural and economic forces which generate change in the rest of the country. Habits of consumption, levels of investment, norms of government spending, all these change in the Region in response to very much the same stimuli as in the nation at large. In fact, as the rest of the nation shifts from farm to metropolis and as the New York area shifts from city to suburb, the tendency for Region and nation to respond in parallel fashion grows even more marked.

There is another aspect to the tie between national change and regional change. About 40 per cent of the Region's employment is in its so-called national-market industries, in which the typical establishment is exposed to the competition of others located at distant points as they ship goods or provide services to far-flung markets in the nation. In such activities the growth or decline of demand in any part of the nation is transmitted to each metropolitan area directly through the currents of trade. As a result a metropolitan area with a "fast-growing mix" of national industries—with industries exhibiting comparatively high national growth rates—is likely to show high rates of growth itself.[1] The outstanding growth rate of the Los Angeles area in the years following the war could have been predicted on this basis, as could the strongly contrasting performance of Boston and the middling record of the New York area itself.

Accordingly, the first hurdle in projecting the future of the New York Metropolitan Region is to project the future of the nation—its birth and death rates, its labor force, its total output, its consumption patterns, its production patterns, and so on. At this stage, there is no

242

need to consider just how this exercise in prescience is achieved; we shall return to that question later.

Once we know how the nation's economy is likely to perform, the next question will be what part the Region is likely to play in that performance. It is the salvation of the seer that inertia plays a major role in ensuring that the growth rate of an area like the New York Metropolitan Region will not differ very much from that of the United States. One need hardly point out that children are born where their mothers live, creating a presumption that the most populous areas will remain so. As the children enter the labor force, a strong disposition exists to look for a job near home rather than take on the costs and pains of migration. In some measure, too, new jobs are generated where the existing jobs are found, for reasons already explored in earlier chapters. Expansion commonly occurs inside the walls of existing plants and offices or close by the existing clusters of jobs and enterprises.

Still, these simple notions scarcely provide an adequate basis for projecting the growth of a metropolitan area. It has already been pointed out that some areas may be endowed with a "mix" of jobs more conducive to growth than other areas. Moreover, pervasive forces like those of transport or labor can greatly alter the competitive position of any area in a few decades. Accordingly, the capacity of any area to provide enough jobs for its labor force—or, for that matter, to provide enough labor force for its job opportunities—is not to be taken for granted.

Indeed, the history of the New York area suggests that there have always been significant discrepancies between the number of people which the area generated and the number of job opportunities it generated —discrepancies bridged by streams of in-migration. In looking at the future of the New York area, therefore, two kinds of questions can be asked: what economic opportunities is the New York area likely to provide? and, where are the people to come from who will fill these opportunities?

To project the Region's job opportunities, we begin with the Region's national-market industries. All sorts of forces are at work in these industries, enlarging the Region's share of national employment in some, reducing its share in others. These forces, spelled out in the underlying books in this series, were reviewed in bold outline in Chapters 4 to 6. They are the raw materials from which we make our guesses about the Region's future share of activity in each of the national-market industries.

With our tentative guesses about the national-market industries set down, there is still the need to gauge the Region's employment in local-market industries. In so huge an area as the New York Metropolitan Region, more people exist by "taking in each other's washing" than by catering to wants which arise outside the Region. Accordingly, it does not do to assume that for every worker in a national-market industry, there is likely to be some predetermined number in local-market industries. New employment-generating forces can appear in the local sector, including local spending by government and local investment by business. Any serious effort at local projection must take these forces into account, blending them with the direct activities of the national-market industries and the ancillary local demands generated out of the national-market industries.

But we cannot take it for granted that the labor force demanded by the Region's needs will automatically be on hand to fill those needs. Streams of in-migration are not infinitely expansible; and a flow of out-migration, if that were needed to achieve a balance between economic opportunity and population currents, would be even less apt to develop quickly. So demographic projections were needed, projections of the population levels likely to be the net result of births, deaths, and aging, plus or minus the maximum believable amounts of in-migration or out-migration. Once a pattern was found which was consistent with our expectations of economic opportunity, we had a projection of jobs and population for the Region.

The scheme of projection for the Region's various parts was even more complex, in some ways, than that for the Region as a whole. Again, however, inertia was on our side; again, we could begin by assuming that whatever was growing in the Region as a whole was likely to grow also in each part of the Region where it was found. But once more, inertia had to be tempered with an appreciation of certain other forces that favor growth in one place in the Region rather than another.

In making these modifications on the existing pattern, we had to take into account such factors as the built-up character of the Region's Core. The fact that open land is scarce inside the Core is, of course, no bar to added growth in many activities. Central-office activity, some kinds of wholesaling, certain financial services, and so on, can move skyward if need be. In other segments of economic activity, however, problems of land availability, transportation, and other factors already noted led us to assume some reduction in the Core's share of the Region's employment and some increase in the shares of areas outside the Core.

In all this manipulation, of course, activities serving neighborhood markets were set aside for later allocation. The locational patterns for these industries, we assumed, would take their cues from the distribution of the jobs already allocated and from the distribution of residences. At this stage, therefore, we turned to the problem of population projections for sub-areas in the Region.

In considering where people might settle among the

competing sections of the Region, we operated against a background of certain well-developed notions. One was a projection of the Region's future housing wants. Another was the analysis, summarized in Chapter 9, of the forces which operate to change the character of neighborhoods. The five-stage concept of neighborhood development provided a way of looking at each sub-area of the Region and gauging its prospective course.*

To apply the concept we could not use the same approach for an area like Manhattan that we used for Queens or Westchester or Nassau; differences in past patterns of habitation, in land availability, and in "access" features of each area had to be taken into account. But, at bottom, the five-stage concept served as the basis for our population projection in all areas. Once this step was completed, it was possible to estimate how the neighborhood-serving activities, such as the food stores and neighborhood banks, would be distributed.

Again putting aside the details until later in the chapter, we come to the last stage of the grand scheme. With the land covered with people, and with the factories and offices in place, we asked ourselves if the pattern we had projected could stand up—if the land in each area could contain its projected uses, if the people could commute to and from their jobs, and so on. Wherever we could, we devised some statistical tests of the internal "viability" of the projection. But we had to recognize that the tests, such as they were, were overly simple and not very rigorous. With our few tests of internal consistency done, the projections

* The five stages, it will be remembered, are (1) the initial development from raw land, (2) the increase of population densities through multifamily dwelling construction, (3) the further increase of densities through down-grading and conversion, (4) the thinning-out of populations, and (5) the redevelopment through public or private action.

of the New York Metropolitan Region for 1965, 1975, and 1985 were final.

CONFESSION AND APOLOGY

A "rational" model of the Region's operations has both its virtues and its pitfalls. It allows the seer to describe, and allows others to reproduce the process by which the projection was generated, but it limits the seer at the same time to an oversimplified concept of the future. Wars, depressions, and acts of God are excluded from his model; great unforeseen changes in technology, analogous to the invention of the automobile, are left out of account; massive shifts in public policy, such as accompanied the New Deal, are excluded.

The strictly "rational" projection that we have described is bound to be unsatisfying on other counts as well. At times, its grossly unsubtle assumptions simply are not complex enough to embrace some major continuing shift in the economy, such as the change in the nature of financial services or the long-run substitution of synthetics for the products of farm and forests.

At times, therefore, we found our own simple assumptions too confining. At critical junctures in the projection process, we had to confess that the results which these asserted relations generated were too improbable to be taken very seriously. When this occurred, we did not hesitate to bend our results away from the answers which our models were producing. Sometimes, the adjustment was intended to reflect some long-term process of a continuing sort such as we have just mentioned. And, sometimes, as we indicated earlier, it was intended to take account of some new event on the horizon which promised to alter past relations, such as the opening of the St. Lawrence Seaway or the building of the Narrows Bridge.*

This is the insubstantial stuff that our projection—that practically any economic projection—is made of. No projection of the economic and demographic characteristics of a metropolitan area can be free of the risk of error; no public or private planner can afford to assume that the potential error is small. From a policy viewpoint, this may suggest that planners and investors should regard the preservation of flexibility as a virtue in itself, a virtue worth paying for at the seeming sacrifice of other standards of performance.

If projections are inherently subject to major error, it is not altogether amiss to ask why we bothered to produce them. There are two answers to the question. First, a careful guess is better than a heedless one; and our guesses may provide a better basis for major business and governmental decisions in the Region than those produced in greater haste or with fewer resources. Second, those who approach the quantitative results with the skepticism they deserve may still find some of our intermediate judgments of some value. Without necessarily accepting the final numbers we generate, they may still find it useful to know what visions the process generates and what stresses and strains the Region may be subjected to in the future. For us, these reasons were sufficient to proceed with the painful process of building a projection. We must leave it to the reader to decide if they are reasons enough for inspecting the results.

* Our departures from rigorous model-building were even more marked than this at times. Here and there in the process we bypassed some expensive machine calculations—even though, conceptually, our model demanded it—simply because it seemed evident that the errors involved in approximating the answers by less rigorous means could not be very large.

One last point before we plunge into an account of
the methodology and results of the projections themselves. The methodology described in this chapter is
little more than a bare outline, stripped of technical detail.° The reader who is disposed to give some weight
to the projections owes it to himself to know at least
as much about the technique as appears between the
covers of this book. Accordingly, we have presented the
technique and the results together in order to reduce
his temptation to seize upon the projections alone. We
relent from this Draconian pattern only to point out that
summary tables embodying the projections will be
found in the Appendix.

THE NATIONAL SCENE

The take-off point for any projection of the New
York Metropolitan Region's future, we observed earlier,
is a projection of the nation. In determining the critical
magnitudes in the nation, we began at the usual start-
ing point: a plausible projection of the nation's population. The Bureau of the Census makes a number of
estimates of future population levels, using various
birth-rate assumptions. One of these estimates assumes
that the birth rates of 1955–1957 for women of any
given age group will remain unchanged over the next
several decades. We accepted the Bureau's estimates for
1965 and 1975 based on this assumption, and we extended the assumption to 1985 with some minor modifications. Needless to say, United States population

° For a fuller description of the projection techniques, see
Barbara R. Berman, Benjamin Chinitz, and Edgar M. Hoover,
Projection of a Metropolis, a technical supplement published
by Harvard University Press.

grows mightily on such a basis—from 165 million in 1955 to 286 million in 1985.*

The next stepping stone to our goal was to guess at the size of the labor force. Past trends in the propensity of men and women to join the labor force are well documented and reasonably well understood. Over the years, men have been tending to enter the labor market at a later age in order to extend their schooling; and they have been tending to leave the labor market at an earlier age in order to enjoy the fruits of their savings. On the other hand, women of most age levels have tended to join the labor force in growing propor- tions, though very young women and some special groups such as urban Negroes have followed their own trends. We assumed that most of the existing trends would continue into the future, and we generated a labor force out of our population figures. Then we set aside some of our hypothetical bodies for the armed forces and for "normal" unemployment. The outcome was a growth in employment from 63 million in 1955 to 106 million in 1985.

Some of the civilian work force, however, only works part time. What we needed for later use was an esti-

* Though estimates of national population for 1965, 1975, and 1985—also of employment and gross national product— were unavoidable, they represented from our viewpoint a hurdle to be overcome rather than an end-product of the study. Accordingly, they are given no prominence in the text and are presented summarily in the Appendix, Table A-1. As a matter of fact, a projection of the national economy could, if permitted, easily swallow up all the research efforts and funds of any group concerned with the analysis of a single metropolitan area. Confronted with this dilemma, we chose the only available compromise. A national projection was done along lines suited to the needs of the New York Study. But it will be evident to the reader that the methodology and assumptions were extremely simple and that, with appropriate resources, more adequate forecasts of the national data are possible.

mate of employment in full-time equivalents. To achieve this result, we assumed that the tendency for part-time jobs to grow faster than full-time jobs would continue into the future. Finally, we made the assumption that the American economy would take a part of its growing production capacity in the form of more leisure—that the normal work week would be reduced or the average vacation period increased (or both)—and we expressed the trend by reducing our full-time work week every decade by a little less than two hours.

It was not enough to estimate employment and the "full-time equivalents" of that employment, however. We also had to know what the employed would be producing. Once more, orthodoxy was the order of the day. The first step was to observe that the nation's aggregate output per full-time equivalent employee has been growing with a reassuring regularity over the past three decades; there have been spurts and slow-downs from time to time but the stability of the nation's total performance has been more evident than the variability. Launching from past trends, we assumed that the comparatively slow growth of very recent years would continue to 1965; to this period, we assigned an annual growth rate per full-time equivalent worker of 2 per cent. On the assumption that the economy is now going through a gestation period in the application of new technology which will eventually lead to more rapid growth rates later on, we assumed that the 1965–1975 decade would enjoy a 2.5 per cent annual rate of growth in output per full-time equivalent worker and the 1975–1985 decade a 3.5 per cent rate. These assumptions produced a tentative set of estimates of the growth in the country's gross national product; according to these estimates, the gross national product, expressed in constant dollars, rises from $397 billion in 1955 to $1,368 billion in 1985.

So enormous growth is envisioned. But growth in

what? So far, we had decided tentatively on the size of the economic box but not of its contents. To fill the box, we first asked how much goods and services were likely to go to the nation's consumers—as distinguished from other claimants such as governments, business, and foreigners; and what goods these consumers would be demanding at their heightened income levels of the future. Numerous empirical studies and theoretical probings of the nature of consumer responses have been made in the United States in recent years. The main lines of these responses are fairly well defined. The growth in consumption of some items like apparel has been quite sluggish; contrariwise, many consumer services, such as those provided by the financial community, have been expanding fast. Our projection of future consumption patterns was based on a fairly simple set of assumptions, characteristic of the approach followed throughout the development of our national projections. We assumed that what was growing slowly would maintain a slow growth, and that fast-growing goods and services would continue to grow fast. Hitching these assumptions to our projections of gross national product, we developed estimates of the goods and services of different types which consumers might be expected to demand.

Having established a bill of goods for consumers, we found it necessary also to gauge how much goods and services government would demand. For this purpose, the long-run trends in the principal items of government expenditure were separately studied and projected into the future. In the process, the state and local sectors were separated from the federal; within each sector, major programs like school expenditures were distinguished; and payrolls were examined separately from business purchases and from new construction. The guiding principle, once again, was one of simple extrapolation: what had grown fast would continue to grow, while laggards would remain laggards. Here and there, however, we took cognizance of major changes in the needs of government such as the shift in the federal government's defense needs from the "transportation equipment industry" (aircraft) to the "metals industry" (missiles and related miscellanea).

With the demands of consumers and governments accounted for, there was still a need to estimate those comparatively small amounts of the nation's goods and services which would go abroad and the amounts which would come from abroad. Of the many possible ways of estimating these figures, we selected one of the cruder approaches in order to conserve research time and money. To fix the aggregate figures for such transactions, the historical relation between gross national product and the nation's foreign transactions on current account was studied and extended into the future. To decide on the composition of the totals, all that we did was to assume that the postwar pattern of imports and exports would generally be continued into the future, at the same time making a few simple adjustments in the pattern to take account of very recent trends.

With the demands of government, the consumer, and the foreign sector now determined, we were almost in a position to estimate everything else that we needed to know about the nation's production of goods and services in 1965, 1975, and 1985. That is to say, having decided what products would be wanted, we could estimate how much steel, leather, machinery, coal, trade services, and so on, would have to be produced in order to fill the bill. Needless to say, "filling the bill" means the production not only of the enumerated refrigerators, automobiles, homes, military hardware, and other items, but also of all the intermediate goods which go into the manufacture of the final products, as well as the production of the machines needed to expand the nation's production capacity to the new high production levels of 1965, 1975, and 1985.

Here, we turned to the use of the so-called inter-industry or input-output tables for our first approximation. These are tables which show, for some stated period, how much of the product of each industry was used by every other industry in the country. Those who are familiar with the use of input-output tables will appreciate at once how they were used to estimate the total production of each industry; for other readers this step may have some of the aspects of black magic. But it should be evident intuitively that, if we know how much every industry requires of the outputs of every other industry in order to turn out its products, there is a basis for an algebraic solution to the question, "how much of everything will be needed to supply a given bundle of final products?"

Of course, the use of these tables as a projection device raises many problems. For one thing, the tables we were obliged to use were based upon United States performance in 1947. In using these tables, we were brushing aside many problems, notably the implications of the unceasing technological changes which inevitably cause shifts in inter-industry relations over time; but we shall return to some of these problems a little later.

For our purposes, estimates of output were not enough; *employment* by industrial sectors was our projection goal. The missing link in passing from production to employment was some estimate of the relation between output and manpower by industries. Here again, the bold approach was followed. Trends in the relation between output and manpower were examined industry by industry for the period since 1929; and it was assumed that these trends would carry on into the future. In other words, it was assumed that industries like chemicals, petroleum products, and machinery would continue to show major gains in the conservation of manpower while industries like apparel production and lumber production would continue to exhibit the productivity sluggishness they had shown in the past.

Each set of assumptions in this chain is pregnant with implications for all the others, and any could be a source of major error. Besides, taken all together, the chain of assumptions does not embody everything we know about the national economy or anticipate for its future. The final step, therefore, was to see where the chain had led and to decide if the magnitudes produced by the process offended our general expectations about the nation's performance. In sector after sector of the economy, we compared the employment trends generated by our model with the recent history of employment trends in the sector and with projections which others had made. In the process, we could fall back on a considerable quantity of knowledge for a few sectors, knowledge generated out of our own industry studies. The effect of this final review was to alter various estimates somewhat: to reduce the relative importance of agricultural employment, to increase the relative importance of financial employment, and so on. The final version of our national estimates reflects a mild relative growth in manufacturing to 1965, and a slight relative decline thereafter. Throughout the period of projection, there is a steady decline in the relative importance of the agriculture, transportation, and utilities groups, and a steady rise in the relative importance of the service groups, construction, finance, and wholesale and retail trades.

FROM NATION TO REGION

In looking at the future of the New York area, we noted earlier, two kinds of questions can be asked: what population is the New York area likely to have? and what economic opportunities is the New York area likely to provide? Having projected the nation's development, we were a step closer to the answers, but there were still some major hurdles to be taken.

THE APPROACH

One can start appraising the Region's future population by asking what numbers are implied by different assumptions about future birth rates, death rates, and migration rates. All sorts of results can be produced as one varies his assumptions; and for some planning purposes the whole range of plausible answers is perhaps more important than any single figure.* But a "most probable" figure is also useful for many purposes. To develop our "most probable" figure, we took off from assumptions we had settled on earlier in the national projection, namely, the assumption that national fertility rates would remain at their 1955–1957 levels and that mortality rates would taper off gradually. The birth rate of the New York Metropolitan Region has characteristically been lower than that of the nation and we assumed that this relation would hold true in the future, though the New York rate would rise a little toward the national rate.

Even on these assumptions alone, that is, without assuming any net migration into the Region, there is a prodigious increase in population to be anticipated—from 15,100,000 in 1955 to 16,800,000 in 1965, 19,000,000 in 1975, and 22,000,000 in 1985. If we could assume that something like historical rates of in-migration would continue in the future, the 1985 total would be even larger, swelling above 25,000,000. But, of course, no serious assumptions about the migration cur-

* Those who would like to see such a range of projections, as well as a much more detailed account of the projection procedures, are referred to the technical supplement, *Projection of a Metropolis,* by Barbara R. Berman, Benjamin Chinitz, and Edgar M. Hoover.

rents can be made without first estimating the job opportunities which the Region seems likely to afford.

Some idea of the future growth patterns in the nation as a whole had already been developed. But we
also needed explicit judgments on how effectively the
New York area would compete with other parts of the
nation, as well as estimates of the consequences of such
growth for the Region's related local activities. Our
studies of the women's apparel industry, the printing
and publishing industry, the electronics industry, and
the financial community, published in earlier books, had
culminated in provisional projections of the amount of
employment which the New York area could be expected to claim in these industries. All told, however,
the national-market employment accounted for in these
studies represented only about 25 per cent of the Region's total national-market employment in a typical
year. For all the rest, projections still had to be made.

In choosing among the variety of seemingly plausible
approaches to a projection, our studies of earlier periods
stood us in good stead. We had already learned, for instance, that it would be dangerous to project the future
performance of any group of industries in the Region
without taking into account the changing "mix" of the
group. We had also learned that, in dealing with questions of competitive change in national-market manufacturing industries, it was essential to distinguish
among different groups of industries, along the lines explored in earlier chapters; that is, to separate the transport-sensitive group from the external-economy and the
labor-oriented groups; to go further within some of these
categories, separating industries "underrepresented"* in

* The reader will remember that the "underrepresented"
industries were simply those in which the Region's share of
national employment was less than its share of national population, while "overrepresented" industries were those in which
the Region's employment share was more than its population
share.

the Region from those "overrepresented"; and to make some added distinctions as well, such as the distinction between port-oriented and other transport-sensitive activities in the Region. For every such group of industries, we had developed a record describing the Region's actual growth and the Region's "expected" growth—the latter term, of course, being our shorthand designation for the growth which the Region would have had if each individual industry's employment in any group had changed in the Region exactly as it did in the nation.

The record showed, for instance, that the national-market transport-oriented industries which were "overrepresented" in the Region had failed (as a group) to increase their employment in the Region as fast as would have been expected on the basis of national growth rates—that from 1929 to 1954 this discrepancy was on the order of 10 to 20 percentage points a decade. We chose to assume that for the future, any industry in this group would grow 16 percentage points per decade slower in the Region than in the nation.*

And so with every other sector of the Region's employment which appeared to be serving national markets. Each sector was subjected to separate scrutiny. In each case, we brought to bear all we knew or thought we knew about the group's competitive position in the Region. There were times, to be sure, when some of the competitive forces which could be verbalized and which are described in other parts of this book could not easily be reflected quantitatively and had to be ignored. There were times, too, when our information suggested no clear implication about future competitive trends in an industry and other times when information was lacking altogether. Where conviction about future trends was lacking, we assumed that the competitive

---

* Actually, the assumption was even a little more complicated. The Region's decline in any industry was slowed up as the degree of "overrepresentation" shrank.

position of the Region would be unaltered; and where guesses were needed about the facts, we guessed. In the nonmanufacturing sectors, assumptions of both these types were particularly plentiful.

With national growth rates determined and with the New York Region's share decided for each national-market industry, we were in a position to calculate the Region's employment in these industries for the years 1965, 1975, and 1985. As was pointed out earlier, however, the national-market activities of the Region represented only about 40 per cent of the Region's total employment in the mid-1950's. All the rest represented activities which catered principally to the local market.[2]

One can think of the Region's local employment as being generated from three main sources: from the demands of the national-market industries or of other local-market industries in the Region; from the current consumption needs of the Region's households; and from private investment and governmental needs in the Region. The technique for putting all these needs together into an internally consistent projection could hardly be described as simple. At its core lay a number of sources of information. One of these sources was the so-called input-output tables for 1947, mentioned earlier, which describe how much of the goods and services produced by each sector of the American economy went to provide the needs of each other sector of the economy and of the country's households. We were in a position to guess, therefore, how much of purely local activity, such as barber shops, would be needed to serve the households and business of the Region.

There were still some hurdles to be overcome, however. For one thing, the national data reflected in the input-output tables did not mirror the particular consumption habits of the Region's households, such as the propensity to spend more of the budget on clothing and less on automobiles. The future consumption propensities of the Region's households had to be estimated, therefore, having in mind the differences between New York and national patterns in the past and the projection of national patterns for the future.

Beyond these difficulties lay the further problem that local industries in the New York Region bearing a given label commonly had input needs which were very different from industries in the nation with exactly the same title. Accordingly, we had to determine how to adjust the nation's 1947 input-output relations for application to the local industries in the Region, a step which was achieved largely by comparing the Region's actual economic performance in 1954 with the performance which would have been generated by the Region if the nation's 1947 inter-industry relations had been operating in these industries. These and numerous other troublesome problems had to be dealt with before we were in a position to say how much employment was likely to be generated in the local segment of the Region's economy.[3] Once the necessary relations were established, however, we had overcome the main obstacles to a simultaneous solution for the desired quantities, namely, employment in the Region by various local economic sectors.

The employment suggested by all these calculations, when compared with the population analysis described earlier, allows us to estimate the migration which would be needed to keep the Region in balance. The prospective economic growth of the Region, according to our calculations, demands a considerable amount of in-migration between 1955 and 1965, on the order of 114,000 persons per year. Thereafter, the net migration flow is seen as falling off rapidly, to only 40,000 in the 1965–1975 decade. In the following ten-year period, there will be net out-migration from the Region—a truly spectacular result, if it can be believed, since it would reverse an historical trend of hundreds of years' standing. But that is a story which needs more discussing.

THE RESULTS

According to our account in Chapters 3 to 6, the economic course of the New York Metropolitan Region has been generated out of a strong mix of growing industries, offset in part by a slipping competitive position in many of them.

For the future, if our projections prove to be related to events, the Region's mix of national-market activities will continue to constitute a source of strength for its economy.

More precisely, our projection suggests that, in manufacturing, if each of the Region's national-market industries were to grow at the rate projected for its United States counterpart, the Region's employment in national-market manufacturing activities as a whole would grow at about the same rate as United States employment in national-market manufacturing industries as a whole. Our projections suggest also that the Region's mix of nonmanufacturing industries would generate much higher nonmanufacturing growth rates than those in the nation; this is largely because the Region has so little agricultural activity, which is a declining sector of the national economy. And, finally, because employment in nonmanufacturing activities tends to grow faster than that in manufacturing and because the Region specializes in nonmanufacturing, the total mix of the Region's employment seems conducive to faster growth than United States employment as a whole. To revert to the somewhat cryptic language of earlier chapters, the Region's "expected" growth rate in national-market activities would be higher than United States growth rates in those activities. The comparison appears in Table 22.

Are these results plausible? We are not sure; we have
a strong suspicion that the New York mix will prove
even stronger than the figures suggest. Part of the reason
for the suspicion has to do with a problem which will
plague every student of metropolitan growth. Our national projections, though done for 28 separate categories of employment—a level of detail which no one
would have attempted ten years ago—was still far cruder
than we would have liked. The New York Metropolitan

TABLE 22   Projections of U. S. Growth Rates and
New York Metropolitan Region's "Expected"[a]
Growth Rates of Employment in National-
Market Activities, 1954–1985

| | Percentage change in employment | | | |
	1954–1985[b]	1954–1965	1965–1975	1975–1985
All national-market activities				
U. S. growth	+60.9	+20.6	+16.5	+14.5
New York "expected"	+95.1	+34.7	+21.5	+19.2
National-market manufacturing				
U. S. growth	+83.0	+34.4	+17.7	+15.6
New York "expected"	+85.9	+34.6	+18.3	+16.8
National-market nonmanufacturing				
U. S. growth	+31.7	+2.5[c]	+14.3	+12.5
New York "expected"	+114.8	+35.0	+28.3	+24.0

[a] To arrive at the Region's future "expected" growth rate,
we projected the Region's and the nation's employment in
each industry or service and then calculated the rate at which
the Region's aggregate employment in a particular category
would grow if each industry or service in the category were
to grow at the projected national rate for the same industry
or service.

[b] The figures for the entire period 1954–1985 were obtained
by linking the percentages for the three sub-periods.

[c] Agricultural employment is projected as declining by 21
per cent in the 1954–1965 period. Nonmanufacturing employment except agriculture is projected as growing by 34.1 per
cent.

Region's industries, as we have pointed out more than once, constitute highly specialized slices of each of these broad groups. One may well ask, therefore, if the growth rates of any broad group can be indiscriminately applied to all the slices which it embraces. And if the answer is no, then one is entitled to speculate that a more finely classified national projection—assuming one were possible—might have given a systematic upward push to the Region's mix. This is the direction, at least, in which our judgment would go.

To move from the "expected" growth rate of the New York Metropolitan Region to the growth which we actually anticipate, one has to add the effects of competitive change projected for each national-market activity. This done, the results in Table 23 emerge.

So much for national-market industries. When the local activity is taken into account—activity running the

TABLE 23 Past and Projected Employment in National-Market Activities, U. S. and New York Metropolitan Region, 1954–1985

	Thousands of employees		Region's share of U. S.
	U. S.	Region	
National-market activities, total			
1954	23,046	2,371	10.3%
1965	27,804	2,981	10.7
1975	32,385	3,405	10.5
1985	37,076	3,839	10.4
Manufacturing			
1954	13,098	1,637	12.5
1965	17,610	2,034	11.6
1975	20,734	2,253	10.9
1985	23,970	2,480	10.3
Nonmanufacturing			
1954	9,948	734	7.4
1965	10,194	947	9.3
1975	11,651	1,152	9.9
1985	13,106	1,359	10.4

gamut from the printing shops which serve the central offices to the local grocers who serve the suburban neighborhoods—we produce a Region whose total employment grows rapidly, though not quite as rapidly as that of the United States. Whereas the Region's total employment of 6,193,000 in 1954 represents 10.1 per cent of the nation, its 7,202,000 jobs in 1965 come to 9.8 per cent of the national total; its 1975 figure of 8,307,000 comes to 9.4 per cent; and its 1985 aggregate of 9,462,000 represents 9.0 per cent.

Chart 18 compares the internal distribution of the New York Metropolitan Region's employment by major categories in 1954 with the projected distribution in 1965, 1975, and 1985.* The pattern of employment shown in the chart is remarkably stable, especially when one considers the long tortuous course of quantitative manipulations which led to the results. The principal changes are the relative growth in the business service group and the relative growth of government. What the chart does not show is the interesting change inside the manufacturing group. The apparel industry, with 23.6 per cent of the Region's manufacturing employment in 1954, is found slipping to 19.5 per cent by 1985. The big relative gainer, meanwhile, is what our classification system calls the metals and metal products group— a group whose employment exceeds that of apparel by 1985. This group includes not only the metal-fabricating industries as we usually define them, but the unclassified and unclassifiable manufacturing industries as well—the sector in which new industries often find their first reflection in Census statistics. If this projection proves valid, the New York Metropolitan Region is evidently in for a change.

These are the jobs we anticipate. Where are the people to fill them? In order for the jobs to be filled, ac-

* For the underlying data, see Appendix, Table A-2.

cording to our calculations, the Region's population will have to go from 15,092,000 in 1955 to 18,033,000 in 1965, 20,810,000 in 1975, and 23,712,000 in 1985.

Stated in relation to total United States population, the Region's share will go from 9.1 per cent in 1955 to 9.2 per cent in 1965, then will fall to 8.8 per cent in 1975 and 8.3 per cent in 1985.

CHART 18 Past and Projected Distribution of Employment in New York Metropolitan Region by Major Economic Groups, 1954–1985

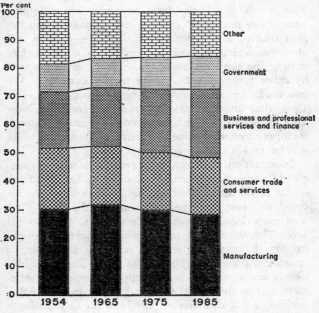

This result, we have already noted, implies that the net flow of people into the Region will continue at a high rate until 1965, but that thereafter the net migration flow will slow down and even reverse itself. Any conclusion like this, moving contrary to everything we have experienced so far, needs the closest attention; its basis needs to be fully understood before it can be given any credibility.

Reviewing the factors that have produced the result, one begins to appreciate that the result is simply a new netting out of old factors—very much like the shift in direction of a tug-of-war as the stronger team's strength gradually wanes and the weaker team's strength gradually grows, until a turning point is reached. In this case, the economic forces have already been reviewed; a favorable mix has finally been overcome by a slipping competitive position to produce net slippage in the Region relative to the nation. This relative—relative, not absolute—decline in economic opportunity in the Region, cutting the need for outside manpower, is augmented by other forces which operate to the same end. We can no longer assume, as one might have assumed in 1900, that immigrants will persist in coming to New York regardless of whether economic opportunity awaits them; nor can we assume that, once in New York, many will be unable to move on.

In-migration, therefore, must be seen as more responsive to economic opportunity than heretofore. And the extent of the economic opportunity must take into account the fact that the birth rate of the New York area each decade moves a little closer to the national level. This means that the Region's capacity to supply its own labor needs, without resort to migration, is growing. At the same time, some of the Region's older people are moving out as they approach or reach retirement and as their need to earn a living in the Region declines. All told, therefore, the basis for anticipating a turnabout in the Region's migration currents does not seem implausible.

INSIDE THE REGION

We indicated earlier that there were many points in the projection process at which it proved impossible to incorporate systematically all that had been learned about the forces at work on the New York Metropolitan Region. This problem loomed especially large in determining what jobs and populations each sub-area of the Region could be expected to contain in the years 1965, 1975, and 1985. How could we crystallize, for instance, the conviction that some parts of Manhattan close to the central business district would increase their high-income populations while other neighborhoods nearby were losing low-income inhabitants; and how could we attach a "scientifically" derived quantity to the expectation that the special amenities of western Suffolk County, close by the open sea, would attract more population than, say, an equally accessible area of Somerset County?

Sometimes we tried to reflect these expectations by assuming the existence of some express set of relations between population growth and the characteristics of a county, drawing heavily on the past development of the Region to define these relations. Sometimes, however, we avoided the problem altogether, by projecting figures for large areas and thus submerging some special trend peculiar to a small sub-area within the overriding trend common to the larger one.

ASSUMPTIONS AND TECHNIQUES

We approached the problem of projecting the distribution of jobs inside the Region with a number of points already well established. First, we had settled on the number of jobs which the Region as a whole would contain, industry by industry, for our target dates 1965,

1975, and 1985.[4] Second, we had pulled apart the structure of the Region's jobs well enough to be able to say that certain types of industries in the Region were behaving quite differently from others in their locational responses and that there was reason to suppose they would continue to do so. Given what we had learned about the factors affecting the movement of jobs, there was no use trying to project the future location of manufacturing employment, for instance, without distinguishing the "nuisance" group from other industries, the growing industries from the declining industries, the large-plant industries from the small-plant categories, the local manufacturing operations from those serving national markets, and so on. Similar distinctions had to be applied for such activities as wholesaling and business services. Disaggregation then was the first need—disaggregation to be followed by piecemeal projection, then by reaggregation into the figures shown in Chart 19.*

The procedure in projecting these disaggregated slices of employment for the Region's sub-areas was roughly as follows. First, there were the industries whose future location in the Region had already been estimated by painstaking industry studies—women's apparel, electronics, printing and publishing, and the financial community.** For the moment, the estimates generated by these studies were accepted at face value. But most of the Region's employment was still to be projected. For this purpose, our first principle was a lesson learned from the analysis of locational behavior in prior periods —that for any group of industries, a projection will not

---

* See Appendix, Tables A-3, A-4, A-5, and A-6, for the underlying data.
** See *Made in New York*, ed. Max Hall (Cambridge: Harvard University Press, 1959); and Sidney M. Robbins and Nestor E. Terleckyj, *Money Metropolis* (Cambridge: Harvard University Press, 1960).

be wide of the mark if it is based on the assumption that each constituent industry will expand or contract in all the Region's sub-areas at the same rate.

We were not content to assume identical rates of change in all sub-areas, however. In manufacturing, New York City's growth rate for the industries in certain groups—the communication-oriented industries and the expanding national-market industries with small plants—was assumed to be lower than that of the Region, in line with past performance. For certain other types of industry, it was assumed that, because of the scarcity of new sites, New York City's 1956 levels of employment represented an absolute ceiling; large-plant industries serving national markets were placed in this class, as were nuisance industries and water-transport-oriented industries. For still others, where New York City's relative performance had been quite stable in the past, the basic assumption was that New York City would continue to retain a stable share of the Region's employment; raw-material-consuming industries and national-market industries with declining employment in the Region fell in this class.

Outside the manufacturing field, the assumptions about New York City's share of the Region's employment also were tailored to fit the past and projected tendencies of different lines of activity. In advertising and contract construction, for instance, it was assumed that New York City would retain its historical shares. In central and administrative offices, however, the assumption was that the City would lose relative to the rest of the Region—that, because of the dispersion of data-processing centers and similar installations, the City's share of the Region's employment would decline by about one-tenth per decade. (Despite this assumption, the City's employment in this category is expected to grow in *absolute* numbers.) New York City's share

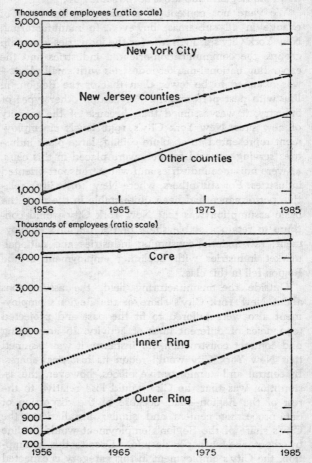

CHART 19 Past and Projected Employment by Parts of New York Metropolitan Region, 1956–1985

Thousands of employees (ratio scale)

New York City

New Jersey counties

Other counties

1956   1965   1975   1985

Thousands of employees (ratio scale)

Core

Inner Ring

Outer Ring

1956   1965   1975   1985

Note: In upper panel, "other counties" means Fairfield County (Connecticut) and the New York State counties of the Region outside New York City. In lower panel, Richmond of wholesale employment also is assumed to drop off as it has in the past, by roughly one-eighth per decade.

Having allocated a portion of the Region's total employment to New York City, we still had the big task of assigning the balance among the remaining counties. Here, we fell back once more on the 1956 pattern plus historical trends. National-market manufacturing industries with large plants, it was assumed, would favor the Outer Ring counties; national-market industries with small plants and the communication-oriented group would favor the Inner Ring counties; and so on. In non-manufacturing activities, office employment would grow somewhat in all counties but with particular vigor in Westchester, Nassau, and Bergen, while wholesaling activity would favor the Inner Ring counties.

In all this manipulation, activities serving neighborhood markets were set aside for later allocation. The locational patterns for these industries, we assumed, would take their cues from the distribution of the jobs already allocated and from the distribution of residences. Indeed, in the various lines of consumer activity, it will be recalled, we had managed to work out some fairly precise relations between county employment in any given line and county population or county jobs. At this stage, therefore, we turned to the information generated out of tentative intraregional population projections, which were based on techniques described below. With these projections in hand, we made use of the historical relations between county employment in each consumer line and county population or other relevant county characteristics, in order to produce a projection for employment in each principal line of consumer activity for 1965, 1975, and 1985.

County, normally in the Inner Ring, could not be separated from the other four counties in New York City and is counted in the Core, which therefore consists here of New York City *in toto* and Hudson County.

In projecting the location of residences, we used some quite different techniques. Here, as indicated earlier, the five-stage concept of neighborhood development underlay our projection. In Manhattan, one could rule out any population changes generated by the development of raw land and could concentrate on the net effect of new apartment houses, the down-grading of existing structures, the thinning-out process, and the altered land use accompanying public and private redevelopment. Crude orders of magnitude had to be assigned to each of these tendencies, a step which required us to review all that we anticipated in the changing economic functions of the Region. Out of this process, we could foresee a continued decline in the population of Manhattan at a pace not very different from the decline of prior decades.

For areas immediately outside Manhattan, the process of projection had to be slightly different. In the Bronx, Brooklyn, and Queens, and in Hudson County, estimates had to be made of the increase in population which might be generated by the building up of some of the last vestiges of open land, in addition to all the other forces suggested in connection with Manhattan. Nor could one afford to assume that any of these forces had identical implications for each of the four counties mentioned. Queens has more open land than Brooklyn or the Bronx; much of Hudson County's open land is peculiarly unsuited to residential development; Brooklyn is built at lower densities than Hudson; the size of family units in Hudson tends to be different from that of the Bronx; and so on. In effect, the peculiarities of past development and present situation were taken systematically into account in each of the four counties and the likely population implications were estimated as each county moved progressively through the cycle of maturation, obsolescence, and redevelopment. Out of this weighting process came figures which foresaw a little added population growth for Queens and declines for each of the three other counties.

With the total population of the Region previously set and the population of Manhattan and the rest of the Core now tentatively determined, we could say what the aggregate population of the rest of the Region —the Inner and Outer Rings—might be. The question still to be faced, however, was that of apportioning the remaining population among the counties of these two widely different zones.

As a preliminary to the apportioning job, a few guesses could be made about the kind of added housing that the growing populations in these areas would demand. Most of the added stock, we assumed, would be single-family structures as in the recent past; multifamily structures would probably increase a little in relative importance as land sites grew scarce in some parts of the Region and as the age distribution of the population shifted, but the single-family structure would still dominate.

After fixing on the totals likely to occupy single-family and multifamily structures, we proceeded to allocate the anticipated growth to the counties of the Inner and Outer Rings, using a somewhat different basis of allocation in each ring.° The Inner Ring, it seems evident, will begin to show marked symptoms of land scarcity during the next twenty-five years, whereas much of the Outer Ring will continue to offer a considerable choice of land alternatives. In each of the Inner Ring counties, land availability was regarded

° Two of the Inner Ring counties, Westchester and Passaic, have northerly portions (beyond their narrow waists) whose characteristics are like the Outer Ring rather than the Inner. Therefore our population projection for each of those counties is the aggregate of two separate projections, in which we used the Inner Ring procedure for the south portion and the Outer Ring procedure for the north portion.

as a restraining upper limit; by setting aside appropriate quantities of land in each county for nonresidential uses, roughly proportionate to the expected growth of the county, and by guessing at the amounts of land likely to be bypassed altogether, we could gauge what might be available for residential use. As land grew more and more scarce in any county from one target date to the next, fewer single-family homes were assigned to the county and more multifamily construction was assumed. In addition to land availability, we also took into account the past and prospective style of development of the county—both its densities of construction and its typical family size. Finally, on top of everything else, we took cognizance of the likelihood that some of the "older" counties, such as Essex, would see the down-grading of their existing structures and the growth of slums, accompanied by crowding in some neighborhoods and thinning out in others. The effects of these processes, as nearly as we could guess them, were also worked into the estimates.

All that was left was to settle upon a plausible basis for projecting the population of the Outer Ring counties. In these areas, it seemed to us, the problem of relative access to the inlying urban mass would begin to play a major hand in the selection and timing of different areas for the development of single-family homes. The first step, therefore, was to allocate the land of the Outer Ring by access zones, a concept which we met earlier, though in somewhat different form. For projection purposes, places in the Outer Ring within ninety minutes of Manhattan were given the highest access rating; those in a band roughly seven or eight miles farther out were given the second highest rating; and so on through a third, fourth, and fifth zone—the fifth being delineated to cover all the remaining land. Our theory was that the vacant land in the most accessible zone would be developed at a rate twice as fast as the land in the zone just beyond, that *that* zone would be developed twice as fast as the next, and so on. On this theory, there would be considerable "leapfrogging" in the development process, since some growth would be taking place in all zones simultaneously, though less in the more remote zones. The likely population density on the settled land was then estimated for each county, with due recognition of past patterns of development in the county. At this stage, too, some modifications were introduced to allow for a small amount of multifamily construction.

The population estimates generated by the process were not permitted to stand, however. Aware of the limitations of so simple an approach, we compared the results with growth trends in the various Outer Ring counties just prior to the 1955 projection date. Though the comparisons were reassuring on the whole, nonetheless they flushed up some significant discrepancies. Suffolk County, for instance, had been showing considerably faster growth than our simple formula implied for the future, while Somerset County was growing more slowly than seemed reconcilable with our formula. Recognizing that discrepancies such as these could have stemmed from a variety of factors, notably the layout of the high-speed highway system and the special amenities provided by nearness to the sea beaches, we modified our projection somewhat in the direction of history, making greater modifications in the 1965 estimates than in the figures for subsequent dates.

With these results in hand, we were tempted to take two further steps. One was to expose the population and job projections to local specialists intimately familiar with each county's prospects, and to modify the projections further in the light of their reactions. The other was to reflect in our projections the implications of population and job statistics which were available for a few counties for years subsequent to our base years of 1955 and 1956. In the end, however, we determined not to take these added steps, for fear that they might undermine the systematic character of the projection to such a degree as largely to negate any claims to internal consistency. It follows, however, that if more detailed consideration of the special features of any area or more recent data on the performance of any area were brought to bear on our projections for that area, the resulting qualifications could conceivably produce more useful projections for the area in question.*

THE RESULTS

The description of the methodology will already have pointed the way to many of the results. Chart 20, depicting the main trends in population within the Region, offers no great surprise. New York City is seen as having a gradually declining population in the long run, the outcome of declines in Manhattan, Brooklyn, and the Bronx, stability in Queens, and increases in Richmond. The Core, consisting of the City's four major boroughs and Hudson County, also is depicted as declining; Hudson's population, if presented separately, would show a comparatively large drop from 1965 to 1985.

In the Inner Ring, population growth continues, though the rate of growth is a little more sedate in some counties than in others. By 1975, for instance, population growth in mushrooming Nassau County apparently will have slowed to a crawl; the growth rate in Essex County will be decelerating rapidly, partly because

---

* After the projections had been completed and most of the book had been set in type, one of those events occurred which make seers grow old prematurely: the preliminary population counts of the 1960 federal Census were made available for counties of the New York Metropolitan Region. When these are compared with our population estimates for 1955 and our projections for 1965 (as shown in the Appendix, Table A-7), a number of discrepancies emerge. See footnote on page 278.

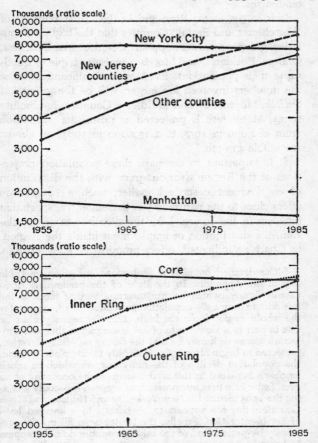

CHART 20 Past and Projected Population by Parts of New York Metropolitan Region, 1955–1985

Thousands (ratio scale)

New York City

New Jersey counties

Other counties

Manhattan

1955   1965   1975   1985

Thousands (ratio scale)

Core

Inner Ring

Outer Ring

1955   1965   1975   1985

Note: "Other counties" means Fairfield County (Connecticut) and the New York State counties of the Region outside New York City.

Newark will long since have stopped adding to its population; and Union County will be showing similar tendencies.

It is in the Outer Ring and in the upper portions of Westchester and Passaic Counties that the highest population growth rates will appear. Counties like Dutchess, Orange, Rockland, and Morris promise to triple or quadruple their populations. Even more significant, because the numbers involved are larger, will be the growth of Suffolk, Monmouth, and Middlesex Counties; in absolute terms, Monmouth is projected as raising its population from 280,000 in 1955 to 1,157,000 in 1985, an almost incredible growth.*

It is important to compare these population projections of the Region's various parts with the distribution of employment described earlier; such a comparison offers clues to the nature of the passenger transportation problem in the future. Like the distribution of population, the distribution of employment inside the Region, as Chart 19 indicated, offers promises of great change.

---

* The detailed population projections are given in Table A-7 in the Appendix. In the light of the preliminary 1960 Census figures, which we are inserting in that table at the last minute, our 1965 population projection of 18,033,000 for the whole Region looks too high. This discrepancy must be due in part to a slower rate of net in-migration than our projection assumed; it may be that the falling off of in-migration, projected to begin after 1965, is already taking place. Second, the population decline of the old cities, on which so much emphasis is placed in this study, seems to be occurring at an even faster rate than our projections suggest, especially affecting the 1965 picture for New York City and Hudson and Essex Counties; this too appears to be related to a lowered level of net in-migration. Finally, the tendency to fill up the previously by-passed land of the inlying counties does not appear to be quite as strong as our projection assumes—witness the comparatively slow growth of Bergen and Richmond Counties. In general, the dispersive population forces in the Region seem even stronger than those built into our model.

The most stable large section of the Region is New York City. Here, total employment moves slowly upward after 1965. Within the City, however, there are signs of considerable shift. The exact dimensions of the shift are not directly evident from our figures, since we had no adequate basis for making any direct guesses of future employment in each of the City's five counties.* Even without county-by-county projections, however, we have no hesitation in saying that the City's projected increase of half a million jobs or so between 1956 and 1985 will occur largely in Manhattan's central business district. This seems clear from the types of employment in which New York City is expected to register its major increases.** Most of the increase appears in the category of finance and the category of business and professional services; only a little of it is found in manufacturing or consumer trade and services.

Once more, we are brought back to speculating whether the commuter transportation facilities, rail and road, will be maintained and expanded sufficiently to realize this growth in Manhattan's central business district. The projected magnitudes are large enough to suggest that present and projected facilities will be under a real strain to bear the expansion in daily commuting. Indeed the projected growth is sufficiently large to permit one to say that public policy in this field may prove a key variable in determining how New York City's central business district develops in the future. Our projection takes it for granted that the strains imposed by such commuting will be met by piecemeal action—by action which keeps the suburban rail commuting system in operation and which significantly expands the facilities for bus and automobile commuting. If this assump-

* Unhappily, the data which are indispensable for projection usually come in the form of a New York City total rather than on a county-by-county basis within the City.

** See Appendix, Tables A-3 and A-6.

tion is not realized in practice, however, another reason will exist for deviations between the projections and reality.

Outside New York City, growth in most of the Region shows a well-balanced future pattern—well-balanced in the sense that employment increases and population increases appear to go hand in hand, with a remarkable degree of consistency. It is important to remember that this result was not an inevitable consequence of the projection technique. Since most categories of employment were projected quite independently of population changes—consumer trades and services being the obvious exception to the rule—considerable disparities in the two projections might have emerged.

The fact that employment trends and population trends do not diverge markedly in most sections of the Region suggests a number of things. It casts doubt on any image of the Region as a giant cluster of human activity held together by a great nub of jobs at the center. Instead, apart from the special problem offered by New York City's projected increase of half a million jobs or so, it affords a picture of a Region in which the centripetal pull is weakening. This, in turn, means a further modification of the oversimplified picture of the Region as a ring of bedroomy communities in the suburbs emptying out their inhabitants every morning to the central city. Incomplete and misleading as that picture is today, it promises to be even more misleading in the decades ahead. Accordingly, the prime transportation "problem" of the Region, so long thought of as that of bringing people to and from the central city, may well be matched by the development of many new and little bottlenecks, arising out of the diffuse cross-hauling and reverse commuting which the future will bring. And the chronic complaint of the outlying areas that they lack an "economic base" may continue to lose some of its realism and force.

TWO VIEWS OF REALITY

The mass of data, analyses, impressions, and hunches which emerges from this study can be viewed in many lights. There are two views, however, which need especially to be understood and contrasted: that of the expert concerned with problems of urban development, and that of the people themselves who live in the New York Metropolitan Region.

To speak of the expert view, of course, is to speak of an abstraction; there are experts and experts. For most of them, however, the projections in these pages carry few surprises. The great growth of our urban areas had long been heralded. The notion that such growth would involve the blanketing of large stretches of land at low densities was already foreseen. The possibility that the old cities inside the urban areas might stop growing and would even lose somewhat in population has been apparent for some time. The wistful notion that middle-income families or older couples might spontaneously return to the cities in such numbers as to reverse the apparent trend has been only a notion, not a real conviction.

For most experts, however, there is cold comfort in this picture. The portrait of a Region developing thinly and patchily at the edges suggests a profligate, planless use of the land. It suggests the eating up of open space, with reduced hopes of capturing large tracts for recreational purposes, little consideration of the traffic implications of the new growth, and the continual rise of incompatible uses of contiguous land. The decline of slum densities in the old cities, though it may ease some problems, is counterpoised by the appearance of slums in the old suburbs, where the mechanisms of government for dealing with the social and physical problems of the slums may be even less adequate than in the old cities. The shift in transportation patterns we envisage still foresees a critical role for suburban rail facilities and still fails to offer any hope that they may pay their way.

If our projections prove to have any validity, however, the perspective in which the expert will see the Region is likely to be somewhat different from that of most of the Region's inhabitants. True, there will be groups of significant size among the Region's heterogeneous populations whose subjective impressions will have something in common with the expert view suggested above. The commuter who makes the long daily haul from a point on the Region's periphery to the central business district of Manhattan or Newark will share some of the expert's views of reality, for instance. The constant encroachment of mass development, the disappearance of open space, and the constant struggle to improve ingress to the central business district involve real problems for those whose jobs are at the center and whose living preferences favor the open spaces.

At the lower end of the income scale we are also likely to find a view which has elements in common with the expert. Squalor and frustration will still be the lot of those disadvantaged groups which are locked into the oldest portions of the urban mass, unable to escape. And even among the middle-income groups one may encounter the occasional suburbanite whose living experience is proving a costly and irritating disappointment.

Much more important in numerical terms, however, are the inhabitants of the Region whose urban environment in the next twenty-five years will represent a major advance over that of their parents, or whose state will be so incomparably different from what went before as to defy comparisons. The offspring of the Jewish or Italian or Greek immigrant of 1900, comfortably established in his Westchester ranch house in 1965, will have the backdrop of his boyhood in the tenements of

Brooklyn or the Bronx against which to compare his surroundings; for him, the disappearance of open space and the decline of the Region's older housing may be largely abstractions running counter to his personal experience. The Negro family, recently established in the forty-year-old apartments of the Grand Concourse in the Bronx, will have the seventy-year-old tenements of teeming Harlem as its prior point of reference. Even the Puerto Rican in-migrants on Manhattan's crowded West Side, while experiencing the restlessness and melancholy of the unhappy migrant, will presumably see something in their environment which they count as superior to life in San Juan or the agricultural back country of Puerto Rico; those who see no redeeming features in their New York environment will presumably have exercised the relatively easy option of returning to the Island.

The difference between the expert view and the subjective view may exist not only with respect to neighborhoods and housing, but also with regard to transportation in the New York area. We have already observed that those who make the long daily haul from a distant point to the central business district are likely to see eye to eye with the experts on the inadequacy of the facilities leading to the central business district. But it has to be remembered that, although this group will grow in absolute numbers it will still constitute a minority, far outweighed by those with other transportation needs.

Those who depend entirely on the New York City subway system will have a different reaction. The system presents no clear signs of deterioration to its users; the intolerable crush at rush-hour peaks is no more marked—it may even be a little less pronounced, on the whole—than twenty or thirty years ago and is unlikely to be much worse in the future. Most automobile commuters may also have a point of view at variance from that of the expert. The great bulk of those who commute from one suburban point to another, rather than travel into the central business district, will probably regard their journey to work as causing no special difficulties and stirring up no special public issues. Some of these commuters will encounter one or another of the little bottlenecks engendered by the new pattern of diffused cross-hauling. On the whole, however, the trips will be comparatively short. The problems of this group may grow as circumferential traffic mounts. But it is quite possible that as a group these daily travelers will not view their existing situation as one of clear deterioration.

The gap between prevalent subjective points of view and the experts' typical evaluation of the Region's problems is easy to understand. The experts compare the Region's development with what it *might* be, given a little better planning; the inhabitants of the Region have little time or opportunity to think of what the Region might be. The experts are always aware of the subtle public costs which society is already bearing because of a lack of advance planning; aware of the land which has been spoiled for industrial development because residences were heedlessly placed nearby; aware of the space which has been blocked for recreation because it is spotted thinly with private uses; of the neighborhoods where crime and disease have grown because of deteriorating environment and inadequate social services; of the local governments whose facilities have gone downhill because their inhabitants cannot carry the load. The experts, in short, are impressed by the problems left behind by the movement of the people in the Region. They note the avoidable burdens which society has assumed as a result of those problems. Most inhabitants, we can be sure, are only vaguely aware of those burdens and even less aware of the ultimate impact that the burdens will make on them.

Before public action can be counted on to alter the

metropolitan environment very much, the experts and the metropolitan dwellers will have to find a way of communicating a little more effectively across the gulf which separates them. If this series of volumes achieves anything, it will be to facilitate that communication. But communication is the beginning of a process, not the end. Once the experts and the public have begun to communicate, the views and goals of both will surely change somewhat, approaching a new common synthesis. That done, we shall have moved a giant step closer to the objective of a more tolerable metropolitan environment.

AUTHOR'S ACKNOWLEDGMENT

The listing of my name as the author of this volume is more than a trifle misleading. A volume whose task is to summarize and synthesize, by its nature, builds largely on the works of others. This book, in particular, draws upon the eight other volumes in this series (listed just before the title page) and upon a myriad of unpublished memoranda and supporting materials produced by my colleagues in this study.

At the same time, I want to acknowledge a special kind of debt to Patricia Noble and Lucille Wu. This book was prepared after most of my collaborators had returned to their academic duties, leaving their manuscripts and their occult and mystifying files. These two were my invaluable link to the rich deposits of records and data on which my summary report relied. Working against pressing deadlines and evaporating funds, they made the production of this book possible.

My final acknowledgment goes to Max Hall, editorial director of the Study. To the everlasting advantage of myself and the other authors in the Study, Mr. Hall persistently pushed beyond the editor's role, distinguishing with uncanny precision between genuine difficulties of communication and intellectual deadwood. All of us who claim authorship in this series owe him a major debt.

Raymond Vernon

Appendix
Tables of Projections

TABLE A-1 Past and Projected U. S. Population, Employment, and Gross National Product, 1955–1985

	Population (millions)	Civilian employment (millions)	Gross national product (billions of 1955 dollars)
1955	165.3	63.2	397
1965	195.7	73.4	580
1975	235.2	88.7	898
1985	286.4	105.6	1,368

Note: The projections of gross national product, being revised estimates, are slightly different from those used in some of the earlier books of the New York Metropolitan Region Study.

Source of 1955 figures: U. S. Bureau of the Census, *Statistical Abstract of the United States: 1959.*

TABLE A-2 Past and Projected Employment in
New York Metropolitan Region by Categories of
Industries, 1954–1985

(in thousands)

	1954	1965	1975	1985
Total employment[a]	6,192.8	7,202.0	8,307.4	9,462.0
Manufacturing*	1,871.9	2,298.9	2,492.4	2,682.7
Food	137.2	168.5	196.5	229.1
Tobacco	4.3	6.2	7.1	8.5
Textiles	51.2	68.3	75.3	83.8
Apparel	446.3	475.4	489.4	528.9
Lumber and timber	11.1	18.2	26.0	35.5
Furniture	31.6	41.7	44.8	47.6
Paper	52.0	46.2	48.0	50.1
Printing and publishing	167.2	200.0	221.0	233.0
Chemicals	108.0	85.2	93.2	95.5
Petroleum and coal	16.4	19.9	23.3	27.7
Rubber products	15.9	11.9	11.7	11.4
Leather and products	45.8	42.8	43.8	45.3
Stone, clay, and glass	26.4	26.1	28.8	32.2
Metals and metal products	346.8	557.6	616.3	672.4
Machinery, exc. electrical	114.8	110.9	120.9	127.8
Electrical machinery	169.8	296.9	314.3	317.1
Transport equipment, exc. auto	104.9	81.9	79.7	69.8
Automobiles and equipment	22.2	41.2	52.3	67.0
Wholesale trade	401.4	461.4	531.7	612.5
Finance[b]	293.3	365.4	451.6	556.5
Consumer trades and services[c]	1,332.9	1,468.7	1,673.3	1,894.0
Business and professional services[d]	946.1	1,132.0	1,436.6	1,748.8
Transportation, communications, and other public utilities	487.7	490.3	530.5	563.1
Contract construction	200.6	187.5	222.5	265.8
Agriculture, forestry, and fisheries	45.3	46.6	49.4	53.1
Government	613.6	751.2	919.4	1,085.5

* The 18 manufacturing categories in this table are not identical with the 2-digit industries used in Census statistics; instead they have been regrouped to correspond to the categories used in our national projections.

For a, b, c, and d, see "Notes for Tables A-3 through A-6," following Table A-6.

TABLE A-3 Employment in Counties of New York Metropolitan Region by Categories of Industries, 1956

(in thousands)

	Total employment[a]	Manufacturing	Wholesale trade	Finance[b]	Consumer trade and services	Business and professional services[d]	Public utilities[e]	Contract construction	Agriculture, forestry and fisheries	Government
Entire Region	6,402.6	1,886.9	443.4	318.8	1,374.6	977.7	493.8	229.2	45.3	633.0
Core, total[f]	4,174.1	1,076.5	352.7	255.3	851.3	748.7	351.2	118.0	5.8	414.6
New York City	3,894.9	942.3	338.8	250.6	808.8	726.9	323.3	111.0	5.2	388.0
Hudson	279.2	134.2	13.9	4.7	42.5	21.8	27.9	7.0	0.6	26.6
Inner Ring, total[f]	1,453.6	508.5	66.5	49.9	348.9	157.9	98.8	72.7	8.7	141.8
Essex	402.1	136.1	23.4	27.8	86.1	44.7	36.1	13.4	1.0	33.5
Nassau	274.2	68.9	9.3	6.5	85.9	29.0	15.4	19.7	1.5	38.0
Westchester	216.9	51.1	8.5	5.7	64.9	30.5	15.4	14.4	2.3	24.1
Bergen	208.1	88.8	8.4	3.1	44.7	17.3	11.1	11.7	2.0	20.9
Union	190.9	86.0	9.7	3.3	35.4	21.9	12.5	7.9	1.0	13.3
Passaic	161.4	77.6	7.1	3.5	31.9	14.4	8.3	5.6	0.9	13.0
Outer Ring, total	775.0	301.9	24.3	13.6	174.3	71.1	43.7	38.6	30.8	76.6
Fairfield	240.7	113.9	8.3	4.4	49.6	22.6	10.4	11.6	3.5	16.4
Middlesex	130.8	64.9	3.9	1.5	20.9	8.7	6.8	5.7	1.9	16.5
Suffolk	105.6	23.9	2.9	2.1	30.0	11.5	6.6	7.9	6.8	13.9
Monmouth	66.1	14.2	2.5	1.6	22.2	6.4	5.4	3.9	5.6	4.2
Morris	58.1	19.7	1.2	1.2	13.4	8.1	2.9	2.5	1.9	7.2
Dutchess	53.6	22.3	1.8	1.0	11.0	4.9	4.2	1.8	3.5	3.2
Orange	49.6	15.8	2.1	1.1	12.7	4.3	3.6	1.6	4.8	3.6
Somerset	35.3	15.6	0.9	0.4	6.8	1.9	1.3	1.8	1.8	4.8
Rockland	29.7	10.8	0.7	0.4	5.9	2.3	1.7	1.5	0.5	6.0
Putnam	5.5	0.8	g	g	1.7	0.4	0.8	0.4	0.5	0.8

Notes follow Table A-6.

TABLE A-4 Projected Employment in Counties of Region by Categories of Industries, 1965

(In thousands)

	Total employment[a]	Manufacturing	Wholesale trade	Finance[b]	Consumer trade and services[c]	Business and professional services[d]	Public utilities[e]	Contract construction	Agriculture, forestry and fisheries	Government
Entire Region	7,202.0	2,298.9	461.4	365.4	1,468.7	1,132.0	490.3	187.5	46.6	751.2
Core, total[f]	4,258.2	1,156.4	340.4	266.8	850.9	797.1	319.5	95.2	6.0	425.7
New York City	3,961.8	1,006.4	322.9	262.3	809.8	774.2	290.8	89.4	5.4	400.5
Hudson	296.4	150.0	17.5	4.5	41.1	22.9	28.7	5.8	0.6	25.2
Inner Ring, total[f]	1,858.7	726.0	88.6	67.6	374.9	217.8	111.2	60.4	9.0	203.4
Essex	461.1	168.5	28.6	29.6	81.3	52.5	42.4	11.3	1.0	45.9
Nassau	325.7	95.8	12.9	9.5	88.7	37.4	13.2	16.1	1.5	50.6
Bergen	298.6	132.4	12.9	7.6	55.1	32.0	13.8	10.1	2.1	32.5
Westchester	287.6	86.4	12.0	9.2	71.4	43.1	15.9	11.6	2.4	35.7
Union	262.7	126.7	12.0	5.8	42.5	31.3	15.5	6.6	1.0	21.3
Passaic	223.0	116.3	10.2	5.9	36.0	21.4	10.3	4.7	0.9	17.4
Outer Ring, total	1,085.2	416.5	32.3	31.0	242.9	117.1	59.6	31.9	31.7	122.1
Fairfield	277.3	130.8	11.5	7.2	51.3	28.4	11.1	9.4	3.6	24.0
Middlesex	193.9	94.9	6.5	4.2	30.7	16.6	10.7	4.9	2.0	23.5
Suffolk	173.6	50.6	4.1	5.9	45.2	21.3	8.0	6.4	7.0	25.2
Monmouth	102.5	24.3	2.3	3.9	33.7	13.2	6.9	3.4	5.8	9.1
Morris	82.2	25.8	1.4	2.6	18.7	12.0	6.7	2.1	1.9	11.1
Dutchess	78.4	35.2	1.4	1.9	16.5	7.8	5.0	1.5	3.6	5.6
Orange	65.6	20.6	2.3	2.1	17.1	6.6	4.6	1.3	4.9	6.0
Somerset	54.8	21.7	1.4	1.3	12.8	4.7	2.2	1.3	1.9	7.3
Rockland	49.4	11.7	1.4	1.7	14.5	6.1	3.3	1.1	0.5	9.1
Putnam	7.6	1.0	g	0.3	2.3	0.6	1.2	0.4	0.5	1.2

Notes follow Table A-6.

TABLE A-5 Projected Employment in Counties of Region by Categories of Industries, 1975

(in thousands)

	Total employment[a]	Manufacturing	Wholesale trade	Finance[b]	Consumer trade and services[b]	Business and professional services[c]	Public utilities[c]	Contract construction	Agriculture, forestry and fisheries	Government
Entire Region	8,307.4	2,492.4	531.7	451.6	1,673.3	1,436.6	530.5	222.5	49.4	919.4
Core, total[f]	4,516.1	1,141.6	367.9	313.0	894.7	921.4	314.6	113.0	6.3	443.5
New York City	4,214.0	995.2	345.6	308.5	854.2	896.1	283.5	106.1	5.7	419.1
Hudson	302.1	146.4	22.3	4.5	40.5	25.3	31.1	6.9	0.6	24.4
Inner Ring, total[f]	2,285.0	845.9	120.2	83.3	434.4	308.1	132.9	71.6	9.5	279.2
Essex	511.1	170.9	18.1	31.8	86.1	64.4	15.5	13.4	1.1	59.1
Nassau	394.3	117.0	18.1	11.5	96.6	52.1	18.0	19.1	1.6	62.9
Bergen	393.5	159.3	18.6	11.7	72.6	53.1	18.0	12.0	2.2	46.0
Westchester	371.9	107.3	16.0	13.0	85.3	64.5	18.2	13.8	2.5	51.4
Union	332.4	152.8	17.0	8.0	50.8	43.6	20.3	7.8	1.1	31.1
Passaic	281.9	138.7	14.4	7.4	43.1	30.4	12.7	5.6	1.0	28.7
Outer Ring, total	1,506.2	505.0	43.6	55.4	344.2	207.1	82.8	37.8	33.6	196.7
Fairfield	345.5	145.5	16.0	10.9	65.4	42.9	13.6	11.1	3.8	36.4
Middlesex	264.4	109.6	9.0	8.2	47.8	31.6	14.6	5.8	2.1	35.7
Suffolk	248.4	69.0	5.8	10.1	61.1	35.5	11.9	7.6	7.4	39.9
Monmouth	158.5	31.2	2.7	7.9	50.8	27.0	10.3	4.0	6.1	18.4
Morris	121.4	33.8	2.1	4.8	26.9	20.6	10.6	2.4	2.1	18.1
Dutchess	105.4	43.6	1.6	3.1	22.6	13.0	6.4	1.8	3.8	9.5
Orange	93.0	25.9	2.6	3.5	24.9	12.4	6.2	1.6	5.2	10.6
Somerset	86.8	29.0	2.1	3.2	21.1	11.6	3.4	1.8	2.0	12.7
Rockland	73.5	16.3	1.6	3.1	21.1	11.5	4.5	1.3	0.5	13.7
Putnam	9.2	1.1	g	0.5	2.6	0.9	1.3	0.5	0.5	1.7

Notes follow Table A-6.

TABLE A-6 Projected Employment in Counties of Region by Categories of Industries, 1985

(in thousands)

	Total employment[a]	Manufacturing	Wholesale trade	Finance[b]	Consumer trade and services[c]	Business and professional services[d]	Public utilities[e]	Contract construction	Agriculture, forestry and fisheries	Government
Entire Region	9,462.0	2,682.7	612.5	556.5	1,894.0	1,748.8	563.1	265.8	53.1	1,085.5
Core, total[f]	4,711.9	1,131.7	392.0	365.7	915.7	1,020.6	304.2	135.1	6.8	440.3
New York City	4,406.5	987.7	386.3	361.2	875.6	994.1	272.2	126.7	6.1	416.7
Hudson	305.4	144.0	25.7	4.5	40.1	26.5	32.0	8.4	0.7	23.6
Inner Ring, total[f]	2,715.7	947.7	161.7	105.2	491.4	416.7	152.5	85.5	10.2	344.8
Essex	569.4	175.8	41.7	39.5	90.8	79.7	53.5	16.0	1.2	71.2
Westchester	478.0	134.5	23.2	16.7	104.3	89.7	20.9	16.5	2.7	69.5
Bergen	470.0	176.7	25.7	15.0	84.0	73.2	21.4	14.2	2.3	57.4
Nassau	460.6	131.4	25.7	14.5	102.5	72.5	16.8	22.8	1.8	72.6
Union	395.0	169.6	24.5	10.6	59.3	57.3	24.6	9.2	1.2	38.7
Passaic	342.6	159.7	20.8	8.9	50.5	44.2	15.2	6.8	1.1	35.4
Outer Ring, total	2,034.5	603.3	58.8	85.7	486.9	311.6	106.4	45.2	36.1	300.4
Fairfield	428.0	156.5	20.8	15.6	88.2	58.5	16.4	13.4	4.1	54.4
Middlesex	348.2	128.8	11.6	12.8	68.4	47.9	18.6	6.9	2.2	50.9
Suffolk	326.7	88.2	8.0	14.5	79.9	49.1	14.4	9.1	8.0	55.6
Monmouth	233.8	40.9	3.7	13.3	74.7	42.5	13.9	4.6	6.6	33.5
Morris	171.5	41.2	3.1	7.8	39.8	31.1	15.2	3.0	2.2	28.2
Dutchess	146.5	55.6	2.5	5.0	33.1	20.5	7.6	2.1	4.1	15.9
Orange	135.6	33.3	3.7	6.1	37.2	21.3	7.7	1.9	5.6	18.9
Somerset	135.3	37.4	3.1	5.6	35.3	21.7	5.7	2.1	2.1	22.2
Rockland	97.6	20.2	2.4	4.4	27.1	17.4	5.5	1.6	0.6	18.3
Putnam	11.4	1.3	g	0.6	3.1	1.5	1.4	0.4	0.6	2.5

Notes on next page.

NOTES FOR TABLES A-3 THROUGH A-6

(Notes a through d apply also to Table A-2)

General note: Because of rounding, detail may not add to totals.

a "Total employment" is actually the total we could allocate by the categories shown, and does not include a number of self-employed and miscellaneous persons.

b Financial totals differ slightly from those in Sidney M. Robbins and Nestor E. Terleckyj, *Money Metropolis* (Cambridge: Harvard University Press, 1960), because of small differences in classification.

c Domestic workers are included with retail trade and consumer services.

d "Business and professional services" consists of central offices; real estate; "miscellaneous business services" (Code 73 in U. S. Bureau of the Budget, *Standard Industrial Classification Manual*, Vol. II, May 1949); radio and television; and professional and nonprofit activities covered by S. I. C. codes 80, 81, 82, 84, 86, and 89.

e Transportation, communications, and other public utilities.

f Richmond County (Staten Island) could not be separated from the rest of New York City in these employment categories; therefore, instead of being placed in the Inner Ring as usual, it is thrown into the Core. Thus, in Tables A-3 through A-6, the Core consists of New York City *in toto* and Hudson County. The placement of Richmond makes little difference numerically, since the county had fewer than 40,-000 jobs in 1956, or less than 1 per cent of the Core total.

g Less than 50 employees.

TABLE A-7 Past and Projected Population in Counties of New York Metropolitan Region, 1955–1985

(in thousands)

	1955	1960[a]	1965	1975	1985
Entire Region	15,092	15,955	18,033	20,810	23,712
New York City ...	7,806	7,650	7,903	7,761	7,685
Core total	8,247	8,037	8,230	7,965	7,810
Brooklyn	2,636	2,585	2,520	2,430	2,350
Manhattan	1,836	1,650	1,750	1,650	1,600
Queens	1,699	1,795	1,910	1,910	1,910
Bronx	1,431	1,400	1,400	1,350	1,350
Hudson	645	607	650	625	600
Inner Ring total ...	4,399	4,919	5,999	7,249	8,093
Nassau	1,033	1,293	1,298	1,444	1,515
Essex	950	912	1,203	1,365	1,486
Westchester	709	806	966	1,247	1,524
South portion .	(593)	n.a.	(741)	(885)	(1,007)
North portion .	(116)	n.a.	(225)	(362)	(517)
Bergen	678	778	1,025	1,315	1,469
Union	450	503	650	811	896
Passaic	375	406	534	646	728
South portion .	(358)	n.a.	(505)	(599)	(657)
North portion .	(17)	n.a.	(29)	(47)	(71)
Richmond	204	220	323	421	475
Outer Ring total ..	2,446	2,999	3,804	5,596	7,809
Fairfield	592	645	790	1,065	1,420
Suffolk	457	660	757	1,055	1,340
Middlesex	335	432	553	845	1,175
Monmouth	280	333	476	771	1,157
Morris	200	260	315	473	667
Orange	170	183	236	350	540
Dutchess	164	175	240	341	481
Somerset	115	143	192	334	562
Rockland	107	136	211	318	409
Putnam	26	31	35	44	58

[a] The 1960 column gives the preliminary results of the U. S. Census, released during the first half of June 1960. These figures were not available when the projections in the last three columns were made. See also footnotes on our pages 276 and 278.

Note: n.a. = not available. Because of rounding, detail will not necessarily add to totals.

NOTES

CHAPTER 1: METROPOLIS TODAY

1. Two of these qualifications are especially important. In the first place, no establishment's location is actually determined by any single locational factor, such as transport or labor; every locational decision is an amalgam of many interacting factors, a netting out of advantages and disadvantages at alternative locations. Second, our classification is based on a body of knowledge which is incomplete in many respects and probably faulty in others.

CHAPTER 3: GROWTH IN THE REGION'S INDUSTRIES

1. With a few arithmetical examples the reader can readily demonstrate to his own satisfaction that an area's *total* employment growth may match or exceed that of the nation even though the area is slipping competitively in every national industry within its borders. In such a case the secret of its total performance will be its strong mix. A declining share of a group of comparatively fast-growing industries can produce a better total record than an increasing share of a group of comparatively slow-growing industries.

2. Table 3 and subsequent tables presenting "expected" employment growth data are based upon a fairly complex technique devised and applied by Robert M. Lichtenberg in another book in this series, *One-Tenth of a Nation* (Cambridge: Harvard University Press, 1960). The description provided here is a deliberate oversimplification of the technique in some respects. For explanation of technique, see Appendix D of Lichtenberg's book.

3. Though a group of plants in the nation may be engaged in some broad category of production such as "chemicals and allied products," those in the New York area similarly labeled can easily have a very different kind of output from those in

Chicago or New Orleans or Kankakee. To be able to say something meaningful about the national growth rates of industry in the New York area, one has to deal with fairly fine slices of industry—fine enough so that the output of plants covered under any industry label represents something like the same range of products from one area to the next. So we are speaking here of fairly fine industry groups—the finest which the Census data provide for the New York area. In our 1929–1939 comparison, 110 industries are involved; in the 1939–1947 comparison, 157 industries; and in the 1947–1954 comparison, 158 industries. For a discussion of the somewhat staggering technical problems involved in piecing together these industry categories so that they maintained their comparability from one Census date to the next, see Lichtenberg, *op. cit.*, Appendix C.

4. What we have been analyzing so far has been the so-called national-market industries—industries whose product is typically distributed over a broad area to many sections of the country. But there are some industries in the New York Metropolitan Region whose distribution pattern, though extending beyond the Region's boundaries, extends no more than a couple of hundred miles or so, not far enough to be called "national-market." Tests similar to those shown in Table 3 indicate that the New York area's mix is strong for these more circumscribed "sectional-market" industries as well. See Lichtenberg, *op. cit.*, Chapter 3.

5. Principally depreciation, advertising, personal services, and interest.

CHAPTER 4: LABOR AND FREIGHT

1. "Value added" data, as such, are not available for wholesaling.

2. Martin Segal, *Wages in the Metropolis* (Cambridge: Harvard University Press, 1960), Chapter 3.

3. Willis D. Weatherford, Jr., *Geographic Differentials of Agricultural Wages in the United States* (Cambridge, Mass., 1957), p. 81.

4. Benjamin Chinitz, *Freight and the Metropolis* (Cambridge: Harvard University Press, 1960), Chapter 3.

5. Chinitz, *op. cit.*

6. These conclusions are bolstered by the results of the Transportation Survey described in Benjamin Chinitz, *op. cit.*, Appendix.

7. A crude reflection of these tendencies is found in the

fact that between 1870 and 1950 the number of persons engaged in agriculture, forestry, fishing, and mining rose only 21 per cent, while those engaged in manufacturing rose 589 per cent. Adapted from Harold Barger, *Distribution's Place in the American Economy* (Princeton: Princeton University Press, 1955), p. 4.

8. Submerged in these figures are a number of transport-sensitive industries whose heavy concentration in the New York area is explained by the existence of the Port; examples are cane sugar refining, primary copper smelting and refining, cork products, and wool carpets and rugs manufacturing. Like the others, most of these industries have also lost ground in the Region relative to the nation. While much of the general argument outlined above applies to these industries along with the others, their decline is also explained in part by the declining importance of the Port itself, discussed earlier.

9. There are a variety of ways to demonstrate that the tendency toward regionalization has been nationwide. For one set of data illustrating the tendency, see Chinitz, *op. cit.*, pp. 114–116.

10. Of course, other factors besides labor, transport, and external economies are taken into account by specific firms in deciding where in the nation to locate an establishment. Some of these factors—taxes, water, and space—are mentioned in Chapter 2 of Robert M. Lichtenberg's book in this series, *One-Tenth of a Nation.* But these factors have a very small relative importance in the competitive shifts of employment as between metropolitan areas or parts of the country.

CHAPTER 5: EXTERNAL ECONOMIES

1. Our estimates are based on data from U. S. Department of Commerce and U. S. Department of Health, Education, and Welfare, *County Business Patterns*, for first quarter of 1947 and 1956.

2. From 1949 to 1954, employment in the states of New York and New Jersey in the central offices of manufacturing firms seems to have risen from 25 per cent of the national total to 28 per cent. U. S. *1954 Census of Manufactures*.

3. For a more extensive treatment of this point, see Sidney M. Robbins and Nestor E. Terleckyj, *Money Metropolis* (Cambridge: Harvard University Press, 1960), pp. 131–136.

CHAPTER 6: FROM JOBS TO PEOPLE TO JOBS AGAIN

1. Louise P. Lerdau, "Some Facets of the Region's Consumer Trade and Service Activities," which is Supplement II in Robert M. Lichtenberg, *One-Tenth of a Nation* (Cambridge: Harvard University Press, 1960).

CHAPTER 7: THE DISTRIBUTION OF JOBS WITHIN THE REGION

1. For more details, see the freight volume in this series, Benjamin Chinitz, *Freight and the Metropolis* (Cambridge: Harvard University Press, 1960), especially pp. 150–152.

CHAPTER 8: JOBS IN MOTION

1. For details see Edgar M. Hoover and Raymond Vernon, *Anatomy of a Metropolis* (Cambridge: Harvard University Press, 1959), pp. 29–30, 53–54. New York: Doubleday, Anchor Books, 1962, pp. 25–26, 48–51.

2. The only significant taxes omitted from the calculations were workmen's compensation taxes. For a description of methods used and some of the underlying data, see Hoover and Vernon, Appendix F.

3. Robert C. Wood, *1400 Governments,* a forthcoming volume in this series.

CHAPTER 9: FROM TENEMENT TO SPLIT LEVEL

1. The 1950 Census showed that in 1949 the median income of managerial workers in the New York Metropolitan Region was $4,062 and that of professional workers $3,866. For craftsmen and foremen, the figure was $3,248; for clerical workers, $2,529; for sales workers, $3,017; for operatives, $2,402; for laborers, $2,348; and for service workers, $1,942. The comparable results of the 1960 Census were not available as this book went to press.

2. Edgar M. Hoover and Raymond Vernon, *Anatomy of a Metropolis* (Cambridge: Harvard University Press, 1959), Chapter 7. New York: Doubleday, Anchor Books, 1962.

3. For some of the formulas descriptive of the relation, see Hoover and Vernon, Appendix I.

CHAPTER 10: CITY HALL AND TOWN HALL

1. Robert C. Wood, *1400 Governments*. The analysis was performed by Vladimir V. Almendinger who collaborated with Professor Wood in this and other phases of the work.

2. U. S. Army Corps of Engineers, *Financing a Delaware Water Resources Program*, preliminary memorandum, April 15, 1959.

3. Wood, *1400 Governments*.

CHAPTER 11: METROPOLIS 1985

1. Compare Robert M. Lichtenberg, *One-Tenth of a Nation* (Cambridge: Harvard University Press, 1960), Chart 6.

2. In making the national projections, the economy had been broken down into 28 categories. The projections for the Region, however, demanded a much more detailed classification. In using the projected national growth rates, we assumed that within any one of the 28 categories the same national growth rate applied to all industries.

3. One especially difficult problem, for instance, was that of shuttling between the value-of-output figures as shown in the input-output tables and the employment figures which our projections required.

4. In the shift from Regional to intraregional projections, problems of industry classification arose again, analogous to those described in note 2 above. Again, we assumed that all the particular parts of any industry category projected for the Region had grown at the same rate.

INDEX

Transport-sensitive industries (*cont'd*)
ployment in national-mar-
ket industries, Region and
nation, 89–91; importance
of rising transport costs,
92; growth rates in New
York area of national-market activities, classified by
area's share of nation's
employment, 94; influence
of truck, 168; estimated
growth rate in national-
market industries in Re-
gion, 257–58
Trolley, 201

Union City, 171, 225
Union County, 141; employment, 140, 292–95; in-
come, 203–4; population,
278, 297
United Automobile Workers
of America, 77
United Rubber, Cork, Linoleum and Plastics Work-
ers of America, 77
United Steel Workers of
America, 77
Utilities industries, 255

Value added, 60; defined,
58; national and Regional
growth rate, by national-
market manufacturing in-
dustries, 59; labor costs,
65; as factor in Region's
economy, 109–10

Wages: Region, 49; New

York area, 66; locational
variations, 65; Region
compared with other parts
of the nation, 66; wage
levels and industrial development in Region, 66–72;
convergence, 72–77, 170;
minimum wage laws, 73;
industrialization growth,
73; labor supply, 74–76;
collective bargaining, 77;
future, 78–79
Warehouses, 88–97
Waterproof outergarments,
55
Water supply, New Jersey,
237–40
West, 43
Westchester County, 141;
employment, 140, 271,
292–95; neighborhood
changes, 181, 182; income,
203–4; future, 229–31;
population, 273, 278, 297
Wholesale trade: employ-
ment in nation and Re-
gion, 22–23; growth, 32–
33; early office activity in
New York area, 37; con-
centration in New York
City, 142; employment in
Region, 154; locational
shift, 159
Women workers, 250
Women's apparel, 70–71,
109
Women's aprons, 37
Women's dresses: importance
to Manhattan, 50; collec-
tive bargaining, 77; as ex-

OTHER ANCHOR BOOKS OF INTEREST

SOCIOLOGY

ALLPORT, GORDON W. The Nature of Prejudice, A149

BARTH, KARL Community, State and Church, A221

BENDIX, REINHARD Max Weber: An Intellectual Portrait, A281

BROWN, ROBERT MCAFEE, & WEIGEL, GUSTAVE, S.J. An American Dialogue, A257

CABLE, GEORGE W. The Negro Question, A144

CHEVALIER, MICHAEL Society, Manners and Politics in the United States, A259

DOLLARD, JOHN Caste and Class in a Southern Town, A95

FORTUNE, EDITORS OF The Exploding Metropolis, A146

GOFFMAN, ERVING Asylums: Essays on the Social Situation of Mental Patients and Other Inmates, A277

——— The Presentation of Self in Everyday Life, A174

GRANICK, DAVID The Red Executive: A Study of the Organization Man in Russian Industry, A246

HANDLIN, OSCAR The Newcomers, A283

——— Race and Nationality in American Life, A110

HERBERG, WILL Protestant-Catholic-Jew, A195

HOOVER, EDGAR M. & VERNON, RAYMOND Anatomy of a Metropolis, A298

MARTINEAU, HARRIET Society in America, Ed. Lipset, A302

NEGLEY, GLENN & PATRICK, J. MAX, eds. The Quest for Utopia, A326

PETERSEN, WILLIAM American Social Patterns, A86

RAAB, EARL, ed. American Race Relations Today, A318

RIEFF, PHILIP Freud: The Mind of the Moralist, A278

RIESMAN, DAVID Constraint and Variety in American Education, A135

——— Selected Essays from Individualism Reconsidered, A58

SCOTT, GEOFFREY The Architecture of Humanism, A33

SIGAL, CLANCY Weekend in Dinlock, A269

SOMERS, HERMAN & ANNE Doctors, Patients and Health Insurance, A309

VICO, GIAMBATTISTA The New Science of Giambattista Vico, Trans. Bergin & Fisch, A254

VIDICH, ARTHUR J., & BENSMAN, JOSEPH Small Town in Mass Society: Class, Power and Religion in a Rural Community, A216

WHYTE, WILLIAM H., JR. The Organization Man, A117

WIENER, NORBERT The Human Use of Human Beings, A34

WILLIAMS, RAYMOND Culture and Society, 1780–1950, A220

OTHER ANCHOR BOOKS OF INTEREST

GOVERNMENT AND POLITICAL SCIENCE

PSYCHOLOGY